Real Estate Appraiser Exam Success

By Lewis Morris

www.insiderswords.com/appraisal

ISBN-13: 978-1728930862

Table of Contents

What is "Insider Language"?

Recent research has confirmed what we have known for decades: The strongest students and leaders in industry have a mastered an Insider Language in their subject and field. This Insider language is made up of the technical terms and vocabulary necessary to communicate effectively in classes or the workplace. For those who master it, learning is easier, faster, and much more enjoyable.

Most students who are surveyed report that the greatest challenge to any course of study is learning the vocabulary. When we examine typical college courses, we discover that there is, on average, 250 Insider Terms a student must learn over the course of a semester. Further, most exams rely heavily on this set of words for assessment purposes. The structure of multiple choice exams lends itself perfectly to the testing of this Insider Language. Students who can differentiate between Insider Language terms can handle challenging exam questions with ease and confidence.

From recent research on learning and vocabulary we have learned:

- Your knowledge of any subject is contained in the content-specific words you know. The more of these terms that you know, the easier it is to understand and recall important information; the easier it will be to communicate your ideas to peers, professors, supervisors, and co-workers. The stronger your content-area vocabulary is, the higher your scores will be on your exams and written assignments.

- Students who develop a strong Insider Language perform better on tests, learn faster, retain more information, and express greater satisfaction in learning.

- Familiarizing yourself with subject-area vocabulary before formal study (pre-learning) is the most effective way to learn this language and reap the most benefit.

- The vocabulary on standardized exams come directly from the stated objectives of the test-makers. This means that the vocabulary found on standardized exams is predictable. Our books focus on this vocabulary.

- Most multiple-choice exams are glorified vocabulary quizzes. Think about the format of a multiple-choice question. The question stem is a definition of a term and the choices (known as distractors) are 4 or 5 similar words. Your task is to differentiate between the meanings of those terms and choose the correct word.

- It takes a person several exposures to a new word to be able to use it with confidence in conversation or in writing. You need to process these words several different ways to make them part of your long-term memory.

The goals of this book are:

- To give you an "Insider Language" for your subject.
- Pre-teach the most important words before you set out on a traditional course of review or study.
- Teach you the most important words in your subject area.
- Teach you strategies for learning subject-area words on your own.
- Boost your confidence in your ability to master this language and support you in your study.
- Reduce the stress of studying and provide you with fun activities that work.

How it works:

The secret to mastering Insider Language is through repetition and exposure. We have eleven steps for you to follow:

1. Read the word and definition in the glossary out loud. "See it, Say it"
2. Identify the part of speech the word belongs to such as noun, verb, adverb, or adjective. This will help you group the word and identify similar words.
3. Place the word in context by using it in a sentence. Write this sentence down and read it aloud.
4. Use "Chunking" to group the words. Make a diagram or word cloud using these groups.
5. Make connections to the words by creating analogies.
6. Create mnemonics that help you recognize patterns and orders of words by substituting the words for more memorable items or actions.
7. Examine the morphology of the word, that is, identify the root, prefix, and suffix that make up the word. Identify similar and related words.
8. Complete word games and puzzles such as crosswords and word searches.
9. Complete matching questions that require you to differentiate between related words.
10. Complete Multiple-choice questions containing the words.
11. Create a visual metaphor or "memory cartoon" to make a mental picture of the word and related processes.

By completing this word study process, you will be exposed to the terminology in various ways that will activate your memory and create a lasting understanding of this language.

The strategies in this book are designed to make you an independent expert at learning insider language. These strategies include:

- Verbalizing the word by reading it and its definition aloud ("See It, Say It"). This allows you to make visual, auditory, and speech connections with its meaning.

- Identifying the type of word (Noun, verb, adverb, and adjective). Making this distinction helps you understand how to visualize the word. It helps you "chunk" the words into groups, and gives you clues on how to use the word.

- Place the word in context by using it in a sentence. Write this sentence down and read it aloud. This will give you an example of how the word is used.

- "Chunking". By breaking down the word list into groups of closely related words, you will learn them better and be able to remember them faster. Once you have group the terms, you can then make word clouds using a free online service. These word clouds provide visual cues to remembering the words and their meanings.

- Analogies. By creating analogies for essential words, you will be making connections that you can see on paper. These connections can trigger your memory and activate your ability to use the word in your writing as you begin to use them. Many of these analogies also use visual cues. In a sense, you can make a mental picture from the analogy.

- Mnemonics. A device such as a pattern of letters, ideas, or associations that assists in remembering something. A mnemonic is especially useful for remembering the order of a set of words or the order of a process.

- Morphology. The study of word roots, prefixes, and suffixes. By examining the structure of the words, you will gain insight into other words that are closely related, and learn how to best use the word.

- Visual metaphors. This is the most sophisticated and entertaining strategy for learning vocabulary. Create a "memory cartoon" using one or more of the vocabulary terms. This activity triggers the visual part of your memory and makes fast, permanent, imprints of the word on your memory. By combining the terms in your visual metaphor, you can "chunk" the entire set of vocabulary terms into several visual metaphors and benefit from the brain's tendency to group these terms.

The activities in this book are designed to imprint the words and their meanings in your memory in different ways. By completing each activity, you will gain the necessary exposures to the word to make it a permanent part of your vocabulary. Each activity uses a different part of your memory. The result is that you will be comfortable using these words and be able to tell the difference between closely related words. The activities include:

A. Crossword Puzzles and Word Searches- These are proven to increase test scores and improve comprehension. Students frequently report that they are fun and engaging, while requiring them to analyze the structure and meaning of the words.

B. Matching- This activity is effective because it forces you to differentiate between many closely related terms.

C. Multiple Choice- This classic question format lends itself to vocabulary study perfectly. Most exams are in this format because they are simple to make, easy to score, and are a reliable type of assessment. (Perfect for the Vocabulary Master!) One strategy to use with multiple choice questions that enhance their effectiveness is to cover the answer choices while you read the question. After reading the question, see if you can answer it before looking at the choices. Then look at the choices to see if you match one of them.

Conducting a thorough "word study" of your insider language will take time and effort, but the rewards will be well worth it. By following this guide and completing the exercises thoughtfully, you will become a stronger, more effective, and satisfied student. Best of luck on your mastery of this Insider Language!

Insider Language Strategies

"See It, Say It!" Reading your Insider Language set aloud

"IT IS BETTER TO FAIL IN ORIGINALITY THAN TO SUCCEED IN IMITATION."
–HERMAN MELVILLE

Reading aloud is the foundation for the development of an Insider Language. It is the single most important thing you can do for vocabulary acquisition. Done correctly, it engages the visual, auditory, and speech centers of the brain and hastens its storage in your long-term memory.

Reading aloud demonstrates the relationship between the printed word and its meaning.

You can read aloud on a higher level than you can initially understand, so reading aloud makes complex ideas more accessible and exposes you to vocabulary and patterns that are not part of your typical speech. Reading aloud helps you understand the complicated text better and makes more challenging text easier to grasp and understand. Reading aloud helps you to develop the "habits of mind" the strongest students use.

Reading aloud will make connections to concepts in the reading that requires you to relate the new vocabulary to things you already know. Go to the glossary at the end of this book and for each word complete the five steps outlined below:

1. Read the word and its definition aloud. Focus on the sound of the word and how it looks on the paper.
2. Read the word aloud again try to say three or four similar words; this will help you build connections to closely related words.
3. Read the word aloud a third time. Try to make a connection to something you have read or heard.
4. Visualize the concept described in the term. Paint a mental picture of the word in use.
5. Try to think of the opposite of the word. Discovering a close antonym will help you place this word in context.

Create a sentence using the word in its proper context

"OPPORTUNITIES DON'T HAPPEN. YOU CREATE THEM." –CHRIS GROSSER

Context means the circumstances that form the setting for an event, statement, or idea, and which it can be fully understood and assessed. Synonyms for context include conditions, factors, situation, background, and setting.

Place the word in context by using it in a sentence. Write this sentence down and read it aloud. By creating sentences, you are practicing using the word correctly. If you strive to make these sentences interesting and creative, they will become more memorable and effective in activating your long-term memory.

Identify the Parts of Speech
"SUCCESS IS NOT FINAL; FAILURE IS NOT FATAL: IT IS THE COURAGE TO CONTINUE THAT COUNTS." –WINSTON S. CHURCHILL

Read through each term in the glossary and make a note of what part of speech each term is. Studying and identifying parts of speech shows us how the words relate to each other. It also helps you create a visualization of each term. Below are brief descriptions of the parts of speech for you to use as a guide.

VERB: A word denoting action, occurrence, or existence. Examples: walk, hop, whisper, sweat, dribbles, feels, sleeps, drink, smile, are, is, was, has.

NOUN: A word that names a person, place, thing, idea, animal, quality, or action. Nouns are the subject of the sentence. Examples: dog, Tom, Florida, CD, pasta, hate, tiger.

ADJECTIVE: A word that modifies, qualifies, or describes nouns and pronouns. Generally, adjectives appear immediately before the words they modify. Examples: smart girl, gifted teacher, old car, red door.

ADVERB: A word that modifies verbs, adjectives and other adverbs. An "ly" ending almost always changes an adjective to an adverb. Examples: ran swiftly, worked slowly, and drifted aimlessly. Many adverbs do not end in "ly." However, all adverbs identify when, where, how, how far, how much, etc. Examples: run hot, lived hard, moved right, study smart.

Chunking

"YOUR POSITIVE ACTION COMBINED WITH POSITIVE THINKING RESULTS IN SUCCESS." SHIV KHERA

Chunking is when you take a set of words and break it down into groups based on a common relationship. Research has shown that our brains learn by chunking information. By grouping your terms, you will be able to recall large sets of these words easily. To help make your chunking go easily use an online word cloud generator to make a set of word clouds representing your chunks.

1. Study the glossary and decide how you want to chunk the set of words. You can group by part of speech, topic, letter of the alphabet, word length, etc. Try to find an easy way to group each term.
2. Once you have your different groups, visit www.wordclouds.com to create a custom word cloud for each group. Print each one of these clouds and post it in a prominent place to serve as constant visual aids for your learning.

Analogies

"CHOOSE THE POSITIVE. YOU HAVE CHOICE, YOU ARE MASTER OF YOUR ATTITUDE, CHOOSE THE POSITIVE, THE CONSTRUCTIVE. OPTIMISM IS A FAITH THAT LEADS TO SUCCESS."– BRUCE LEE

An analogy is a comparison in which an idea or a thing is compared to another thing that is quite different from it. Analogies aim at explaining an idea by comparing it to something that is familiar. Metaphors and similes are tools used to create analogies.

Analogies are useful for learning vocabulary because they require you to analyze a word (or words), and then transfer that analysis to another word. This transfer reinforces the understanding of all the words.

As you analyze the relationships between the analogies you are creating, you will begin to understand the complex relationships between the seemingly unrelated words.

_A__ is to __B_ as __C_ is to __D_

This can be written using colons in place of the terms "is to" and "as."

 A:B::C:D

The two items on the left (items A & B) describe a relationship and are separated by a single colon. The two items on the right (items C & D) are shown on the right and are also separated by a colon. Together, both sides are then separated by two colons in the middle, as shown here: Tall: Short :: Skinny: Fat. The relationship used in this analogy is the antonym.

How to create an analogy

Start with the basic formula for an analogy:

____ : ____ :: ____ : ____

Next, we will examine a simple synonym analogy:

automobile : car :: box : crate

The key to figuring out a set of word analogies is determining the relationship between the paired set of words.

Here is a list of the most common types of Analogies and examples

Synonym	Scream : Yell :: Push : Shove
Antonym	Rich : Poor :: Empty : Full
Cause is to Effect	Prosperity : Happiness :: Success : Joy
A Part is to its Whole	Toe : Foot :: Piece : Set
An Object to its Function	Car : Travel :: Read : Learn
A Item is to its Category	Tabby : House Cat :: Doberman : Dog
Word is a symptom of the other	Pain : Fracture :: Wheezing : Allergy
An object and it's description	Glass : Brittle :: Lead : Dense
The word is lacking the second word	Amputee : Limb :: Deaf : Hearing
The first word Hinders the second word	Shackles : Movement :: Stagger : Walk
The first word helps the action of the second	Knife : Bread :: Screwdriver : Screw
This word is made up of the second word	Sweater : Wool :: Jeans : Denim
A word and it's definition	Cede: Break Away :: Abolish : To get rid of

Using words from the glossary, make a set of analogies using each one. As a bonus, use more than one glossary term in a single analogy.

_____ : _____ :: _____ : _____

Name the relationship between the words in your analogy:_____

_____ : _____ :: _____ : _____

Name the relationship between the words in your analogy:_____

_____ : _____ :: _____ : _____

Name the relationship between the words in your analogy:_____

Mnemonics

"IT ISN'T THE MOUNTAINS AHEAD TO CLIMB THAT WEAR YOU OUT; IT'S THE PEBBLE IN YOUR SHOE."   —MUHAMMAD ALI

A mnemonic is a learning technique that helps you retain and remember information. Mnemonics are one of the best learning methods for remembering lists or processes in order. Mnemonics make the material more meaningful by adding associations and creating patterns. Interestingly, mnemonics may work better when they utilize absurd, startling, or shocking examples and references. Mnemonics help organize the information so that you can easily retrieve it later. By giving you associations and cues, mnemonics allow you to form a mental structure ordering a list or process to help you remember it better. This mental structure allows you to create a structure of association between items that may not appear to have any relationship. Mnemonics typically use references that are easy to visualize and thus easier to remember. Through visualization of vivid images and references, the information is much easier to imprint into long-term memory. The power of making mnemonics lies in converting dull, inert and uninspiring information into something vibrant and memorable.

How to make simple and effective mnemonics
Some of the best mnemonics help us remember simple rules or lists in order.

Step 1. Take a list of terms you are trying to remember in order. For example, we will use the scientific method:

observation, question, hypothesis, methods, results, and conclusion.

Next, we will replace each word on the list with a new word that starts with the same letter. These new words will together form a vivid sentence that is easy to remember:

Objectionable Queens Haunted Macho Rednecks Creatively.

As silly as the above sentence seems, it is easy to remember, and now we can call on this sentence to remind us of the order of the scientific method.

Visit http://www.mnemonicgenerator.com/ and try typing in a list of words. It is fun to see the mnemonics that it makes and shows how easy it is to make great mnemonics to help your studying.

Using vivid words in your mnemonics allows you to see the sentence you are making. Words that are gross, scary, or name interesting animals are helpful. Profanity is also useful because the shock value can trigger memory. The following are lists of vivid words to use in your mnemonics:

Gross words

Moist, Gurgle, Phlegm, Fetus, Curd, Smear, Squirt, Chunky, Orifice, Maggots, Viscous, Queasy, Bulbous, Pustule, Putrid, Fester, Secrete, Munch, Vomit, Ooze, Dripping, Roaches, Mucus, Stink, Stank, Stunk, Slurp, Pus, Lick, Salty, Tongue, Fart, Flatulence, Hemorrhoid.

Interesting Animals

Aardvark, Baboon, Chicken, Chinchilla, Duck, Dragonfly, Emu, Electric Eel, Frog, Flamingo, Gecko, Hedgehog, Hyena, Iguana, Jackal, Jaguar, Leopard, Lynx, Minnow, Manatee, Mongoose, Neanderthal, Newt, Octopus, Oyster, Pelican, Penguin, Platypus, Quail, Racoon, Rattlesnake, Rhinoceros, Scorpion, Seahorse, Toucan, Turkey, Vulture, Weasel, Woodpecker, Yak, Zebra.

Superhero Words

Diabolical, Activate, Boom, Clutch, Dastardly, Dynamic, Dynamite, Shazam, Kaboom, Zip, Zap, Zoom, Zany, Crushing, Smashing, Exploding, Ripping, Tearing.

Scary Words

Apparition, Bat, Chill, Demon, Eerie, Fangs, Genie, Hell, Lantern, Macabre, Nightmare, Owl, Ogre, Phantasm, Repulsive, Scarecrow, Tarantula, Undead, Vampire, Wraith, Zombie.

There are several types of mnemonics that can help your memory.

1. Images

Visual mnemonics are a type of mnemonic that works by associating an image with characters or objects whose name sounds like the item that must be memorized. This is one of the easiest ways to create effective mnemonics. An example would be to use the shape of numbers to help memorize a long list of them. Numbers can be memorized by their shapes, so that: 0 -looks like an egg; 1 -a pencil, or a candle; 2 -a snake; 3 -an ear; 4 -a sailboat; 5 -a key; 6 -a comet; 7 -a knee; 8 -a snowman; 9 -a comma.

Another type of visual mnemonic is the word-length mnemonic in which the number of letters in each word corresponds to a digit. This simple mnemonic gives pi to seven decimal places:

3.141582 becomes "How I wish I could calculate pi."

Of course, you could use this type of mnemonic to create a longer sentence showing the digits of an important number. Some people have used this type of mnemonic to memorize thousands of digits.

Using the hands is also an important tool for creating visual objects. Making the hands into specific shapes can help us remember the pattern of things or the order of a list of things.

2. Rhyming

Rhyming mnemonics are quick ways to make things memorable. A classic example is a mnemonic for the number of days in each month:
"30 days hath September, April, June, and November.
All the rest have 31
Except February, my dear son.
It has 28, and that is fine
But in Leap Year it has 29."

Another example of a rhyming mnemonic is a common spelling rule:
"I before e except after c
or when sounding like a
in neighbor and weigh."

Use **rhymer.com** to get large lists of rhyming words.

3. Homonym

A homonym is one of a group of words that share the same pronunciation but have different meanings, whether spelled the same or not.

Try saying what you're attempting to remember out loud or very quickly, and see if anything leaps out. If you know other languages, using similar-sounding words from those can be effective.

You could also browse this list of homonyms
at http://www.cooper.com/alan/homonym_list.html.

4. Onomatopoeia

An Onomatopeia is a word that phonetically imitates, resembles or suggests the source of the sound that it describes. Are there any noises made by the thing you're trying to memorize? Is it often associated with some other sound? Failing that, just make up a noise that seems to fit.

Achoo, ahem, baa, bam, bark, beep, beep beep, belch, bleat, boo, boo hoo, boom, burp, buzz, chirp, click clack, crash, croak, crunch, cuckoo, dash, drip, ding dong, eek, fizz, flit, flutter, gasp, grrr, ha ha, hee hee, hiccup, hiss, hissing, honk, icky, itchy, jiggly, jangle, knock knock, lush, la la la, mash, meow, moan, murmur, neigh, oink, ouch, plop, pow, quack, quick, rapping, rattle, ribbit, roar, rumble, rustle, scratch, sizzle, skittering, snap crackle pop, splash, splish splash, spurt, swish, swoosh, tap, tapping, tick tock, tinkle, tweet, ugh, vroom, wham, whinny, whip, whooping, woof.

5. Acronyms

An acronym is a word or name formed as an abbreviation from the initial components of a word, such as NATO, which stands for North Atlantic Treaty Organization. If you're trying to memorize something involving letters, this is often a good bet. A lot of famous mnemonics are acronyms, such as ROYGBIV which stands for the order of colors in the light spectrum (Red, Orange, Yellow, Green, Blue, Indigo, and Violet).

A great acronym generator to try is: www.all-acronyms.com.

A different spin on an acronym is a backronym. A **backronym** is a specially constructed phrase that is supposed to be the source of a word that is an acronym. A backronym is constructed by creating a new phrase to fit an already existing word, name, or acronym.

The word is a combination of *backward* and *acronym*, and has been defined as a "reverse acronym." For example, the United States Department of Justice assigns to their Amber Alert program the meaning "**A**merica's **M**issing: **B**roadcast **E**mergency **R**esponse." The process can go either way to make good mnemonics.

Visit: https://arthurdick.com/projects/backronym/ to try out a simple backronym generator.

6. Anagrams

An anagram is a direct word switch or word play, the result of rearranging the letters of a word or phrase to produce a new word or phrase, using all the original letters exactly once; for example, the word anagram can be rearranged into nag-a-ram.

Try re-arranging letters or components and see if anything memorable emerges. Visit http://www.nameacronym.net/ to use a simple anagram generator.

One particularly memorable form of anagram is the spoonerism, where you swap the initial syllables or letters of words to make new phrases. These are usually humorous, and this makes them easier to remember. Here are some examples:

"Is it kisstomary to cuss the bride?" (as opposed to "customary to kiss")
"The Lord is a shoving leopard." (instead of "a loving shepherd")
"A blushing crow." ("crushing blow")
"A well-boiled icicle" ("well-oiled bicycle")
"You were fighting a liar in the quadrangle." ("lighting a fire")
"Is the bean dizzy?" (as opposed to "is the dean busy?")

7. Stories

Make up quick stories or incidents involving the material you want to memorize. For larger chunks of information, the stories can get more elaborate. Structured stories are particularly good for remembering lists or other sequenced information. Have a look at https://en.wikipedia.org/wiki/Method_of_loci for a more advanced memory sequencing technique.

Visual Metaphors

"LIMITS, LIKE FEAR, IS OFTEN AN ILLUSION." –MICHAEL JORDAN

What is a Metaphor?

A metaphor is a figure of speech that refers to one thing by mentioning another thing. Metaphors provide clarity and identify hidden similarities between two seemingly unrelated ideas. A visual metaphor is an image that creates a link between different ideas.

Visual metaphors help us use our understanding of the world to learn new concepts, skills, and ideas. Visual metaphors help us relate new material to what we already know. Visual metaphors must be clear and simple enough to spark a connection and understanding. Visual metaphors should use familiar things to help you be less fearful of new, complex, or challenging topics. Metaphors trigger a sense of familiarity so that you are more accepting of the new idea. Metaphors work best when you associate a familiar, easy to understand idea with a challenging, obscure, or abstract concept.

How to make a visual metaphor

1. Brainstorm using the words of the concept. Use different fonts, colors, or shapes to represent parts of the concept.

2. Merge these images together

3. Show the process using arrows, accents, etc.

4. Think about the story line your metaphor projects.

Examples of visual metaphors:

A skeleton used to show a framework of something.

A cloud showing an outline.

A bodybuilder whose muscles represent supporting ideas and details.

A sandwich where the meat, tomato, and lettuce represent supporting ideas.

A recipe card to show a process.

Your metaphor should be accurate. It should be complex enough to convey meaning, but simple and clear enough to be easily understood.

Morphology
"SCIENCE IS THE CAPTAIN, AND PRACTICE THE SOLDIERS." LEONARDO DA VINCI

Morphology is the study of the origin, roots, suffixes, and prefixes of the words. Understanding the meaning of prefixes, suffixes, and roots make it easier to decode the meaning of new vocabulary. Having the ability to decode using morphology increases text comprehension when initially reading as well.

The capability of identifying meaningful parts of words (morphemes), including prefixes, suffixes, and roots can be helpful. Identifying morphemes improves decoding accuracy and fluency. Reading speed improves when you can decode larger chunks of text quickly. When you can recognize morphemes in words, you will be better able to make sense of new words in context. Below are charts containing the most common prefixes, suffixes, and root words. Use them to help you decode your vocabulary terms.

Prefixes

Prefix	Meaning	Example words and meanings	
a, ab, abs	away from	absent	not to be present, to give
		abdicate	up an office or throne.
ad, a, ac, af, ag, an, ar, at, as	to, toward	Advance	To move forward
		advantage	To have the upper hand
anti	against	Antidote	To repair poisoning
		antisocial	refers to someone who's
		antibiotic	not social
bi, bis	two	bicycle	two-wheeled cycle
		binary	two number system
		biweekly	every two weeks
circum, cir	around	circumnavigate	Travel around the world
		circle	a figure that goes all around
com, con, co, col	with, together	Complete	To finish
		Complement	To go along with
de	away from, down, the opposite of	depart	to go away from
		detour	to go out of your way
dis, dif, di	apart	dislike	not to like
		dishonest	not honest
		distant	away
En-, em-	Cause to	Entrance	the way in.
epi	upon, on top of	epitaph	writing upon a tombstone
		epilogue	speech at the end, on top
		epidemic	of the rest
equ, equi	equal	equalize	to make equal
		equitable	fair, equal
ex, e, ef	out, from	exit	to go out
		eject	to throw out
		exhale	to breathe out
Fore-	Before	Forewarned	To have prior warning

Prefix	Meaning	Example Words and Meanings	
in, il, ir, im, en	in, into	Infield Imbibe	The inner playing field to take part in
in, il, ig, ir, im	not	inactive ignorant irreversible irritate	not active not knowing not reversible to put into discomfort
inter	between, among	international interact	among nations to mix with
mal, male	bad, ill, wrong	malpractice malfunction	bad practice fail to function, bad function
Mid	Middle	Amidships	In the middle of a ship
mis	wrong, badly	misnomer	The wrong name
mono	one, alone, single	monocle	one lensed glasses
non	not, the reverse of	nonprofit	not making a profit
ob	in front, against, in front of, in the way of	Obsolete	No longer needed
omni	everywhere, all	omnipresent omnipotent	always present, everywhere all powerful
Over	On top	Overdose	Take too much medication
Pre	Before	Preview	Happens before a show.
per	through	Permeable pervasive	to pass through, all encompassing
poly	many	Polygamy polygon	many spouses figure with many sides
post	after	postpone postmortem	to do after after death
pre	before, earlier than	Predict Preview	To know before To view before release
pro	forward, going ahead of, supporting	proceed pro-war promote	to go forward supporting the war to raise or move forward
re	again, back	retell recall reverse	to tell again to call back to go back
se	apart	secede seclude	to withdraw, become apart to stay apart from others
Semi	Half	Semipermeable	Half-permeable

Prefix	Meaning	Example Words and Meanings	
Sub	under, less than	Submarine	under water
super	over, above, greater	superstar superimpose	a start greater than her stars to put over something else
trans	across	transcontinental transverse	across the continent to lie or go across
un, uni	one	unidirectional unanimous unilateral	having one direction sharing one view having one side
un	not	uninterested unhelpful unethical	not interested not helpful not ethical

Roots

Root	Meaning	Example words & meanings	
act, ag	to do, to act	Agent Activity	One who acts as a representative Action
Aqua	Water	Aquamarine	The color of water
Aud	To hear	Auditorium	A place to hear music
apert	open	Aperture	An opening
bas	low	Basement Basement	Something that is low, at the bottom A room that is low
Bio	Living thing	Biological	Living matter
cap, capt, cip, cept, ceive	to take, to hold, to seize	Captive Receive Capable Recipient	One who is held To take Able to take hold of things One who takes hold or receives
ced, cede, ceed, cess	to go, to give in	Precede Access Proceed	To go before Means of going to To go forward
Cogn	Know	Cognitive	Ability to think
cred, credit	to believe	Credible Incredible Credit	Believable Not believable Belief, trust
curr, curs, cours	to run	Current Precursory Recourse	Now in progress, running Running (going) before To run for aid
Cycle	Circle	Lifecycle	The circle of life
dic, dict	to say	Dictionary Indict	A book explaining words (sayings)

Root	Meaning	Examples and meanings	
duc, duct	to lead	Induce	To lead to action
		Conduct	To lead or guide
		Aqueduct	Pipe that leads water somewhere
equ	equal, even	Equality	Equal in social, political rights
		Equanimity	Evenness of mind, tranquility
fac, fact, fic, fect, fy	to make, to do	Facile	Easy to do
		Fiction	Something that is made up
		Factory	Place that makes things
		Affect	To make a change in
fer, ferr	to carry, bring	Defer	To carry away
		Referral	Bring a source for help/information
Gen	Birth	Generate	To create something
graph	write	Monograph	A writing on a particular subject
		Graphite	A form of carbon used for writing
Loc	Place	Location	A place
Mater	Mother	Maternity	Expecting birth
Mem	Recall	Memory	The recall experiences
mit, mis	to send	Admit	To send in
		Missile	Something sent through the air
Nat	Born	Native	Born in a place
par	equal	Parity	Equality
		Disparate	No equal, not alike
Ped	Foot	Podiatrist	Foot doctor
Photo	Light	Photograph	A picture
plic	to fold, to bend, to turn	Complicate	To fold (mix) together
		Implicate	To fold in, to involve
pon, pos, posit, pose	to place	Component	A part placed together with others
		Transpose	A place across
		Compose	To put many parts into place
		Deposit	To place for safekeeping
scrib, script	to write	Describe	To write about or tell about
		Transcript	A written copy
		Subscription	A written signature or document
sequ, secu	to follow	Sequence	In following order

Root	Meaning	Examples and Meanings	
Sign	Mark	Signal	to alert somebody
spec, spect, spic	to appear, to look, to see	Specimen Aspect	An example to look at One way to see something
sta, stat, sist,	to stand, or make stand	Constant	Standing with
stit, sisto	Stable, steady	Status Stable Desist	Social standing Steady (standing) To stand away from
Struct	To build	Construction	To build a thing
tact	to touch	Contact Tactile	To touch together To be able to be touched
ten, tent, tain	to hold	Tenable Retentive Maintain	Able to be held, holding Holding To keep or hold up
tend, tens, tent	to stretch	Extend Tension	To stretch or draw out Stretched
Therm	Temperature	Thermometer	Detects temperature
tract	to draw	Attract Contract	To draw together An agreement drawn up
ven, vent	to come	Convene Advent	To come together A coming
Vis	See	Invisible	Cannot be seen
ver, vert, vers	to turn	Avert Revert Reverse	To turn away To turn back To turn around

Crossword Puzzles

1. Using the Across and Down clues, write the correct words in the numbered grid below.

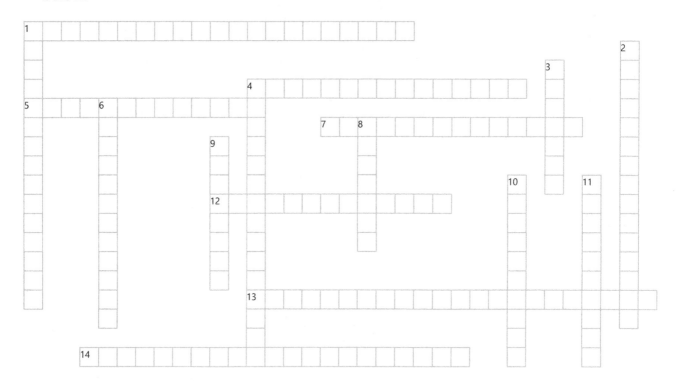

ACROSS

1. A market-derived figure that represents the amount an entrepreneur receives for their contribution.
4. The price at which the property would change hands between a willing buyer and a willing seller and both having reasonable knowledge of relevant facts.
5. The date on which the analyses, opinions, and advice in an appraisal, review, or consulting service apply.
7. The price of a property with above- or below-market financing expressed in terms of the price that would have been paid in an all-cash sale.
12. A borrower has possession of the property.
13. Sum of all fixed and variable operating expenses and reserve for replacement.
14. The ratio of total operating expenses to effective gross income

DOWN

1. An agreement put into words (written or spoken).
2. Total area of finished above-grade residential space
3. A tangible or intangible benefit of real property that enhances its attractiveness or increases the satisfaction of the user.
4. Absolute ownership unencumbered by any other interest or estate.
6. an estimate of replacement cost of a structure, less depreciation, plus land value.
8. Zoning regulations that designate the distance a building must be set back from the front, rear, and sides of the property lines.
9. The periodic income attributable to the interests in real property.
10. Annual crops and plantings such as corn, wheat, and vegetables.
11. Value a specific property has to a specific person or firm for a specific use.

A. Effective Date
D. Setback
G. Fair Market Value
J. Gross Living Area
M. Fee Simple Estate
P. Hypothication

B. Total Operating Expenses
E. Express contract
H. Amenity
K. Cost Approach
N. Entrepreneurial profit

C. Cash Equivalent
F. Emblements
I. Cash Flow
L. Value in use
O. Operating Expense Ratio

2. Using the Across and Down clues, write the correct words in the numbered grid below.

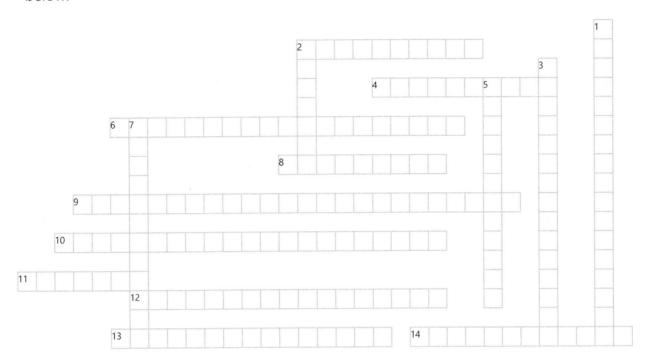

ACROSS

2. Value of a superior property is adversely affected by its association with an inferior property of the same type.
4. Value a specific property has to a specific person or firm for a specific use.
6. A letter or statement that serves as a notice of delivery from the appraiser to the client of a report containing an opinion or conclusion concerning real estate
8. Stage in market area's life cycle. The market area experiences equilibrium without market gains or losses.
9. The process by which all roads are grouped into classes or systems according to the character of service they are intended to provide.
10. The wear and tear that begins with the building is completed and placed into service.
11. Principle that real property value is created and sustained when contrasting, opposing, or interacting elements are in a state of equilibrium.
12. An appraiser's opinions or conclusions developed specific to an assignment.
13. A limitation that passes with the land regardless of the owner.
14. The right for the construction, maintenance, and operation of a rail line on a property.

DOWN

1. A condition that limits the use of a report.
2. A remainder that has negligible economic utility or value due to its size, shape, or other detrimental characteristics.
3. Absolute ownership unencumbered by any other interest or estate.
5. Complementary land uses; inhabitants, buildings, or business enterprises.
7. The difference between an improvements total economic life and its remaining economic life.

A. Deed restriction
D. Functional Classification
G. Remnant
J. Limiting Condition
M. Letter of Transmittal

B. Rail Easement
E. Balance
H. Regression
K. Effective age
N. Fee Simple Estate

C. Physical Deterioration
F. Neighborhood
I. Stability
L. Value in use
O. Assignment Results

3. Using the Across and Down clues, write the correct words in the numbered grid below.

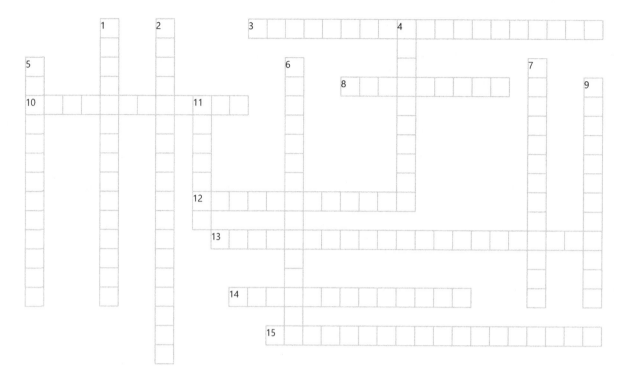

ACROSS

3. Easement that is attached to, benefits, and passes with the conveyance of the dominant estate. Burdens the servient estate.
8. The condition of dying without a will.
10. The right for the construction, maintenance, and operation of a rail line on a property.
12. Something that has been added or appended to a property and has since become an inherent part of the property.
13. The estimated period during which improvements will continue to represent the highest and best use of the property.
14. An agreement in which all the elements of a contract are present and, therefore, legally enforceable.
15. Only one party makes a promise

DOWN

1. An agreement put into words (written or spoken).
2. A statistical measure that attempts to determine the strength of the relationship between one dependent variable and a series of other changing variables.
4. The combining of 2 or more parcels into one ownership (tract).
5. Voluntary and one of the most common types of liens.
6. A limitation that passes with the land regardless of the owner.
7. In accounting, a category for property under the modified accelerated cost recovery system.
9. One cause of depreciation.
11. Going to the State. The process that should a property be abandoned, it reverts back to the state.

A. Deed restriction
B. Remaining Economic Life
C. Obsolescence
D. Regression Analysis
E. Intestate
F. Unilateral contract
G. Easement appurtenant
H. Express contract
I. Mortgage liens
J. Rail Easement
K. Escheat
L. Valid contract
M. Assemblage
N. Property Class
O. Appurtenance

4. Using the Across and Down clues, write the correct words in the numbered grid below.

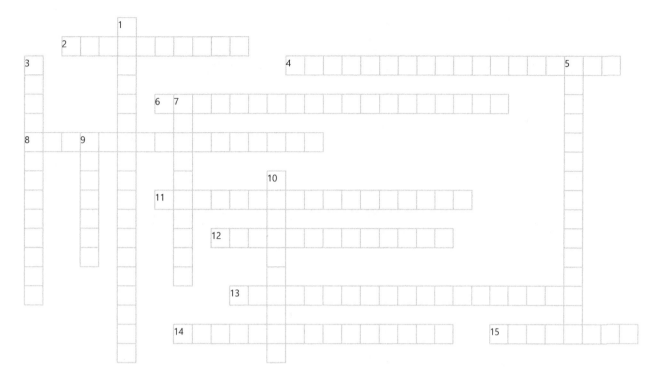

ACROSS

2. Seizure of property by court order.
4. Right to undisturbed use and control of designated air space above a specific land area within stated elevations.
6. The last phase in the development of the value opinion in which two or more value indications derived from market data are resolved into a value opinion.
8. Dollar amount required to construct an exact duplicate of the subject improvements, at current prices.
11. A promise made in exchange for another promise.
12. Newly constructed housing units; includes both single-family and multifamily domiciles.
13. The opinion of value derived from the reconciliation of value indications and stated in the appraisal report
14. Value to a particular individual. The present worth of anticipated future benefits.
15. An increase in value when extra utility is created by combining smaller parcels under single ownership.

DOWN

1. Two or more sales are compared to derive an indication of the size of the adjustment for a single characteristic.
3. Soft cost expenditures that are necessary components but are not typically part of the construction contract.
5. A right granted or taken for the construction, maintenance, and operation of the highway.
7. Temporary use to which a site or improved property is put until it is ready to be put to its future highest and best use.
9. A remainder that has negligible economic utility or value due to its size, shape, or other detrimental characteristics.
10. A transaction in which the buyers and sellers of a product act independently and have no relationship to each other.

A. Supra surface rights
B. Final Opinion of Value
C. Arms Length
D. Housing Starts
E. Attachment
F. Final Reconciliation
G. Highway Easement
H. Bilateral contract
I. Remnant
J. Interim use
K. Reproduction Cost
L. Investment Value
M. Indirect costs
N. Paired data analysis
O. Plottage

5. Using the Across and Down clues, write the correct words in the numbered grid below.

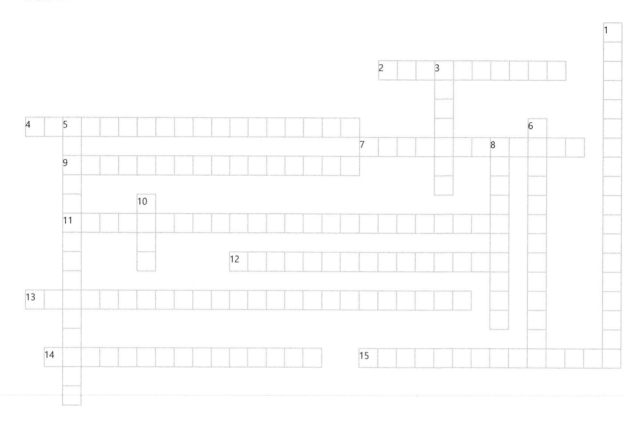

ACROSS

2. The combining of 2 or more parcels into one ownership (tract).
4. Only one party makes a promise
7. Data that is analyzed through the process of comparison.
9. The right to construct, operate, and maintain a pipeline over the lands of others within prescribed geographical limits.
11. The amount entrepreneur expects to receive for his or her contribution to the project.
12. Price an economic good will attract in the competitive market.
13. The process by which all roads are grouped into classes or systems according to the character of service they are intended to provide.
14. Divided or undivided rights in real estate that represent less than the whole.
15. Created intentionally by property owner's actions. i.e. mortgage

DOWN

1. The parties involved in the transfer of property rights. Includes buyers, sellers, lessors, lessees, and brokers and their agents.
3. The wearing away of surface land by natural causes.
5. Ann agreement that is presumed to exist because of the parties' actions.
6. The process of valuing a universe of properties as of a given date using standard methodology, employing common data, and allowing for statistical testing.
8. The state of having the requisite or adequate ability or qualities to perform the specific assignment and produce credible assignment results.
10. Written, legal instrument that conveys an estate or interest in real property to someone else, assuming it is executed and delivered.

A. Erosion
B. Competence
C. Mass Appraisal
D. Implied contract
E. Specific Data
F. Voluntary liens
G. Partial Interest
H. Entrepreneurial Incentive
I. Assemblage
J. Deed
K. Unilateral contract
L. Functional Classification
M. Pipeline Easement
N. Market Participants
O. Value in Exchange

6. Using the Across and Down clues, write the correct words in the numbered grid below.

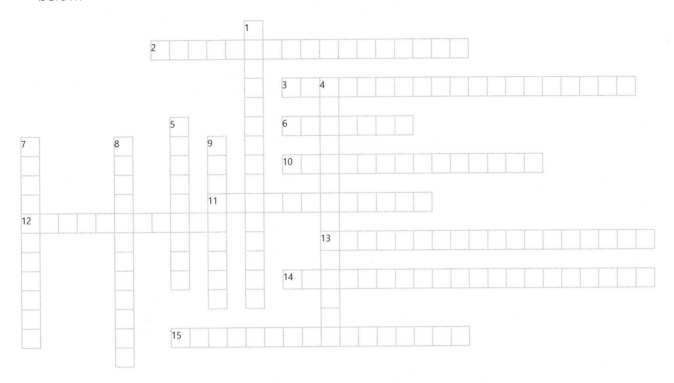

ACROSS

2. Annual amount of total revenue that a property would generate if it were occupied all throughout the year.
3. One of the four criteria the highest and best use of a property must meet.
6. The employment of a site or holding to produce revenue or other benefits.
10. Study of real estate market conditions for specific types of property.
11. In final reconciliation, the range in which the final market value opinion of a property may fall; usually stated as the interval between a high and low value limit.
12. The most probable price at which real estate would sell.
13. Income-producing property such as office and retail buildings.
14. The annualized yield or rate of return on capital that is generated or capable of being generated within an investment or portfolio over a period of ownership.
15. A systematic set of procedures an appraiser follows to provide answers to a client's questions about real property value.

DOWN

1. Ann agreement that is presumed to exist because of the parties' actions.
4. Neighborhood phenomenon in which middle- and upper-income persons purchase neighborhood properties and renovate or rehabilitate them.
5. Stage in market area's life cycle. The market area experiences equilibrium without market gains or losses.
7. Any claim or liability that affects our limits the title to property.
8. The degree, nature, or extent of interest that a person has in land.
9. An increase in dry land created by the gradual accumulation of waterborne solid material over formerly riparian land.

A. Valuation process
D. Encumbrance
G. Estate in land
J. Stability
M. Internal Rate of Return

B. Legal Permissibility
E. Accretion
H. Gross Market Income
K. Implied contract
N. Range of Value

C. Gentrification
F. Commercial Property
I. Land Use
L. Market Value
O. Market Analysis

7. Using the Across and Down clues, write the correct words in the numbered grid below.

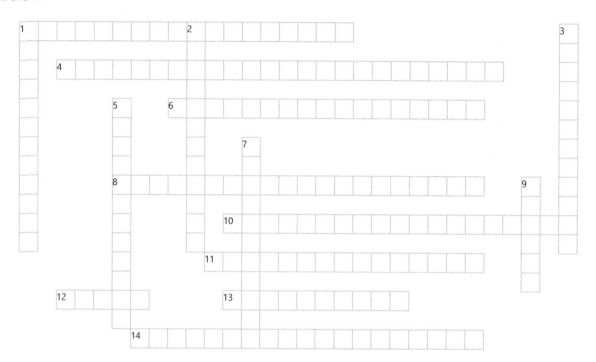

ACROSS

1. The readjustment of the value of an appreciated asset for tax purposes upon inheritance.
4. The process by which all roads are grouped into classes or systems according to the character of service they are intended to provide.
6. Ratio of NOI to annual debt service.
8. An allowance that provides for the periodic replacement of building components that wear out more rapidly than the building itself.
10. A study of the cost-benefit relationships of an economic endeavor.
11. The price at which the property would change hands between a willing buyer and a willing seller and both having reasonable knowledge of relevant facts.
12. Amount a particular purchaser agrees to pay and a particular seller agrees to accept under the circumstances surrounding their transaction.
13. One who owns an interest in real property for his or her own lifetime.
14. A vacant or in proof parcel of land devoted to or available for use as a residence.

DOWN

1. The price expected for a whole property (e.g., a house) or a part of a property (e.g., a plumbing fixture) that is removed from the premises usually for use elsewhere.
2. In final reconciliation, the range in which the final market value opinion of a property may fall; usually stated as the interval between a high and low value limit.
3. Operating expenses that generally do not vary with occupancy and that prudent management will pay whether the properties occupied or vacant.
5. Something that has been added or appended to a property and has since become an inherent part of the property.
7. A rivalry between buyers or between sellers.
9. One who conveys the rights of occupancy and use to others under lease agreement.

A. Competition
B. Fair Market Value
C. Lessor
D. Functional Classification
E. Appurtenance
F. Debt coverage ratio
G. Fixed Expense
H. Price
I. Residential Property
J. Replacement Allowance
K. Salvage Value
L. Range of Value
M. Life tenant
N. Feasibility Analysis
O. Step Up Depreciation

8. Using the Across and Down clues, write the correct words in the numbered grid below.

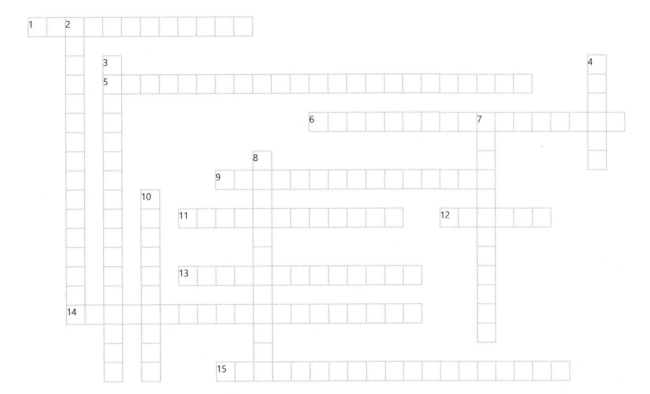

ACROSS

1. One cause of depreciation.
5. An element of comparison in the sales comparison approach.
6. Total floor area of a building, excluding unenclosed area, measured from the exterior of the walls of the above-grade area.
9. An agreement put into words (written or spoken).
11. Has no legal force or binding effect and cannot be enforced in a court of law.
12. A series of related changes brought about by a chain of causes and effects.
13. A part of an appraisal report in which the appraiser certifies that the work was completed according to the applicable standards.
14. Net income that is left after the 4 agents of production have been paid.
15. Is used for elements that cannot be given a numerical value.

DOWN

2. Rights to the use and profits of the underground portion of a designated property.
3. Person who is entitled to an estate after a prior estate or interest has expired
4. The party of parties who engage an appraiser in a specific assignment.
7. A sale involving a seller acting under undue distress.
8. Data that is analyzed through the process of comparison.
10. A type of renovation that involves modification or updating of existing improvements.

A. Express contract
D. Client
G. Qualitative analysis
J. Economic Characteristics
M. Specific Data

B. Remainder interest
E. Certification
H. Obsolescence
K. Gross Building Area
N. Subsurface rights

C. Remodeling
F. Trends
I. Surplus Productivity
L. Distress Sale
O. Void contract

9. Using the Across and Down clues, write the correct words in the numbered grid below.

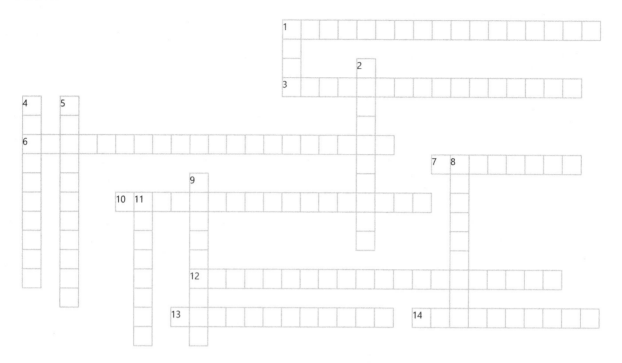

ACROSS

1. Flow of savings account money from savings and loans accounts to higher yield investments.
3. An appraisal report in which the scope of work includes an exterior-only viewing of the subject property.
6. Damage to property arising as a consequence of a taking over and above direct damages.
7. A projected income and expense statement for proposed development.
10. Price per cubic foot, front foot, and per apartment.
12. The total annual income the rental property produces after subtracting vacancy losses and adding miscellaneous income.
13. Part of the purchase price given to bind a bargain.
14. The more a property or its components are in harmony with the surrounding properties or components, the greater the contributory value.

DOWN

1. Written, legal instrument that conveys an estate or interest in real property to someone else, assuming it is executed and delivered.
2. Value of a superior property is adversely affected by its association with an inferior property of the same type.
4. Land that is not needed to serve or support the existing improvement.
5. Items of information on value influences that derive from social, economic, governmental, and environmental forces and originate outside the property being appraised.
8. A lump sum benefit that an investor receives or expects to receive upon the termination of an investment; also called reversionary benefit.
9. A tax on the estate or wealth of the deceased person that is usually computed as a percentage of the market value of the assets of the estate.
11. A lease in which the landlord passes on all expenses to the tenant.

A. Regression
D. General Data
G. Net Lease
J. Earnest money
M. Effective Gross Income

B. Pro Forma
E. Deed
H. Consequential Damages
K. Units of comparison
N. Excess Land

C. Disintermediation
F. Reversion
I. Drive by Appraisal
L. Conformity
O. Estate Tax

10. Using the Across and Down clues, write the correct words in the numbered grid below.

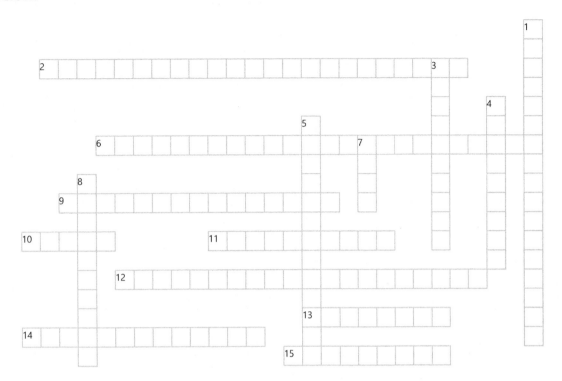

ACROSS

2. A category of elements of comparison in the sales comparison approach
6. The amount entrepreneur expects to receive for his or her contribution to the project.
9. Total area of finished above-grade residential space
10. A contract in which the rights to use and occupy land or structures are transferred by the owner to another for a specified period of time in return for specified rent.
11. The most probable rent the property should bring in a competitive and open market reflecting all conditions and restrictions of the lease agreement.
12. Relevant characteristics used to compare and adjust the property prices.
13. The sudden removal of land from the property of one owner to that of another, e.g., change in the course of a river.
14. Voluntary and one of the most common types of liens.
15. A tax on the estate or wealth of the deceased person that is usually computed as a percentage of the market value of the assets of the estate.

DOWN

1. Involuntary transfer of property takes place when a party makes a property claim by taking possession over a period of years.
3. The state of having the requisite or adequate ability or qualities to perform the specific assignment and produce credible assignment results.
4. The amount of money borrowed from lender (mortgagee).
5. In accounting, a category for property under the modified accelerated cost recovery system.
7. first thing a developer considers in developing a property is the cost of land.
8. A transaction in which the buyers and sellers of a product act independently and have no relationship to each other.

A. Entrepreneurial Incentive
D. Adverse possession
G. Elements of comparison
J. Physical Characteristics
M. Competence

B. Avulsion
E. Gross Living Area
H. Principle
K. Mortgage liens
N. Lease

C. Property Class
F. Land
I. Arms Length
L. Estate Tax
O. Market Rent

11. Using the Across and Down clues, write the correct words in the numbered grid below.

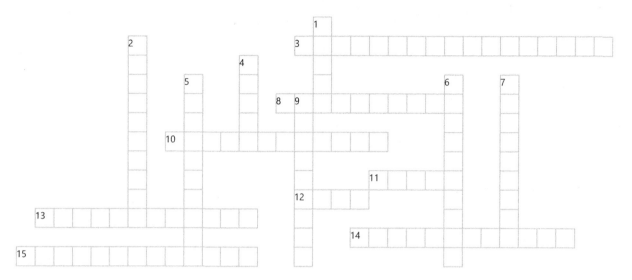

ACROSS

3. The tenant's possessory interest created by a lease.
8. The period of time over which a structure may reasonably be expected to perform the function for which it was designed.
10. In appraising, a loss in property value from any cause
11. Amount a particular purchaser agrees to pay and a particular seller agrees to accept under the circumstances surrounding their transaction.
12. first thing a developer considers in developing a property is the cost of land.
13. The price expected for a whole property (e.g., a house) or a part of a property (e.g., a plumbing fixture) that is removed from the premises usually for use elsewhere.
14. One cause of depreciation.
15. A part of an appraisal report in which the appraiser certifies that the work was completed according to the applicable standards.

DOWN

1. A contract in which the rights to use and occupy land or structures are transferred by the owner to another for a specified period of time in return for specified rent.
2. The entire taking of the full real property interest of a parcel for public use under the power of eminent domain; requires the payment of compensation.
4. Combination of all elements that constitute proof of ownership.
5. One who owns an interest in real property for his or her own lifetime.
6. An appraisal review in which the reviewer's scope of work does not include an inspection of the subject property.
7. The condition of dying without a will.
9. Stage in market area's life cycle. The market area experiences equilibrium without market gains or losses.

A. Useful life	B. Title
E. Life tenant	F. Intestate
I. Leasehold Interest	J. Obsolescence
M. Lease	N. Land

C. Price	D. Stability
G. Certification	H. Depreciation
K. Full Taking	L. Salvage Value
O. Desk Review	

12. Using the Across and Down clues, write the correct words in the numbered grid below.

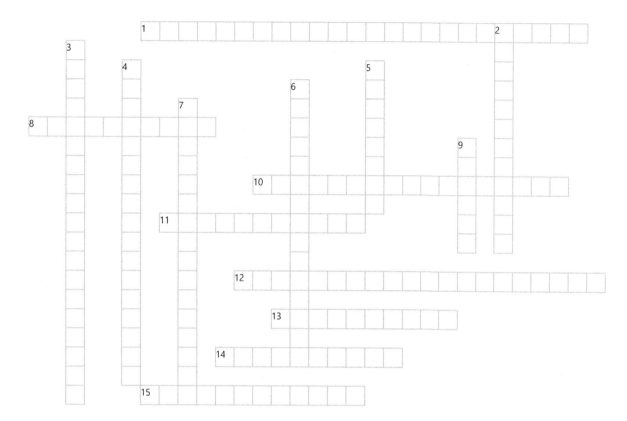

ACROSS

1. The process by which all roads are grouped into classes or systems according to the character of service they are intended to provide.
8. The most probable rent the property should bring in a competitive and open market reflecting all conditions and restrictions of the lease agreement.
10. When the value of a business plus the amount of real property is sought.
11. Any claim or liability that affects our limits the title to property.
12. A method used to convert an estimate of a single year's income expectancy into an indication of value in one direct step
13. The cost to restore an item of deferred maintenance to new or reasonably new condition.
14. One who owns an interest in real property for his or her own lifetime.
15. Depriving an abutting owner of the inherent rights of ingress and to egress from the highway or street.

DOWN

2. Something that has been added or appended to a property and has since become an inherent part of the property.
3. Needed repairs or replacement of items that should have taken place during the course of normal maintenance.
4. The change in the value of a property as a whole, resulting from the addition or deletion of a property component.
5. Right of government to raise revenue through assessments on valuable goods, products, and rights.
6. The written or oral communication of an appraisal.
7. Created by law, rather than by choice. i.e. property tax lien.
9. Public regulation of the character and extent of real estate use though police power.

A. Life tenant
D. Functional Classification
G. Involuntary liens
J. Direct Capitalization
M. Loss of Access

B. Contributory Value
E. Zoning
H. Cost to Cure
K. Market Rent
N. Appraisal Report

C. Encumbrance
F. Deferred Maintenance
I. Going concern value
L. Appurtenance
O. Taxation

13. Using the Across and Down clues, write the correct words in the numbered grid below.

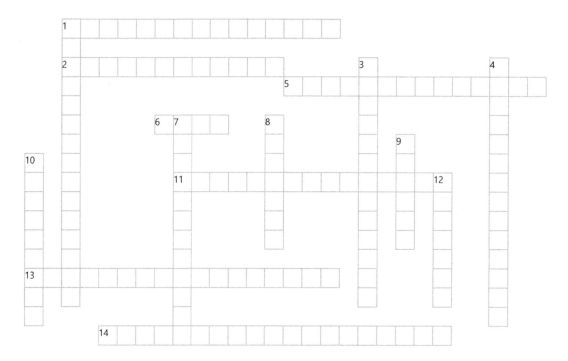

ACROSS

1. An agreement put into words (written or spoken).
2. The value of a future payment or series of future payments discounted to the current date or to time period zero.
5. The price of a property with above- or below-market financing expressed in terms of the price that would have been paid in an all-cash sale.
6. Written, legal instrument that conveys an estate or interest in real property to someone else, assuming it is executed and delivered.
11. An ordinal technique for analyzing data, commonly used in the analysis of comparable sales.
13. The dwelling that is designated for occupancy by one family.
14. The impairment of functional capacity of a property according to market tastes and standards.

DOWN

1. Testimony of persons who are presumed to have special knowledge of, or skill in, a particular field due to education, experience, or study.
3. The development or improvement of cleared or undeveloped land in an urban renewal area.
4. A stage in a market area's life cycle characterized by renewal, redevelopment, modernization, and increasing demand.
7. Trespassing on the domain of another.
8. A remainder that has negligible economic utility or value due to its size, shape, or other detrimental characteristics.
9. One who is the right to occupancy and use of the property of another for a period of time according to a lease agreement.
10. The act or process of developing an opinion of value.
12. Zoning regulations that designate the distance a building must be set back from the front, rear, and sides of the property lines.

A. Encroachment
D. Remnant
G. Appraisal
J. Redevelopment
M. Revitalization

B. Ranking Analysis
E. Deed
H. Setback
K. Functional Obsolesce
N. Single Family House

C. Cash Equivalent
F. Express contract
I. Expert Testimony
L. Lessee
O. Present Value

14. Using the Across and Down clues, write the correct words in the numbered grid below.

ACROSS

2. The parties involved in the transfer of property rights. Includes buyers, sellers, lessors, lessees, and brokers and their agents.
4. The type and extent of research and analyses in appraisal or appraisal review assignment.
6. The amount entrepreneur expects to receive for his or her contribution to the project.
8. Only one party makes a promise
10. The present or anticipated undersupply of an item relative to the demand for it. Conditions of scarcity contribute to value.
11. The legal process of settling an estate after a person has died.
14. Easement that is attached to, benefits, and passes with the conveyance of the dominant estate. Burdens the servient estate.
15. A future possessor read interest in real estate that is given to a third-party and matures upon the termination of a limited or determinable be.

DOWN

1. A systematic set of procedures an appraiser follows to provide answers to a client's questions about real property value.
3. The period over time which a structure may be competitive in the market.
5. A form of ownership in which each owner possesses the exclusive right to use and occupy an allotted unit plus an undivided interest in common areas.
7. Right of government to raise revenue through assessments on valuable goods, products, and rights.
9. The relative position of the property to competitive properties and other value influences in its market area
12. Right or interest in property.
13. The result of the cause and effect relationship among the forces that influence real property value.

A. Entrepreneurial Incentive
D. Easement appurtenant
G. Scarcity
J. Market Participants
M. Taxation

B. Remainder
E. Economic life
H. Change
K. Estate
N. Location

C. Condominium
F. Probate
I. Unilateral contract
L. Scope of Work
O. Valuation process

15. Using the Across and Down clues, write the correct words in the numbered grid below.

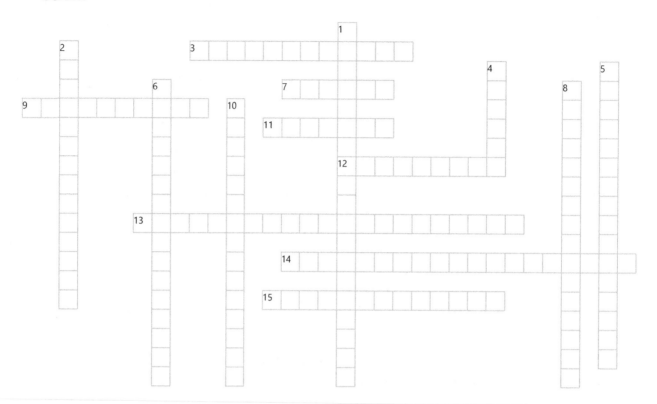

ACROSS

3. The value of a future payment or series of future payments discounted to the current date or to time period zero.
7. Public regulation of the character and extent of real estate use though police power.
9. The period of time over which a structure may reasonably be expected to perform the function for which it was designed.
11. The employment of a site or holding to produce revenue or other benefits.
12. The amount of money borrowed from lender (mortgagee).
13. Adjustments for differences between the subject and comparable properties expressed as a percentage of the sale price of the comparable property.
14. The impairment of functional capacity of a property according to market tastes and standards.
15. Newly constructed housing units; includes both single-family and multifamily domiciles.

DOWN

1. One of the four criteria the highest and best use of a property must meet; the selected land-use must yield the highest value of the possible uses.
2. Property taxes or special assessments, has priority over other liens.
4. Purchaser's wish for an item to satisfy human needs or individual wants beyond essential life-support needs.
5. The number of years since a structure or bldg. was originally built (birth).
6. The right to construct, operate, and maintain a pipeline over the lands of others within prescribed geographical limits.
8. Buyers and sellers of particular real estate and the transactions that occur among them.
10. Price an economic good will attract in the competitive market.

A. Useful life
B. Percentage Adjustments
C. Functional Obsolesce
D. Present Value
E. Real Estate Market
F. Housing Starts
G. Maximum Productivity
H. Land Use
I. Zoning
J. Chronological age
K. Desire
L. Value in Exchange
M. Principle
N. Pipeline Easement
O. Government lien

16. Using the Across and Down clues, write the correct words in the numbered grid below.

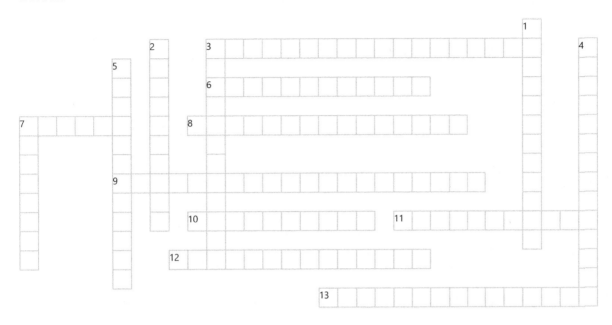

ACROSS

3. Any rate used to convert income into value.
6. Lien against a particular property owned by the debtor.
7. One who conveys the rights of occupancy and use to others under lease agreement.
8. The price at which the property would change hands between a willing buyer and a willing seller and both having reasonable knowledge of relevant facts.
9. An interest in real property restricting future land-use to preservation, conservation, wildlife habitat, or some combination of those uses.
10. A comprehensive, long-range official plan that guides the physical growth and development of the community.
11. A private or public partnership that pools funds for the acquisition and development of real estate projects or other business ventures.
12. The repair and restoration of existing improvements that are in poor condition to a state that makes the property competitive again.
13. Value to a particular individual. The present worth of anticipated future benefits.

DOWN

1. The interests, benefits, and rights inherent in ownership of real estate.
2. The state of having the requisite or adequate ability or qualities to perform the specific assignment and produce credible assignment results.
3. an estimate of replacement cost of a structure, less depreciation, plus land value.
4. Estimate of the rate at which a particular class of properties will sell in a particular geographic area.
5. Trespassing on the domain of another.
7. The relative position of the property to competitive properties and other value influences in its market area

A. Cost Approach
D. Master Plan
G. Capitalization Rate
J. Investment Value
M. Specific Lien

B. Absorption rate
E. Real Property
H. Lessor
K. Rehabilitation
N. Encroachment

C. Fair Market Value
F. Competence
I. Conservation Easement
L. Location
O. Syndication

17. Using the Across and Down clues, write the correct words in the numbered grid below.

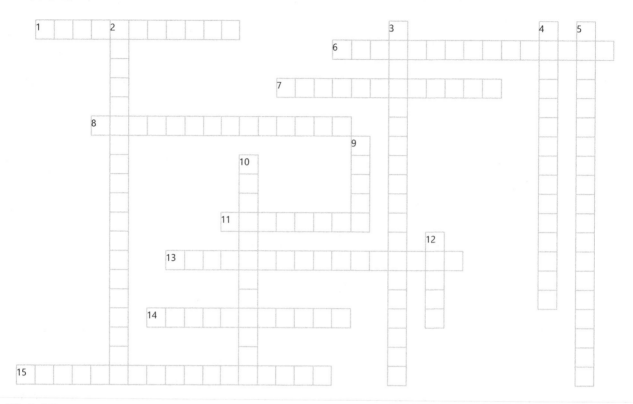

ACROSS

1. The type and extent of research and analyses in appraisal or appraisal review assignment.
6. Value to a particular individual. The present worth of anticipated future benefits.
7. Depriving an abutting owner of the inherent rights of ingress and to egress from the highway or street.
8. The repair and restoration of existing improvements that are in poor condition to a state that makes the property competitive again.
11. Pledge of a described property interest as collateral or security for the repayment of a loan under certain terms and conditions.
13. An appraisal report in which the scope of work includes an exterior-only viewing of the subject property.
14. Value of an inferior property is enhanced by its association with better properties of the same type.
15. The periodic expenditures necessary to maintain the real property and continue production of the effective gross income, assuming prudent and competent management.

DOWN

2. Easement that is attached to, benefits, and passes with the conveyance of the dominant estate. Burdens the servient estate.
3. One of the four criteria the highest and best use of a property must meet.
4. An ordinal technique for analyzing data, commonly used in the analysis of comparable sales.
5. Net income that is left after the 4 agents of production have been paid.
9. Amount a particular purchaser agrees to pay and a particular seller agrees to accept under the circumstances surrounding their transaction.
10. One cause of depreciation.
12. Monetary worth of a property, good, or service to buyers and sellers at a given time.

A. Scope of Work	B. Price	C. Loss of Access
D. Operating Expenses	E. Drive by Appraisal	F. Mortgage
G. Investment Value	H. Obsolescence	I. Legal Permissibility
J. Ranking Analysis	K. Easement appurtenant	L. Rehabilitation
M. Progression	N. Surplus Productivity	O. Value

18. Using the Across and Down clues, write the correct words in the numbered grid below.

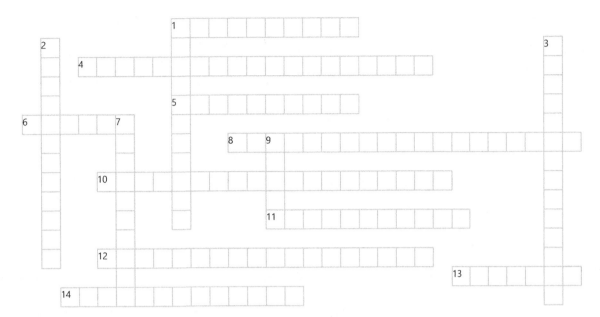

ACROSS

1. The most probable rent the property should bring in a competitive and open market reflecting all conditions and restrictions of the lease agreement.
4. A letter or statement that serves as a notice of delivery from the appraiser to the client of a report containing an opinion or conclusion concerning real estate
5. Annual crops and plantings such as corn, wheat, and vegetables.
6. The result of the cause and effect relationship among the forces that influence real property value.
8. The legal responsibility of a plaintiff to make reasonable efforts, after an injury or breach of contract, to alleviate the effects of the injury or breach.
10. A study of the cost-benefit relationships of an economic endeavor.
11. Any claim or liability that affects our limits the title to property.
12. Two or more sales are compared to derive an indication of the size of the adjustment for a single characteristic.
13. Ability of a product to satisfy a human want, need, or desire.
14. A lease in which an intermediate, or sandwich, leaseholder is the lessee of one party and the lessor of another.

DOWN

1. Amount paid for an income producing property.
2. Complementary land uses; inhabitants, buildings, or business enterprises.
3. The rights of an owner to possess, control, enjoy, sell, lease, mortgage, and dispose of the property.
7. Land that is not needed to serve or support the existing improvement.
9. Combination of all elements that constitute proof of ownership.

A. Excess Land
D. Encumbrance
G. Paired data analysis
J. Bundle of rights
M. Market Rent

B. Utility
E. Change
H. Neighborhood
K. Mitigation of Damages
N. Sandwich lease

C. Title
F. Market Price
I. Feasibility Analysis
L. Emblements
O. Letter of Transmittal

19. Using the Across and Down clues, write the correct words in the numbered grid below.

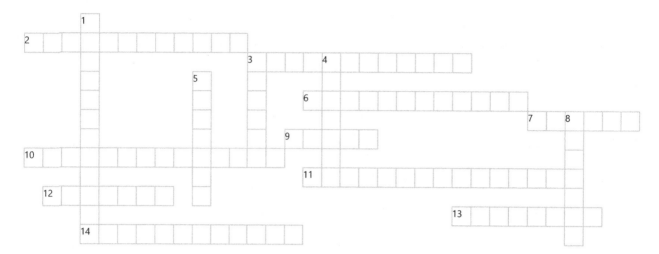

ACROSS

2. The ratio of income or yield to the original investment.
3. The interests, benefits, and rights inherent in ownership of real estate.
6. an estimate of replacement cost of a structure, less depreciation, plus land value.
7. The result of the cause and effect relationship among the forces that influence real property value.
9. A contract in which the rights to use and occupy land or structures are transferred by the owner to another for a specified period of time in return for specified rent.
10. Rights pertaining to properties touching a river or stream.
11. Estate owned by 2 or more persons, each of whom has an equal undivided interest. Unlike Joint Tenancy and Tenancy by Entirety, No right of survivorship.
12. Ability of a product to satisfy a human want, need, or desire.
13. The minimum rate of return on invested capital.
14. Complementary land uses; inhabitants, buildings, or business enterprises.

DOWN

1. In appraising, a loss in property value from any cause
3. Any communication, written or oral, of an appraisal or appraisal review that is transmitted to the client upon completion of an assignment.
4. The legal process of settling an estate after a person has died.
5. A stage of diminishing demand in a market areas life cycle.
8. A tangible or intangible benefit of real property that enhances its attractiveness or increases the satisfaction of the user.

A. Real Property
E. Cost Approach
I. Utility
M. Tenancy in Common

B. Riparian rights
F. Lease
J. Rate of return
N. Decline

C. Report
G. Amenity
K. Neighborhood
O. Depreciation

D. Probate
H. Change
L. Safe Rate

20. Using the Across and Down clues, write the correct words in the numbered grid below.

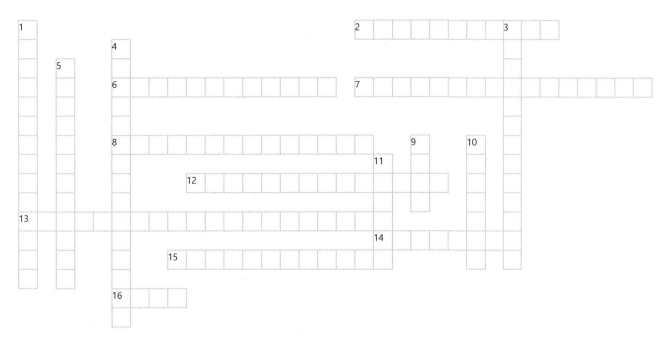

ACROSS

2. A shortened term for similar property sales, rentals, or operating expenses used for comparison in the valuation process.
6. When a property has the lowest asking price and the same utility as other properties, yet attracts the greatest demand.
7. The number of years since a structure or bldg. was originally built (birth).
8. Supply and demand for housing, economic activity.
12. Property taxes or special assessments, has priority over other liens.
13. An element of depreciation; and diminution in value caused by negative externalities and generally incurable on the part of the owner, landlord, or tenant.
14. A lease in which the landlord passes on all expenses to the tenant.
15. Trespassing on the domain of another.
16. land that is improved so that is ready to be used for a specific purpose.

DOWN

1. The manner in which a transaction was financed.
3. A building component with an expected remaining economic life that is the same as the remaining economic life of the entire structure.
4. Easement that is not attached or appurtenant to any particular estate; does not run with the land nor is it transferred through the conveyance of title.
5. The value of a particular component is measured in terms of the amount it adds to the value of the whole property.
9. Charge against property in which the property is the security for payment of the debt.
10. goods, such as equipment (machinery and tools), bldgs., and infrastructure.
11. The party of parties who engage an appraiser in a specific assignment.

A. Capital
D. Site
G. Net Lease
J. Government lien
M. Contribution
P. Economic Forces

B. Substitution
E. Financing Terms
H. Client
K. Easement in gross
N. Long Lived Item

C. Encroachment
F. Comparables
I. Lien
L. Chronological age
O. External Obsolescence

21. Using the Across and Down clues, write the correct words in the numbered grid below.

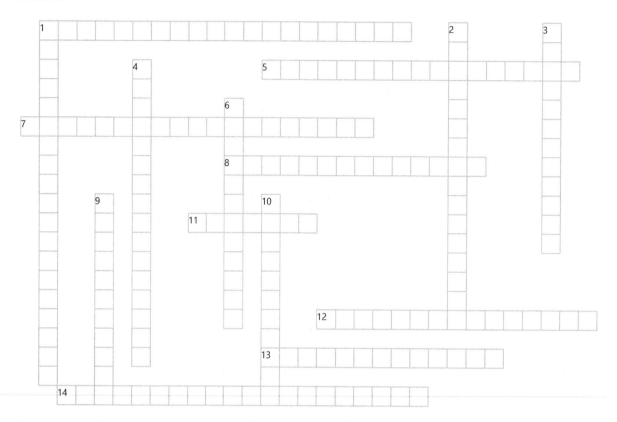

ACROSS

1. One of the four criteria the highest and best use of a property must meet.
5. An appraiser's opinions or conclusions developed specific to an assignment.
7. The last phase in the development of the value opinion in which two or more value indications derived from market data are resolved into a value opinion.
8. The conversion of income into value.
11. Time and distance relationships between a particular use and supporting facilities.
12. Price an economic good will attract in the competitive market.
13. Soft cost expenditures that are necessary components but are not typically part of the construction contract.
14. Analyzing value of a property based on numerical data.

DOWN

1. The impairment of functional capacity of a property according to market tastes and standards.
2. The number of years since a structure or bldg. was originally built (birth).
3. Value is a function of expected benefits to get from the ownership of the property.
4. An easement for the construction, maintenance, and operation of a full line, usually for the transmission of electric power.
6. The yield rate used to convert future payments or receipts into present value; usually considered to be a synonym for yield rate.
9. Items of information on value influences that derive from social, economic, governmental, and environmental forces and originate outside the property being appraised.
10. Amount paid for an income producing property.

A. Discount Rate
D. Market Price
G. Pole Line Easement
J. Value in Exchange
M. Indirect costs

B. Capitalization
E. Quantitative Analysis
H. Functional Obsolesce
K. Assignment Results
N. Financial Feasibility

C. Linkage
F. Anticipation
I. Final Reconciliation
L. Chronological age
O. General Data

22. Using the Across and Down clues, write the correct words in the numbered grid below.

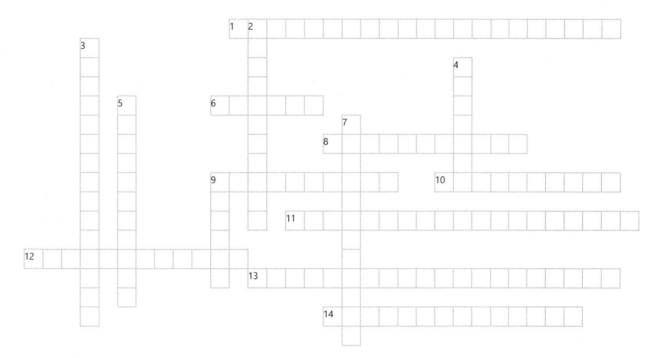

ACROSS

1. A process for examining the productive attributes of the specific property, its demand and supply, and its geographic market area.
6. One who is the right to occupancy and use of the property of another for a period of time according to a lease agreement.
8. Any claim or liability that affects our limits the title to property.
9. The more a property or its components are in harmony with the surrounding properties or components, the greater the contributory value.
10. The process in which older structures or historic buildings are modernized, remodeled, or restored.
11. One of the four criteria the highest and best use of a property must meet; the selected land-use must yield the highest value of the possible uses.
12. Trespassing on the domain of another.
13. The total income attributable to real property at full occupancy before vacancy and operating expenses are deducted.
14. Guiding control of the money supply in the economy.

DOWN

2. Changes made to basic data to facilitate comparison or understanding.
3. Easement that is not attached or appurtenant to any particular estate; does not run with the land nor is it transferred through the conveyance of title.
4. Time and distance relationships between a particular use and supporting facilities.
5. Information that is gathered in its original form by the analyst.
7. Value is a function of expected benefits to get from the ownership of the property.
9. The party of parties who engage an appraiser in a specific assignment.

A. Renovation
D. Marketability Analysis
G. Client
J. Monetary Policy
M. Lessee

B. Anticipation
E. Linkage
H. Conformity
K. Potential Gross Income
N. Encroachment

C. Adjustments
F. Encumbrance
I. Primary Data
L. Easement in gross
O. Maximum Productivity

23. Using the Across and Down clues, write the correct words in the numbered grid below.

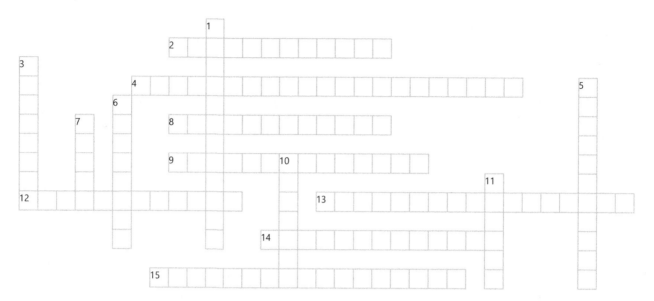

ACROSS

2. Has no legal force or binding effect and cannot be enforced in a court of law.
4. A process for examining the productive attributes of the specific property, its demand and supply, and its geographic market area.
8. The value of a future payment or series of future payments discounted to the current date or to time period zero.
9. The conversion of income into value.
12. Trespassing on the domain of another.
13. Flow of savings account money from savings and loans accounts to higher yield investments.
14. Typically result from a lawsuit in which a monetary judgment is awarded.
15. An appraiser's opinions or conclusions developed specific to an assignment.

DOWN

1. Operating expenses that generally do not vary with occupancy and that prudent management will pay whether the properties occupied or vacant.
3. The annual rate of return on capital that is commensurate with the risk assumed by the investor; the rate of interest or yield necessary to attract capital.
5. A form of ownership in which each owner possesses the exclusive right to use and occupy an allotted unit plus an undivided interest in common areas.
6. Pledge of a described property interest as collateral or security for the repayment of a loan under certain terms and conditions.
7. comprises of all costs required to construct and market the product as land alone or with improvements.
10. The employment of a site or holding to produce revenue or other benefits.
11. One who is the right to occupancy and use of the property of another for a period of time according to a lease agreement.

A. Assignment Results
D. Marketability Analysis
G. Labor
J. Condominium
M. Lessee

B. Void contract
E. Risk Rate
H. Fixed Expense
K. Present Value
N. Land Use

C. Disintermediation
F. Capitalization
I. Judgment liens
L. Mortgage
O. Encroachment

24. Using the Across and Down clues, write the correct words in the numbered grid below.

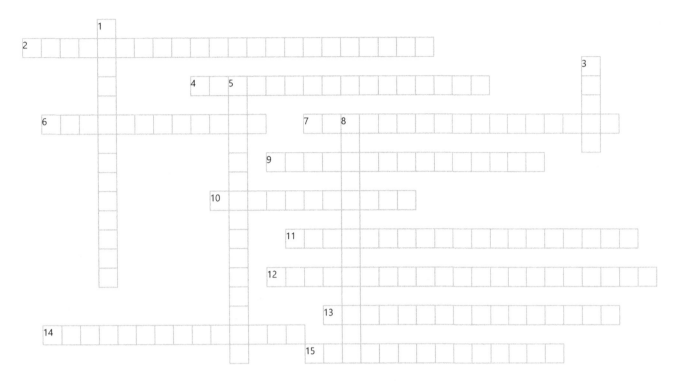

ACROSS

2. An individual or other legal person designated in a will to settle the estate of a deceased person.
4. Created by law, rather than by choice. i.e. property tax lien.
6. A sale involving a seller acting under undue distress.
7. Flow of savings account money from savings and loans accounts to higher yield investments.
9. A limitation that passes with the land regardless of the owner.
10. Any claim or liability that affects our limits the title to property.
11. Needed repairs or replacement of items that should have taken place during the course of normal maintenance.
12. The wear and tear that begins with the building is completed and placed into service.
13. The number of years since a structure or bldg. was originally built (birth).
14. Rights pertaining to properties touching a river or stream.
15. Estimate of the rate at which a particular class of properties will sell in a particular geographic area.

DOWN

1. Created intentionally by property owner's actions. i.e. mortgage
3. comprises of all costs required to construct and market the product as land alone or with improvements.
5. Price an economic good will attract in the competitive market.
8. Land, water, and anything attached to the land-either naturally or placed by human hands.

A. Deferred Maintenance
D. Personal Representative
G. Riparian rights
J. Involuntary liens
M. Physical Deterioration

B. Value in Exchange
E. Encumbrance
H. Surface rights
K. Absorption rate
N. Chronological age

C. Distress Sale
F. Labor
I. Voluntary liens
L. Deed restriction
O. Disintermediation

25. Using the Across and Down clues, write the correct words in the numbered grid below.

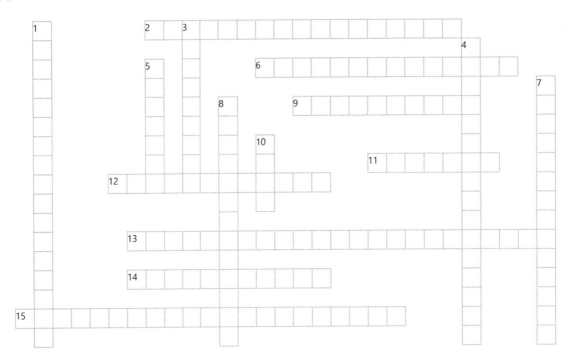

ACROSS

2. The amount of vacant space needed in a market for its orderly operation.
6. A stage in a market area's life cycle characterized by renewal, redevelopment, modernization, and increasing demand.
9. The cost to restore an item of deferred maintenance to new or reasonably new condition.
11. A remainder that has negligible economic utility or value due to its size, shape, or other detrimental characteristics.
12. The value of a future payment or series of future payments discounted to the current date or to time period zero.
13. A category of elements of comparison in the sales comparison approach
14. Amount paid for an income producing property.
15. The estimated period during which improvements will continue to represent the highest and best use of the property.

DOWN

1. Total floor area of a building, excluding unenclosed area, measured from the exterior of the walls of the above-grade area.
3. The condition of dying without a will.
4. The right to construct, operate, and maintain a pipeline over the lands of others within prescribed geographical limits.
5. The legal process of settling an estate after a person has died.
7. arise from construction and other improvements to real estate.
8. A borrower has possession of the property.
10. A plan, map, or chart of a city, town, section, or subdivision indicating the location and boundaries of individual properties.

A. Present Value
D. Probate
G. Market Price
J. Gross Building Area
M. Intestate

B. Remaining Economic Life
E. Revitalization
H. Mechanics liens
K. Hypothication
N. Cost to Cure

C. Remnant
F. Frictional Vacancy
I. Physical Characteristics
L. Pipeline Easement
O. Plat

26. Using the Across and Down clues, write the correct words in the numbered grid below.

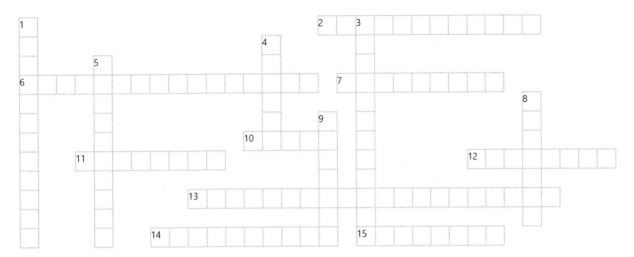

ACROSS

2. Management of government receipts and expenditures.
6. An appraisal report in which the scope of work includes an exterior-only viewing of the subject property.
7. An increase in dry land created by the gradual accumulation of waterborne solid material over formerly riparian land.
10. Amount a particular purchaser agrees to pay and a particular seller agrees to accept under the circumstances surrounding their transaction.
11. Right of government to raise revenue through assessments on valuable goods, products, and rights.
12. The sudden removal of land from the property of one owner to that of another, e.g., change in the course of a river.
13. An interest in real property restricting future land-use to preservation, conservation, wildlife habitat, or some combination of those uses.
14. Seizure of property by court order.
15. A lease in which the landlord passes on all expenses to the tenant.

DOWN

1. Has no legal force or binding effect and cannot be enforced in a court of law.
3. Lien against a particular property owned by the debtor.
4. One who conveys the rights of occupancy and use to others under lease agreement.
5. The process in which older structures or historic buildings are modernized, remodeled, or restored.
8. A stage of diminishing demand in a market areas life cycle.
9. A remainder that has negligible economic utility or value due to its size, shape, or other detrimental characteristics.

A. Net Lease
D. Accretion
G. Decline
J. Price
M. Renovation

B. Conservation Easement
E. Lessor
H. Drive by Appraisal
K. Attachment
N. Avulsion

C. Remnant
F. Specific Lien
I. Void contract
L. Taxation
O. Fiscal Policy

27. Using the Across and Down clues, write the correct words in the numbered grid below.

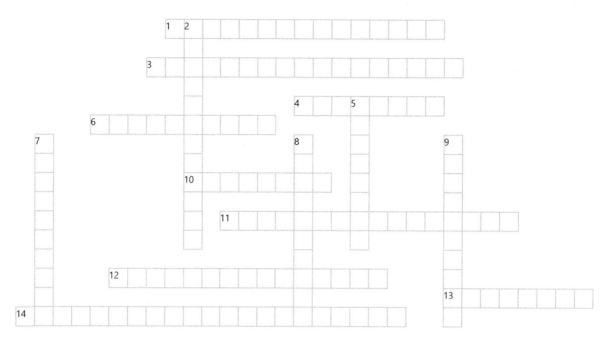

ACROSS

1. Damages that is caused by the remainder's proximity to the improvement being constructed.
3. The change in the value of a property as a whole, resulting from the addition or deletion of a property component.
4. An individual or other legal person designated in a will to settle the estate of the deceased person.
6. An exception to the general zoning regulations; permits specific, usually small, parcels of land to be zone for a use that is not permitted in the surrounding area.
10. The sudden removal of land from the property of one owner to that of another, e.g., change in the course of a river.
11. The number of years since a structure or bldg. was originally built (birth).
12. Divided or undivided rights in real estate that represent less than the whole.
13. Right of government to raise revenue through assessments on valuable goods, products, and rights.
14. A condition which is contrary to what is known by the appraiser to exist on the effective date of the assignment results, but is used for the purpose of analysis.

DOWN

2. In final reconciliation, the range in which the final market value opinion of a property may fall; usually stated as the interval between a high and low value limit.
5. The periodic income attributable to the interests in real property.
7. The more a property or its components are in harmony with the surrounding properties or components, the greater the contributory value.
8. Industrial or commercial site that is abandoned or underused because it suffers from real or perceived continuing contamination.
9. A transaction in which the buyers and sellers of a product act independently and have no relationship to each other.

A. Spot Zoning
D. Avulsion
G. Cash Flow
J. Brownfield
M. Chronological age

B. Hypothetical Condition
E. Executor
H. Proximity Damage
K. Arms Length
N. Range of Value

C. Partial Interest
F. Taxation
I. Conformity
L. Contributory Value

28. Using the Across and Down clues, write the correct words in the numbered grid below.

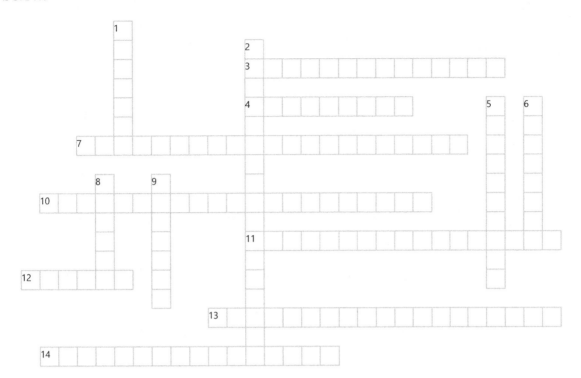

ACROSS

3. A tax on the right to receive property by inheritance; as distinguished from estate tax.
4. The act or process of developing an opinion of value.
7. The wear and tear that begins with the building is completed and placed into service.
10. A condition which is contrary to what is known by the appraiser to exist on the effective date of the assignment results, but is used for the purpose of analysis.
11. The periodic expenditures necessary to maintain the real property and continue production of the effective gross income, assuming prudent and competent management.
12. The result of the cause and effect relationship among the forces that influence real property value.
13. A report that is transmitted orally.
14. Technically valid but gives one or more parties the power to legally void the agreement and thus cancel performance.

DOWN

1. Ability of a product to satisfy a human want, need, or desire.
2. A promise made in exchange for another promise.
5. The state of having the requisite or adequate ability or qualities to perform the specific assignment and produce credible assignment results.
6. Pledge of a described property interest as collateral or security for the repayment of a loan under certain terms and conditions.
8. Public regulation of the character and extent of real estate use though police power.
9. A remainder that has negligible economic utility or value due to its size, shape, or other detrimental characteristics.

A. Bilateral contract
D. Zoning
G. Appraisal
J. Hypothetical Condition
M. Voidable contract

B. Mortgage
E. Competence
H. Physical Deterioration
K. Operating Expenses
N. Utility

C. Change
F. Remnant
I. Inheritance Tax
L. Oral Appraisal Report

29. Using the Across and Down clues, write the correct words in the numbered grid below.

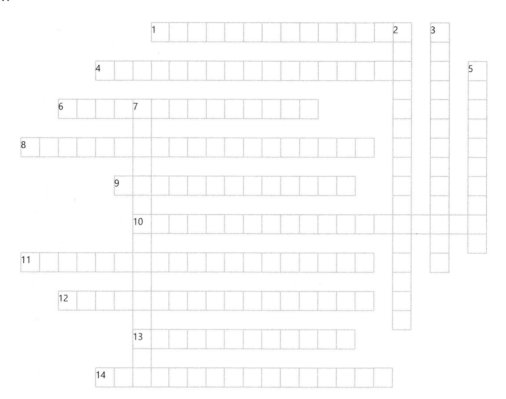

ACROSS

1. Supply and demand for housing, economic activity.
4. Total floor area of a building, excluding unenclosed area, measured from the exterior of the walls of the above-grade area.
6. Rights pertaining to properties touching a river or stream.
8. A report that is transmitted orally.
9. The overall vacancy rate that occurs as a result of the interaction of supply and demand of a particular property type in a particular region or market.
10. Easement that is attached to, benefits, and passes with the conveyance of the dominant estate. Burdens the servient estate.
11. One of the four criteria the highest and best use of a property must meet.
12. A condition that limits the use of a report.
13. One cause of depreciation.
14. Improvements on and off the site that make it suitable for its intended use or development.

DOWN

2. A dwelling not intended for year-round use, e.g., a vacation home.
3. A lease in which an intermediate, or sandwich, leaseholder is the lessee of one party and the lessor of another.
5. The more a property or its components are in harmony with the surrounding properties or components, the greater the contributory value.
7. Dollar amount required to reconstruct a bldg. or other improvement, which have the same or equivalent utility as the original.

A. Easement appurtenant
D. Seasonal Dwelling
G. Sandwich lease
J. Limiting Condition
M. Legal Permissibility

B. Market Vacancy
E. Site Improvements
H. Conformity
K. Economic Forces
N. Obsolescence

C. Replacement Cost
F. Oral Appraisal Report
I. Gross Building Area
L. Riparian rights

30. Using the Across and Down clues, write the correct words in the numbered grid below.

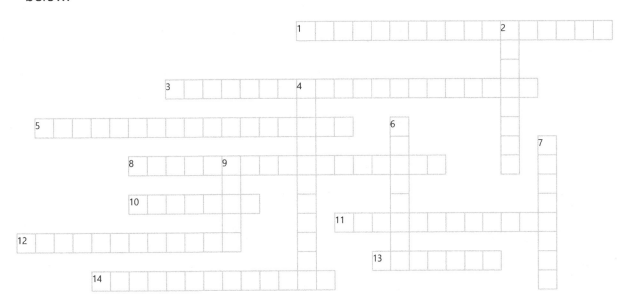

ACROSS

1. An appraiser's opinions or conclusions developed specific to an assignment.
3. An allowance that provides for the periodic replacement of building components that wear out more rapidly than the building itself.
5. Total floor area of a building, excluding unenclosed area, measured from the exterior of the walls of the above-grade area.
8. The periodic expenditures necessary to maintain the real property and continue production of the effective gross income, assuming prudent and competent management.
10. The legal process of settling an estate after a person has died.
11. The standard method of measurement for office buildings as defined by the Building Owners and Managers Association.
12. Operating expenses that generally do not vary with occupancy and that prudent management will pay whether the properties occupied or vacant.
13. Zoning regulations that designate the distance a building must be set back from the front, rear, and sides of the property lines.
14. A building component with an expected remaining economic life that is the same as the remaining economic life of the entire structure.

DOWN

2. An individual or other legal person designated in a will to settle the estate of the deceased person.
4. The most probable price at which real estate would sell.
6. The annual rate of return on capital that is commensurate with the risk assumed by the investor; the rate of interest or yield necessary to attract capital.
7. The quantity left over.
9. Combination of all elements that constitute proof of ownership.

A. Fixed Expense
B. Long Lived Item
C. Assignment Results
D. Operating Expenses
E. Gross Building Area
F. Replacement Allowance
G. Residual
H. Title
I. BOMA Standard
J. Risk Rate
K. Market Value
L. Setback
M. Probate
N. Executor

31. Using the Across and Down clues, write the correct words in the numbered grid below.

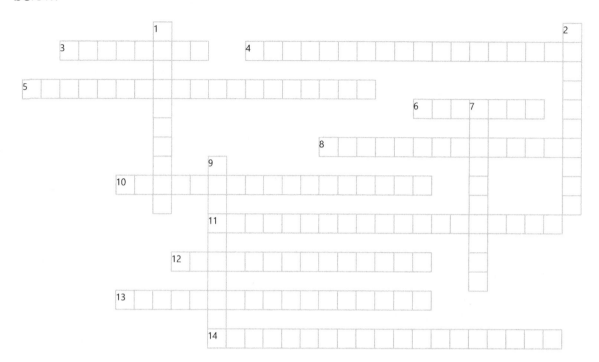

ACROSS

3. The quantity left over.
4. The readjustment of the value of an appreciated asset for tax purposes upon inheritance.
5. A study of the cost-benefit relationships of an economic endeavor.
6. Zoning regulations that designate the distance a building must be set back from the front, rear, and sides of the property lines.
8. Estimate of the rate at which a particular class of properties will sell in a particular geographic area.
10. The change in the value of a property as a whole, resulting from the addition or deletion of a property component.
11. One of the criteria for highest and best use of a property must meet.
12. The manner in which a transaction was financed.
13. The dwelling that is designated for occupancy by one family.
14. Net income that is left after the 4 agents of production have been paid.

DOWN

1. The entire taking of the full real property interest of a parcel for public use under the power of eminent domain; requires the payment of compensation.
2. The rental is based on a common index (i.e. Consumer Price Index or the Wholesale Price Index.
7. Industrial or commercial site that is abandoned or underused because it suffers from real or perceived continuing contamination.
9. Legal term signifying pending litigation that can affect ownership title to real estate.

A. Lis Pendens
B. Financing Terms
C. Full Taking
D. Residual
E. Brownfield
F. Absorption rate
G. Physical Possibility
H. Single Family House
I. Feasibility Analysis
J. Surplus Productivity
K. Setback
L. Index lease
M. Step Up Depreciation
N. Contributory Value

32. Using the Across and Down clues, write the correct words in the numbered grid below.

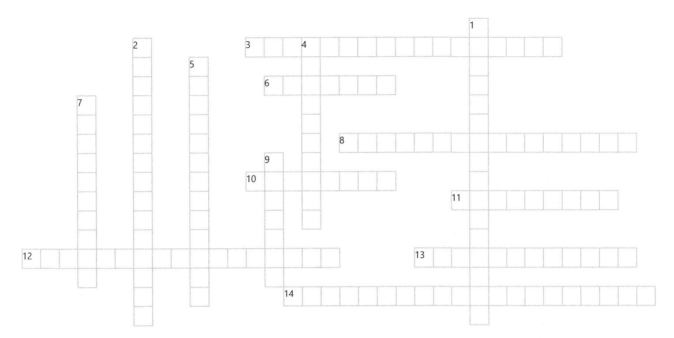

ACROSS

3. The tenant's possessory interest created by a lease.
6. The legal process of settling an estate after a person has died.
8. Technically valid but gives one or more parties the power to legally void the agreement and thus cancel performance.
10. The quantity left over.
11. The amount of money borrowed from lender (mortgagee).
12. Annual amount of total revenue that a property would generate if it were occupied all throughout the year.
13. The actual rental income specified in a lease.
14. An interest in real property restricting future land-use to preservation, conservation, wildlife habitat, or some combination of those uses.

DOWN

1. A description of land that identifies the real estate according to a system established or approved by law.
2. The price at which the property would change hands between a willing buyer and a willing seller and both having reasonable knowledge of relevant facts.
4. An exception to the general zoning regulations; permits specific, usually small, parcels of land to be zone for a use that is not permitted in the surrounding area.
5. The development or improvement of cleared or undeveloped land in an urban renewal area.
7. Temporary use to which a site or improved property is put until it is ready to be put to its future highest and best use.
9. Zoning regulations that designate the distance a building must be set back from the front, rear, and sides of the property lines.

A. Spot Zoning
D. Residual
G. Redevelopment
J. Conservation Easement
M. Legal Description

B. Probate
E. Gross Market Income
H. Setback
K. Fair Market Value
N. Interim use

C. Voidable contract
F. Leasehold Interest
I. Principle
L. Contract rent

33. Using the Across and Down clues, write the correct words in the numbered grid below.

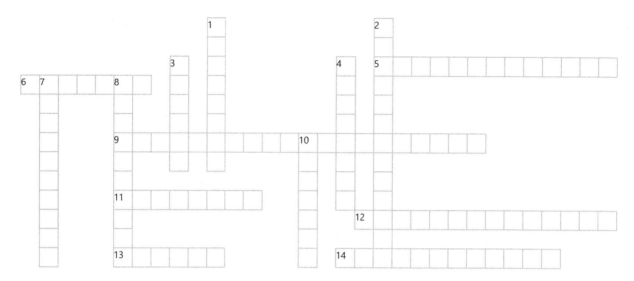

ACROSS

5. The development or improvement of cleared or undeveloped land in an urban renewal area.
6. In condemnation, the loss in value to the remainder in a partial taking of property.
9. The total annual income the rental property produces after subtracting vacancy losses and adding miscellaneous income.
11. The relative position of the property to competitive properties and other value influences in its market area
12. Rights pertaining to properties abutting a lake or pond.
13. Purchaser's wish for an item to satisfy human needs or individual wants beyond essential life-support needs.
14. Data that is analyzed through the process of comparison.

DOWN

1. The minimum rate of return on invested capital.
2. Time it takes an interest in real property to sell on the market subsequent to the date of an appraisal.
3. One who is the right to occupancy and use of the property of another for a period of time according to a lease agreement.
4. The sudden removal of land from the property of one owner to that of another, e.g., change in the course of a river.
7. Seizure of property by court order.
8. Land that is not needed to serve or support the existing improvement.
10. A remainder that has negligible economic utility or value due to its size, shape, or other detrimental characteristics.

A. Damages
D. Desire
G. Littoral rights
J. Avulsion
M. Excess Land

B. Attachment
E. Location
H. Safe Rate
K. Lessee
N. Specific Data

C. Redevelopment
F. Marketing time
I. Remnant
L. Effective Gross Income

34. Using the Across and Down clues, write the correct words in the numbered grid below.

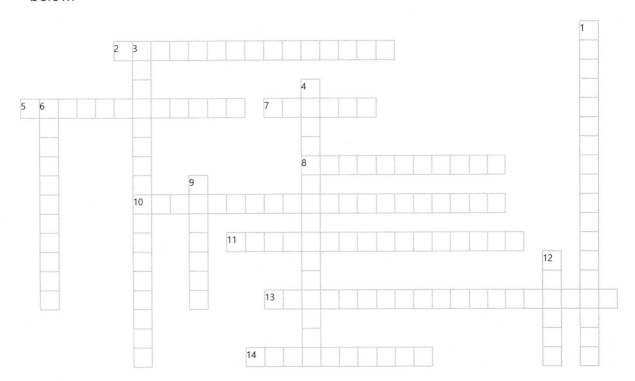

ACROSS

2. Price an economic good will attract in the competitive market.
5. The period over time which a structure may be competitive in the market.
7. Public regulation of the character and extent of real estate use though police power.
8. The type and extent of research and analyses in appraisal or appraisal review assignment.
10. Total payment is insufficient to pay interest due.
11. The number of years since a structure or bldg. was originally built (birth).
13. A report that is transmitted orally.
14. The rental is based on a common index (i.e. Consumer Price Index or the Wholesale Price Index.

DOWN

1. Any rate used to convert income into value.
3. An appraiser's opinions or conclusions developed specific to an assignment.
4. Value to a particular individual. The present worth of anticipated future benefits.
6. A shortened term for similar property sales, rentals, or operating expenses used for comparison in the valuation process.
9. Land on which no improvements have been made
12. Any communication, written or oral, of an appraisal or appraisal review that is transmitted to the client upon completion of an assignment.

A. Oral Appraisal Report
B. Zoning
C. Capitalization Rate
D. Negative Amortization
E. Comparables
F. Index lease
G. Chronological age
H. Economic life
I. Report
J. Raw Land
K. Investment Value
L. Assignment Results
M. Scope of Work
N. Value in Exchange

35. Using the Across and Down clues, write the correct words in the numbered grid below.

ACROSS

2. An appraisal report in which the appraiser's scope of work does not include an inspection of the subject property or comparables.
4. An element of comparison in the sales comparison approach.
6. Industrial or commercial site that is abandoned or underused because it suffers from real or perceived continuing contamination.
8. Time it takes an interest in real property to sell on the market subsequent to the date of an appraisal.
10. Total rights of use, occupancy and control, limited to the lifetime of the designated party, i.e. life tenant.
11. The process of valuing a universe of properties as of a given date using standard methodology, employing common data, and allowing for statistical testing.
12. The most probable rent the property should bring in a competitive and open market reflecting all conditions and restrictions of the lease agreement.
13. Ability of a product to satisfy a human want, need, or desire.
14. A limitation that passes with the land regardless of the owner.

DOWN

1. Most commonly found in retail business. This lease has a base rent which is fixed and an excess rent, this is most commonly based on the percentage of the sales.
3. The combining of 2 or more parcels into one ownership (tract).
5. The present or anticipated undersupply of an item relative to the demand for it. Conditions of scarcity contribute to value.
7. An increase in dry land created by the gradual accumulation of waterborne solid material over formerly riparian land.
9. Money paid to an owner of real property or mineral rights for the right to deplete natural resource.

A. Marketing time
D. Accretion
G. Scarcity
J. Market Rent
M. Mass Appraisal

B. Economic Characteristics
E. Percentage lease
H. Deed restriction
K. Royalty
N. Assemblage

C. Brownfield
F. Utility
I. Life estate
L. Desktop Appraisal

36. Using the Across and Down clues, write the correct words in the numbered grid below.

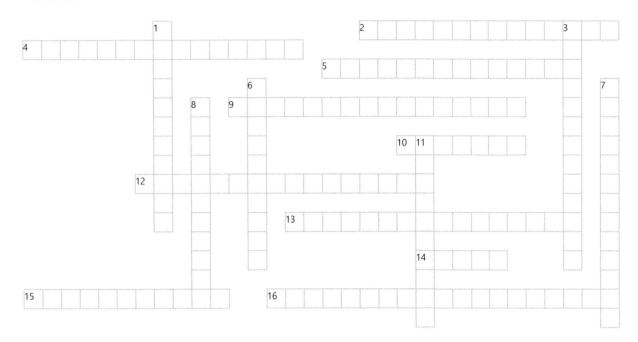

ACROSS

2. Estimate of the rate at which a particular class of properties will sell in a particular geographic area.
4. A right granted or taken for the construction, maintenance, and operation of the highway.
5. Rights pertaining to properties abutting a lake or pond.
9. A description of land that identifies the real estate according to a system established or approved by law.
10. A stage of diminishing demand in a market areas life cycle.
12. The right to construct, operate, and maintain a pipeline over the lands of others within prescribed geographical limits.
13. Data and analyses used in the assignment are summarized (i.e. less detail).
14. Combination of all elements that constitute proof of ownership.
15. A shortened term for similar property sales, rentals, or operating expenses used for comparison in the valuation process.
16. The last phase in the development of the value opinion in which two or more value indications derived from market data are resolved into a value opinion.

DOWN

1. A lien against all of the property owned by the debtor.
3. The value of a property according to the tax rolls in ad valorem taxation.
6. In law, just, rational, appropriate, ordinary, or usual in the circumstances.
7. Voluntary and one of the most common types of liens.
8. The most probable price at which real estate would sell.
11. A method of estimating value in which the depreciated cost of the improvements on the improved property is calculated and deducted from the total sale price

A. Decline
B. Market Value
C. Summary appraisal
D. Assessed Value
E. Absorption rate
F. General Lien
G. Reasonable
H. Final Reconciliation
I. Mortgage liens
J. Comparables
K. Littoral rights
L. Extraction
M. Title
N. Legal Description
O. Highway Easement
P. Pipeline Easement

37. Using the Across and Down clues, write the correct words in the numbered grid below.

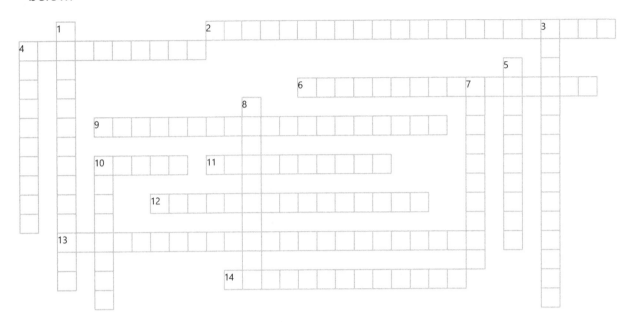

ACROSS

2. An individual or other legal person designated in a will to settle the estate of a deceased person.
4. An identified parcel or tract of land, including improvements.
6. The number of years since a structure or bldg. was originally built (birth).
9. One of the four criteria the highest and best use of a property must meet; the selected land-use must yield the highest value of the possible uses.
10. Amount a particular purchaser agrees to pay and a particular seller agrees to accept under the circumstances surrounding their transaction.
11. An appraisal review in which the reviewer's scope of work does not include an inspection of the subject property.
12. Total area of finished above-grade residential space
13. An element of comparison in the sales comparison approach.
14. Impairment of condition; because of depreciation that reflects the loss in value due to wear and tear, disintegration, use in service, and the action of the elements.

DOWN

1. The price of a property with above- or below-market financing expressed in terms of the price that would have been paid in an all-cash sale.
3. Estate owned by 2 or more persons, each of whom has an equal undivided interest. Unlike Joint Tenancy and Tenancy by Entirety, No right of survivorship.
4. A type of renovation that involves modification or updating of existing improvements.
5. The most probable rent the property should bring in a competitive and open market reflecting all conditions and restrictions of the lease agreement.
7. Temporary use to which a site or improved property is put until it is ready to be put to its future highest and best use.
8. When the lessee (tenant) does not pay any costs of ownership and pays a given amount of rent per period.
10. A projected income and expense statement for proposed development.

A. Price
D. Remodeling
G. Maximum Productivity
J. Cash Equivalent
M. Economic Characteristics
P. Deterioration

B. Market Rent
E. Gross Living Area
H. Real Estate
K. Chronological age
N. Gross lease

C. Interim use
F. Personal Representative
I. Pro Forma
L. Desk Review
O. Tenancy in Common

38. Using the Across and Down clues, write the correct words in the numbered grid below.

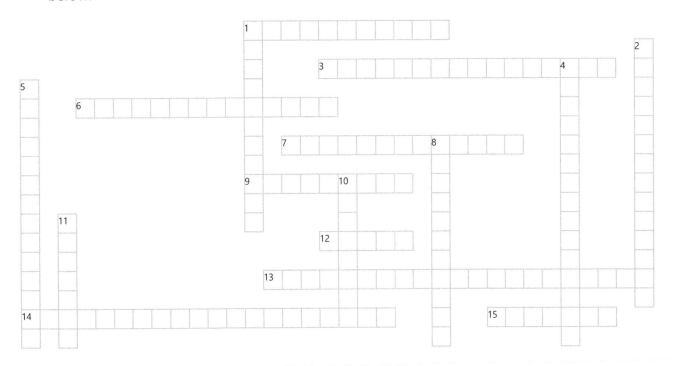

ACROSS

1. When the government regulates the land use for the good of the public.
3. A description of land that identifies the real estate according to a system established or approved by law.
6. The process of reducing a range of value indications into an appropriate conclusion for that analysis.
7. The process of valuing a universe of properties as of a given date using standard methodology, employing common data, and allowing for statistical testing.
9. An increase in dry land created by the gradual accumulation of waterborne solid material over formerly riparian land.
12. comprises of all costs required to construct and market the product as land alone or with improvements.
13. The wear and tear that begins with the building is completed and placed into service.
14. An element of depreciation; and diminution in value caused by negative externalities and generally incurable on the part of the owner, landlord, or tenant.
15. The employment of a site or holding to produce revenue or other benefits.

DOWN

1. Information that is gathered in its original form by the analyst.
2. Created intentionally by property owner's actions. i.e. mortgage
4. Value to a particular individual. The present worth of anticipated future benefits.
5. Supply and demand for housing, economic activity.
8. Changes made to basic data to facilitate comparison or understanding.
10. Right of government to raise revenue through assessments on valuable goods, products, and rights.
11. Money paid to an owner of real property or mineral rights for the right to deplete natural resource.

A. Adjustments
D. Voluntary liens
G. Police power
J. Physical Deterioration
M. Mass Appraisal
P. Labor

B. Land Use
E. Taxation
H. External Obsolescence
K. Reconciliation
N. Royalty

C. Investment Value
F. Accretion
I. Legal Description
L. Primary Data
O. Economic Forces

39. Using the Across and Down clues, write the correct words in the numbered grid below.

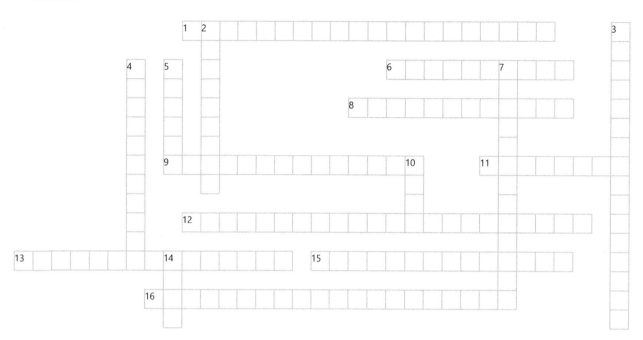

ACROSS

1. A voluntary legal agreement that becomes part of the chain of title thereby protecting a historic, archaeological, or cultural resource.
6. Legal term signifying pending litigation that can affect ownership title to real estate.
8. Value is a function of expected benefits to get from the ownership of the property.
9. Supply and demand for housing, economic activity.
11. Type of market are characterized by homogeneous land use. e.g., apt., commercial, industrial, agricultural
12. An individual or other legal person designated in a will to settle the estate of a deceased person.
13. The written or oral communication of an appraisal.
15. arise from construction and other improvements to real estate.
16. Total payment is insufficient to pay interest due.

DOWN

2. A lump sum benefit that an investor receives or expects to receive upon the termination of an investment; also called reversionary benefit.
3. Created by law, rather than by choice. i.e. property tax lien.
4. A shortened term for similar property sales, rentals, or operating expenses used for comparison in the valuation process.
5. The result of the cause and effect relationship among the forces that influence real property value.
7. Impairment of condition; because of depreciation that reflects the loss in value due to wear and tear, disintegration, use in service, and the action of the elements.
10. land that is improved so that is ready to be used for a specific purpose.
14. Charge against property in which the property is the security for payment of the debt.

A. Comparables
D. Deterioration
G. Economic Forces
J. Mechanics liens
M. Lis Pendens
P. Preservation Easement

B. Personal Representative
E. Involuntary liens
H. Negative Amortization
K. Site
N. Appraisal Report

C. District
F. Anticipation
I. Change
L. Lien
O. Reversion

40. Using the Across and Down clues, write the correct words in the numbered grid below.

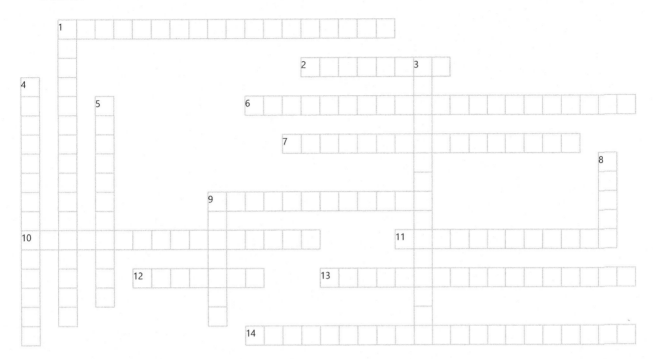

ACROSS

1. Income-producing property such as office and retail buildings.
2. Right of government to raise revenue through assessments on valuable goods, products, and rights.
6. The wear and tear that begins with the building is completed and placed into service.
7. An appraisal report in which the scope of work includes an exterior-only viewing of the subject property.
9. The ratio of income or yield to the original investment.
10. Buyers and sellers of particular real estate and the transactions that occur among them.
11. A sale involving a seller acting under undue distress.
12. Land on which no improvements have been made
13. When the value of a business plus the amount of real property is sought.
14. A market-derived figure that represents the amount an entrepreneur receives for their contribution.

DOWN

1. The number of years since a structure or bldg. was originally built (birth).
3. Income derived from the operation of a business or real property
4. The rights of an owner to possess, control, enjoy, sell, lease, mortgage, and dispose of the property.
5. Changes made to basic data to facilitate comparison or understanding.
8. Monetary worth of a property, good, or service to buyers and sellers at a given time.
9. A remainder that has negligible economic utility or value due to its size, shape, or other detrimental characteristics.

A. Remnant
D. Commercial Property
G. Entrepreneurial profit
J. Adjustments
M. Taxation
P. Chronological age

B. Physical Deterioration
E. Real Estate Market
H. Drive by Appraisal
K. Operating Income
N. Going concern value

C. Raw Land
F. Distress Sale
I. Bundle of rights
L. Rate of return
O. Value

1. Using the Across and Down clues, write the correct words in the numbered grid below.

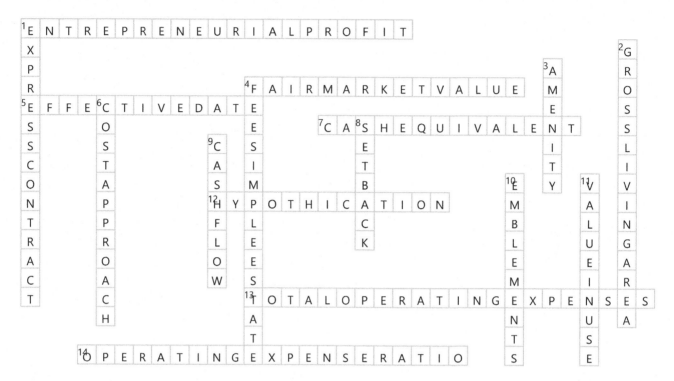

ACROSS

1. A market-derived figure that represents the amount an entrepreneur receives for their contribution.
4. The price at which the property would change hands between a willing buyer and a willing seller and both having reasonable knowledge of relevant facts.
5. The date on which the analyses, opinions, and advice in an appraisal, review, or consulting service apply.
7. The price of a property with above- or below-market financing expressed in terms of the price that would have been paid in an all-cash sale.
12. A borrower has possession of the property.
13. Sum of all fixed and variable operating expenses and reserve for replacement.
14. The ratio of total operating expenses to effective gross income

DOWN

1. An agreement put into words (written or spoken).
2. Total area of finished above-grade residential space
3. A tangible or intangible benefit of real property that enhances its attractiveness or increases the satisfaction of the user.
4. Absolute ownership unencumbered by any other interest or estate.
6. an estimate of replacement cost of a structure, less depreciation, plus land value.
8. Zoning regulations that designate the distance a building must be set back from the front, rear, and sides of the property lines.
9. The periodic income attributable to the interests in real property.
10. Annual crops and plantings such as corn, wheat, and vegetables.
11. Value a specific property has to a specific person or firm for a specific use.

A. Effective Date
D. Setback
G. Fair Market Value
J. Gross Living Area
M. Fee Simple Estate
P. Hypothication

B. Total Operating Expenses
E. Express contract
H. Amenity
K. Cost Approach
N. Entrepreneurial profit

C. Cash Equivalent
F. Emblements
I. Cash Flow
L. Value in use
O. Operating Expense Ratio

2. Using the Across and Down clues, write the correct words in the numbered grid below.

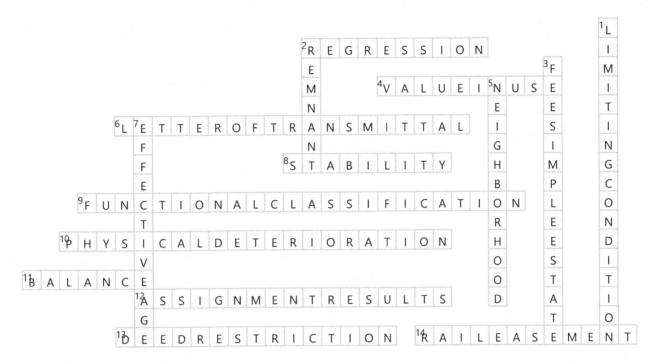

ACROSS

2. Value of a superior property is adversely affected by its association with an inferior property of the same type.
4. Value a specific property has to a specific person or firm for a specific use.
6. A letter or statement that serves as a notice of delivery from the appraiser to the client of a report containing an opinion or conclusion concerning real estate
8. Stage in market area's life cycle. The market area experiences equilibrium without market gains or losses.
9. The process by which all roads are grouped into classes or systems according to the character of service they are intended to provide.
10. The wear and tear that begins with the building is completed and placed into service.
11. Principle that real property value is created and sustained when contrasting, opposing, or interacting elements are in a state of equilibrium.
12. An appraiser's opinions or conclusions developed specific to an assignment.
13. A limitation that passes with the land regardless of the owner.
14. The right for the construction, maintenance, and operation of a rail line on a property.

DOWN

1. A condition that limits the use of a report.
2. A remainder that has negligible economic utility or value due to its size, shape, or other detrimental characteristics.
3. Absolute ownership unencumbered by any other interest or estate.
5. Complementary land uses; inhabitants, buildings, or business enterprises.
7. The difference between an improvements total economic life and its remaining economic life.

A. Deed restriction
B. Rail Easement
C. Physical Deterioration
D. Functional Classification
E. Balance
F. Neighborhood
G. Remnant
H. Regression
I. Stability
J. Limiting Condition
K. Effective age
L. Value in use
M. Letter of Transmittal
N. Fee Simple Estate
O. Assignment Results

3. Using the Across and Down clues, write the correct words in the numbered grid below.

Grid answers:

- 3 Across: EASEMENT APPURTENANT
- 8 Across: INTESTATE
- 10 Across: RAIL EASEMENT
- 12 Across: APPURTENANCE
- 13 Across: REMAINING ECONOMIC LIFE
- 14 Across: VALID CONTRACT
- 15 Across: UNILATERAL CONTRACT
- 1 Down: EXPRESS CONTRACT
- 2 Down: REGRESSION ANALYSIS
- 4 Down: ASSEMBLAGE
- 5 Down: MORTGAGE LIENS
- 6 Down: DEED RESTRICTION
- 7 Down: PROPERTY CLASS
- 9 Down: OBSOLESCENCE

ACROSS

3. Easement that is attached to, benefits, and passes with the conveyance of the dominant estate. Burdens the servient estate.
8. The condition of dying without a will.
10. The right for the construction, maintenance, and operation of a rail line on a property.
12. Something that has been added or appended to a property and has since become an inherent part of the property.
13. The estimated period during which improvements will continue to represent the highest and best use of the property.
14. An agreement in which all the elements of a contract are present and, therefore, legally enforceable.
15. Only one party makes a promise

DOWN

1. An agreement put into words (written or spoken).
2. A statistical measure that attempts to determine the strength of the relationship between one dependent variable and a series of other changing variables.
4. The combining of 2 or more parcels into one ownership (tract).
5. Voluntary and one of the most common types of liens.
6. A limitation that passes with the land regardless of the owner.
7. In accounting, a category for property under the modified accelerated cost recovery system.
9. One cause of depreciation.
11. Going to the State. The process that should a property be abandoned, it reverts back to the state.

A. Deed restriction
D. Regression Analysis
G. Easement appurtenant
J. Rail Easement
M. Assemblage

B. Remaining Economic Life
E. Intestate
H. Express contract
K. Escheat
N. Property Class

C. Obsolescence
F. Unilateral contract
I. Mortgage liens
L. Valid contract
O. Appurtenance

4. Using the Across and Down clues, write the correct words in the numbered grid below.

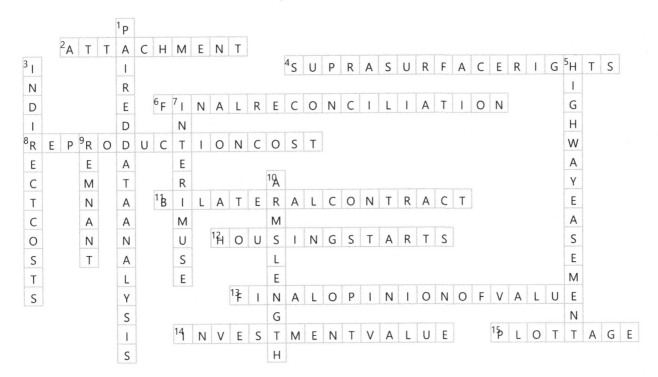

ACROSS

2. Seizure of property by court order.
4. Right to undisturbed use and control of designated air space above a specific land area within stated elevations.
6. The last phase in the development of the value opinion in which two or more value indications derived from market data are resolved into a value opinion.
8. Dollar amount required to construct an exact duplicate of the subject improvements, at current prices.
11. A promise made in exchange for another promise.
12. Newly constructed housing units; includes both single-family and multifamily domiciles.
13. The opinion of value derived from the reconciliation of value indications and stated in the appraisal report
14. Value to a particular individual. The present worth of anticipated future benefits.
15. An increase in value when extra utility is created by combining smaller parcels under single ownership.

DOWN

1. Two or more sales are compared to derive an indication of the size of the adjustment for a single characteristic.
3. Soft cost expenditures that are necessary components but are not typically part of the construction contract.
5. A right granted or taken for the construction, maintenance, and operation of the highway.
7. Temporary use to which a site or improved property is put until it is ready to be put to its future highest and best use.
9. A remainder that has negligible economic utility or value due to its size, shape, or other detrimental characteristics.
10. A transaction in which the buyers and sellers of a product act independently and have no relationship to each other.

A. Supra surface rights
D. Housing Starts
G. Highway Easement
J. Interim use
M. Indirect costs

B. Final Opinion of Value
E. Attachment
H. Bilateral contract
K. Reproduction Cost
N. Paired data analysis

C. Arms Length
F. Final Reconciliation
I. Remnant
L. Investment Value
O. Plottage

5. Using the Across and Down clues, write the correct words in the numbered grid below.

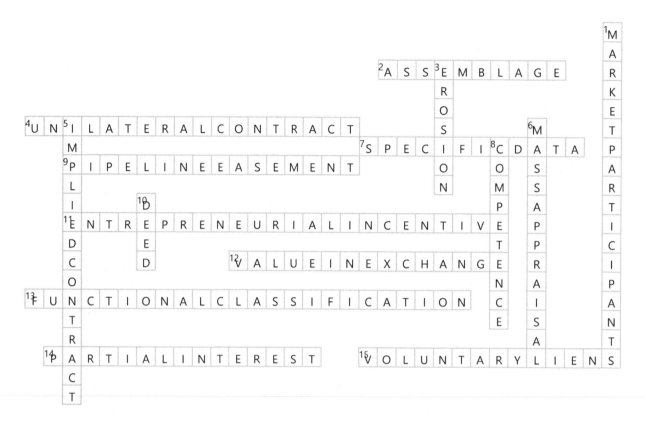

ACROSS

2. The combining of 2 or more parcels into one ownership (tract).
4. Only one party makes a promise
7. Data that is analyzed through the process of comparison.
9. The right to construct, operate, and maintain a pipeline over the lands of others within prescribed geographical limits.
11. The amount entrepreneur expects to receive for his or her contribution to the project.
12. Price an economic good will attract in the competitive market.
13. The process by which all roads are grouped into classes or systems according to the character of service they are intended to provide.
14. Divided or undivided rights in real estate that represent less than the whole.
15. Created intentionally by property owner's actions. i.e. mortgage

DOWN

1. The parties involved in the transfer of property rights. Includes buyers, sellers, lessors, lessees, and brokers and their agents.
3. The wearing away of surface land by natural causes.
5. Ann agreement that is presumed to exist because of the parties' actions.
6. The process of valuing a universe of properties as of a given date using standard methodology, employing common data, and allowing for statistical testing.
8. The state of having the requisite or adequate ability or qualities to perform the specific assignment and produce credible assignment results.
10. Written, legal instrument that conveys an estate or interest in real property to someone else, assuming it is executed and delivered.

A. Erosion
D. Implied contract
G. Partial Interest
J. Deed
M. Pipeline Easement

B. Competence
E. Specific Data
H. Entrepreneurial Incentive
K. Unilateral contract
N. Market Participants

C. Mass Appraisal
F. Voluntary liens
I. Assemblage
L. Functional Classification
O. Value in Exchange

6. Using the Across and Down clues, write the correct words in the numbered grid below.

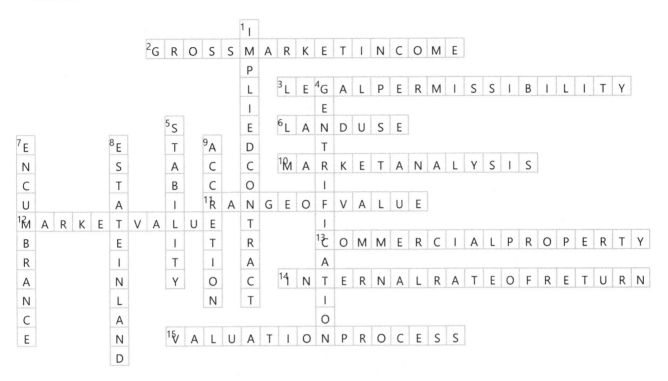

ACROSS

2. Annual amount of total revenue that a property would generate if it were occupied all throughout the year.
3. One of the four criteria the highest and best use of a property must meet.
6. The employment of a site or holding to produce revenue or other benefits.
10. Study of real estate market conditions for specific types of property.
11. In final reconciliation, the range in which the final market value opinion of a property may fall; usually stated as the interval between a high and low value limit.
12. The most probable price at which real estate would sell.
13. Income-producing property such as office and retail buildings.
14. The annualized yield or rate of return on capital that is generated or capable of being generated within an investment or portfolio over a period of ownership.
15. A systematic set of procedures an appraiser follows to provide answers to a client's questions about real property value.

DOWN

1. Ann agreement that is presumed to exist because of the parties' actions.
4. Neighborhood phenomenon in which middle- and upper-income persons purchase neighborhood properties and renovate or rehabilitate them.
5. Stage in market area's life cycle. The market area experiences equilibrium without market gains or losses.
7. Any claim or liability that affects our limits the title to property.
8. The degree, nature, or extent of interest that a person has in land.
9. An increase in dry land created by the gradual accumulation of waterborne solid material over formerly riparian land.

A. Valuation process
B. Legal Permissibility
C. Gentrification
D. Encumbrance
E. Accretion
F. Commercial Property
G. Estate in land
H. Gross Market Income
I. Land Use
J. Stability
K. Implied contract
L. Market Value
M. Internal Rate of Return
N. Range of Value
O. Market Analysis

7. Using the Across and Down clues, write the correct words in the numbered grid below.

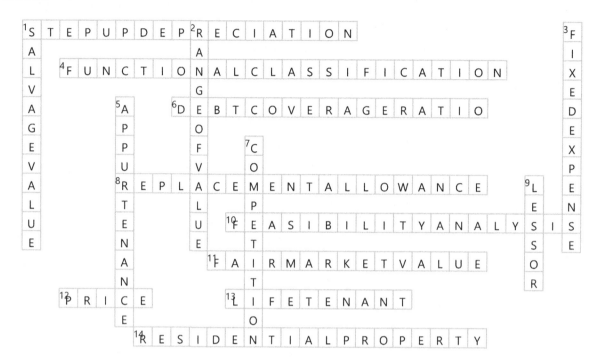

ACROSS

1. The readjustment of the value of an appreciated asset for tax purposes upon inheritance.
4. The process by which all roads are grouped into classes or systems according to the character of service they are intended to provide.
6. Ratio of NOI to annual debt service.
8. An allowance that provides for the periodic replacement of building components that wear out more rapidly than the building itself.
10. A study of the cost-benefit relationships of an economic endeavor.
11. The price at which the property would change hands between a willing buyer and a willing seller and both having reasonable knowledge of relevant facts.
12. Amount a particular purchaser agrees to pay and a particular seller agrees to accept under the circumstances surrounding their transaction.
13. One who owns an interest in real property for his or her own lifetime.
14. A vacant or in proof parcel of land devoted to or available for use as a residence.

DOWN

1. The price expected for a whole property (e.g., a house) or a part of a property (e.g., a plumbing fixture) that is removed from the premises usually for use elsewhere.
2. In final reconciliation, the range in which the final market value opinion of a property may fall; usually stated as the interval between a high and low value limit.
3. Operating expenses that generally do not vary with occupancy and that prudent management will pay whether the properties occupied or vacant.
5. Something that has been added or appended to a property and has since become an inherent part of the property.
7. A rivalry between buyers or between sellers.
9. One who conveys the rights of occupancy and use to others under lease agreement.

A. Competition
D. Functional Classification
G. Fixed Expense
J. Replacement Allowance
M. Life tenant

B. Fair Market Value
E. Appurtenance
H. Price
K. Salvage Value
N. Feasibility Analysis

C. Lessor
F. Debt coverage ratio
I. Residential Property
L. Range of Value
O. Step Up Depreciation

8. Using the Across and Down clues, write the correct words in the numbered grid below.

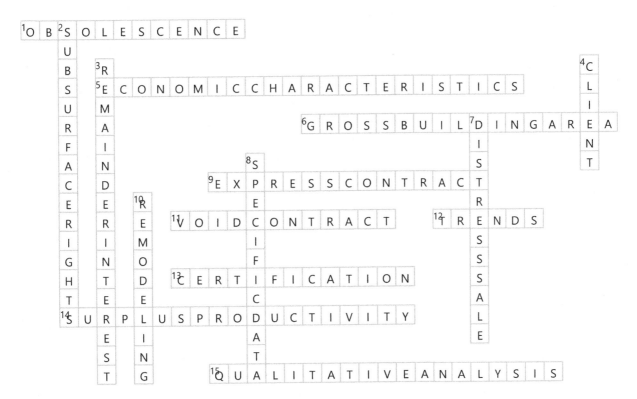

ACROSS

1. One cause of depreciation.
5. An element of comparison in the sales comparison approach.
6. Total floor area of a building, excluding unenclosed area, measured from the exterior of the walls of the above-grade area.
9. An agreement put into words (written or spoken).
11. Has no legal force or binding effect and cannot be enforced in a court of law.
12. A series of related changes brought about by a chain of causes and effects.
13. A part of an appraisal report in which the appraiser certifies that the work was completed according to the applicable standards.
14. Net income that is left after the 4 agents of production have been paid.
15. Is used for elements that cannot be given a numerical value.

DOWN

2. Rights to the use and profits of the underground portion of a designated property.
3. Person who is entitled to an estate after a prior estate or interest has expired
4. The party of parties who engage an appraiser in a specific assignment.
7. A sale involving a seller acting under undue distress.
8. Data that is analyzed through the process of comparison.
10. A type of renovation that involves modification or updating of existing improvements.

A. Express contract
D. Client
G. Qualitative analysis
J. Economic Characteristics
M. Specific Data

B. Remainder interest
E. Certification
H. Obsolescence
K. Gross Building Area
N. Subsurface rights

C. Remodeling
F. Trends
I. Surplus Productivity
L. Distress Sale
O. Void contract

9. Using the Across and Down clues, write the correct words in the numbered grid below.

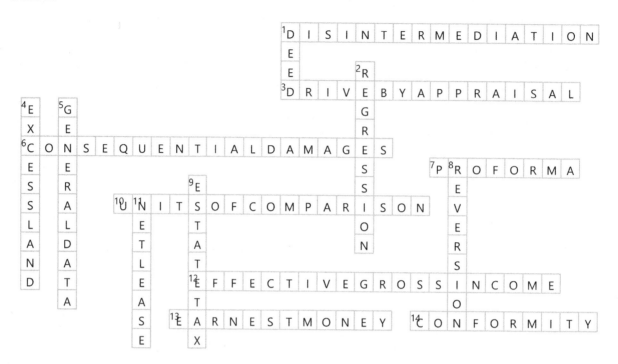

ACROSS

1. Flow of savings account money from savings and loans accounts to higher yield investments.
3. An appraisal report in which the scope of work includes an exterior-only viewing of the subject property.
6. Damage to property arising as a consequence of a taking over and above direct damages.
7. A projected income and expense statement for proposed development.
10. Price per cubic foot, front foot, and per apartment.
12. The total annual income the rental property produces after subtracting vacancy losses and adding miscellaneous income.
13. Part of the purchase price given to bind a bargain.
14. The more a property or its components are in harmony with the surrounding properties or components, the greater the contributory value.

DOWN

1. Written, legal instrument that conveys an estate or interest in real property to someone else, assuming it is executed and delivered.
2. Value of a superior property is adversely affected by its association with an inferior property of the same type.
4. Land that is not needed to serve or support the existing improvement.
5. Items of information on value influences that derive from social, economic, governmental, and environmental forces and originate outside the property being appraised.
8. A lump sum benefit that an investor receives or expects to receive upon the termination of an investment; also called reversionary benefit.
9. A tax on the estate or wealth of the deceased person that is usually computed as a percentage of the market value of the assets of the estate.
11. A lease in which the landlord passes on all expenses to the tenant.

A. Regression
D. General Data
G. Net Lease
J. Earnest money
M. Effective Gross Income

B. Pro Forma
E. Deed
H. Consequential Damages
K. Units of comparison
N. Excess Land

C. Disintermediation
F. Reversion
I. Drive by Appraisal
L. Conformity
O. Estate Tax

10. Using the Across and Down clues, write the correct words in the numbered grid below.

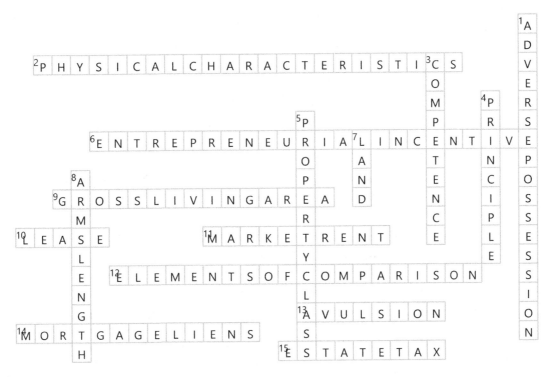

ACROSS

2. A category of elements of comparison in the sales comparison approach
6. The amount entrepreneur expects to receive for his or her contribution to the project.
9. Total area of finished above-grade residential space
10. A contract in which the rights to use and occupy land or structures are transferred by the owner to another for a specified period of time in return for specified rent.
11. The most probable rent the property should bring in a competitive and open market reflecting all conditions and restrictions of the lease agreement.
12. Relevant characteristics used to compare and adjust the property prices.
13. The sudden removal of land from the property of one owner to that of another, e.g., change in the course of a river.
14. Voluntary and one of the most common types of liens.
15. A tax on the estate or wealth of the deceased person that is usually computed as a percentage of the market value of the assets of the estate.

DOWN

1. Involuntary transfer of property takes place when a party makes a property claim by taking possession over a period of years.
3. The state of having the requisite or adequate ability or qualities to perform the specific assignment and produce credible assignment results.
4. The amount of money borrowed from lender (mortgagee).
5. In accounting, a category for property under the modified accelerated cost recovery system.
7. first thing a developer considers in developing a property is the cost of land.
8. A transaction in which the buyers and sellers of a product act independently and have no relationship to each other.

A. Entrepreneurial Incentive
D. Adverse possession
G. Elements of comparison
J. Physical Characteristics
M. Competence

B. Avulsion
E. Gross Living Area
H. Principle
K. Mortgage liens
N. Lease

C. Property Class
F. Land
I. Arms Length
L. Estate Tax
O. Market Rent

11. Using the Across and Down clues, write the correct words in the numbered grid below.

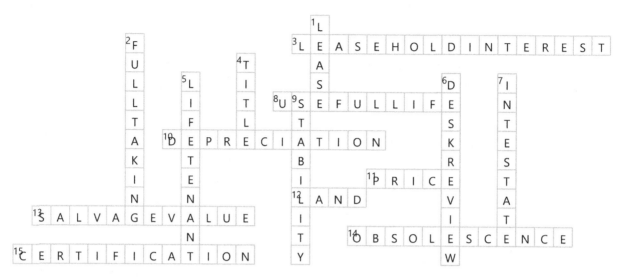

ACROSS

3. The tenant's possessory interest created by a lease.
8. The period of time over which a structure may reasonably be expected to perform the function for which it was designed.
10. In appraising, a loss in property value from any cause
11. Amount a particular purchaser agrees to pay and a particular seller agrees to accept under the circumstances surrounding their transaction.
12. first thing a developer considers in developing a property is the cost of land.
13. The price expected for a whole property (e.g., a house) or a part of a property (e.g., a plumbing fixture) that is removed from the premises usually for use elsewhere.
14. One cause of depreciation.
15. A part of an appraisal report in which the appraiser certifies that the work was completed according to the applicable standards.

DOWN

1. A contract in which the rights to use and occupy land or structures are transferred by the owner to another for a specified period of time in return for specified rent.
2. The entire taking of the full real property interest of a parcel for public use under the power of eminent domain; requires the payment of compensation.
4. Combination of all elements that constitute proof of ownership.
5. One who owns an interest in real property for his or her own lifetime.
6. An appraisal review in which the reviewer's scope of work does not include an inspection of the subject property.
7. The condition of dying without a will.
9. Stage in market area's life cycle. The market area experiences equilibrium without market gains or losses.

A. Useful life	B. Title	C. Price	D. Stability
E. Life tenant	F. Intestate	G. Certification	H. Depreciation
I. Leasehold Interest	J. Obsolescence	K. Full Taking	L. Salvage Value
M. Lease	N. Land	O. Desk Review	

12. Using the Across and Down clues, write the correct words in the numbered grid below.

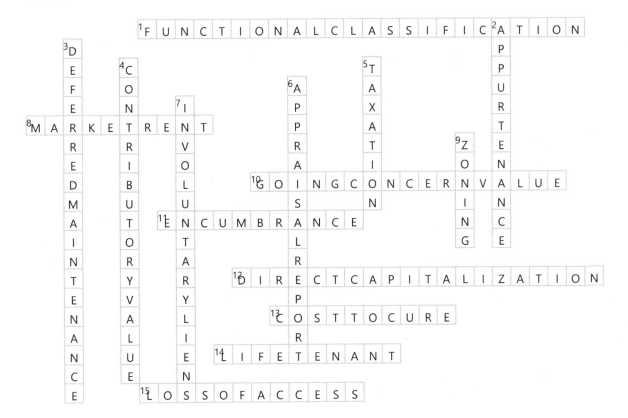

ACROSS

1. The process by which all roads are grouped into classes or systems according to the character of service they are intended to provide.
8. The most probable rent the property should bring in a competitive and open market reflecting all conditions and restrictions of the lease agreement.
10. When the value of a business plus the amount of real property is sought.
11. Any claim or liability that affects our limits the title to property.
12. A method used to convert an estimate of a single year's income expectancy into an indication of value in one direct step
13. The cost to restore an item of deferred maintenance to new or reasonably new condition.
14. One who owns an interest in real property for his or her own lifetime.
15. Depriving an abutting owner of the inherent rights of ingress and to egress from the highway or street.

DOWN

2. Something that has been added or appended to a property and has since become an inherent part of the property.
3. Needed repairs or replacement of items that should have taken place during the course of normal maintenance.
4. The change in the value of a property as a whole, resulting from the addition or deletion of a property component.
5. Right of government to raise revenue through assessments on valuable goods, products, and rights.
6. The written or oral communication of an appraisal.
7. Created by law, rather than by choice. i.e. property tax lien.
9. Public regulation of the character and extent of real estate use though police power.

A. Life tenant
D. Functional Classification
G. Involuntary liens
J. Direct Capitalization
M. Loss of Access

B. Contributory Value
E. Zoning
H. Cost to Cure
K. Market Rent
N. Appraisal Report

C. Encumbrance
F. Deferred Maintenance
I. Going concern value
L. Appurtenance
O. Taxation

13. Using the Across and Down clues, write the correct words in the numbered grid below.

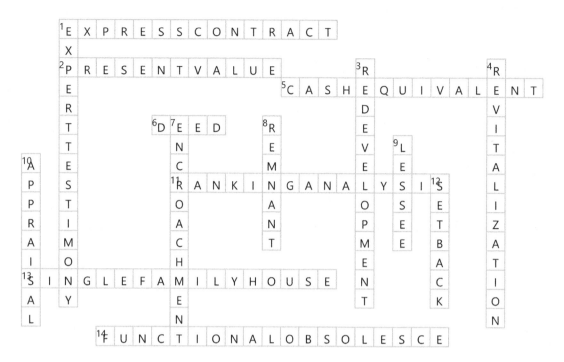

ACROSS

1. An agreement put into words (written or spoken).
2. The value of a future payment or series of future payments discounted to the current date or to time period zero.
5. The price of a property with above- or below-market financing expressed in terms of the price that would have been paid in an all-cash sale.
6. Written, legal instrument that conveys an estate or interest in real property to someone else, assuming it is executed and delivered.
11. An ordinal technique for analyzing data, commonly used in the analysis of comparable sales.
13. The dwelling that is designated for occupancy by one family.
14. The impairment of functional capacity of a property according to market tastes and standards.

DOWN

1. Testimony of persons who are presumed to have special knowledge of, or skill in, a particular field due to education, experience, or study.
3. The development or improvement of cleared or undeveloped land in an urban renewal area.
4. A stage in a market area's life cycle characterized by renewal, redevelopment, modernization, and increasing demand.
7. Trespassing on the domain of another.
8. A remainder that has negligible economic utility or value due to its size, shape, or other detrimental characteristics.
9. One who is the right to occupancy and use of the property of another for a period of time according to a lease agreement.
10. The act or process of developing an opinion of value.
12. Zoning regulations that designate the distance a building must be set back from the front, rear, and sides of the property lines.

A. Encroachment
D. Remnant
G. Appraisal
J. Redevelopment
M. Revitalization

B. Ranking Analysis
E. Deed
H. Setback
K. Functional Obsolesce
N. Single Family House

C. Cash Equivalent
F. Express contract
I. Expert Testimony
L. Lessee
O. Present Value

14. Using the Across and Down clues, write the correct words in the numbered grid below.

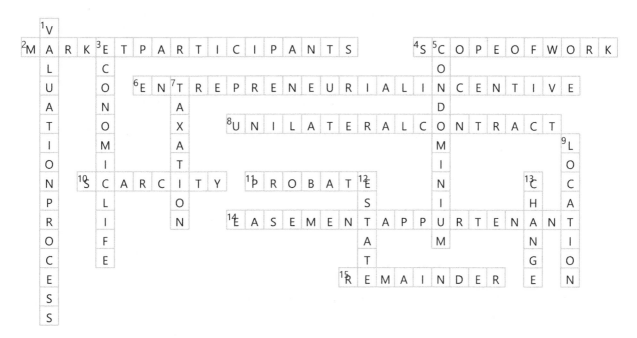

ACROSS

2. The parties involved in the transfer of property rights. Includes buyers, sellers, lessors, lessees, and brokers and their agents.
4. The type and extent of research and analyses in appraisal or appraisal review assignment.
6. The amount entrepreneur expects to receive for his or her contribution to the project.
8. Only one party makes a promise
10. The present or anticipated undersupply of an item relative to the demand for it. Conditions of scarcity contribute to value.
11. The legal process of settling an estate after a person has died.
14. Easement that is attached to, benefits, and passes with the conveyance of the dominant estate. Burdens the servient estate.
15. A future possessor read interest in real estate that is given to a third-party and matures upon the termination of a limited or determinable be.

DOWN

1. A systematic set of procedures an appraiser follows to provide answers to a client's questions about real property value.
3. The period over time which a structure may be competitive in the market.
5. A form of ownership in which each owner possesses the exclusive right to use and occupy an allotted unit plus an undivided interest in common areas.
7. Right of government to raise revenue through assessments on valuable goods, products, and rights.
9. The relative position of the property to competitive properties and other value influences in its market area
12. Right or interest in property.
13. The result of the cause and effect relationship among the forces that influence real property value.

A. Entrepreneurial Incentive
B. Remainder
C. Condominium
D. Easement appurtenant
E. Economic life
F. Probate
G. Scarcity
H. Change
I. Unilateral contract
J. Market Participants
K. Estate
L. Scope of Work
M. Taxation
N. Location
O. Valuation process

15. Using the Across and Down clues, write the correct words in the numbered grid below.

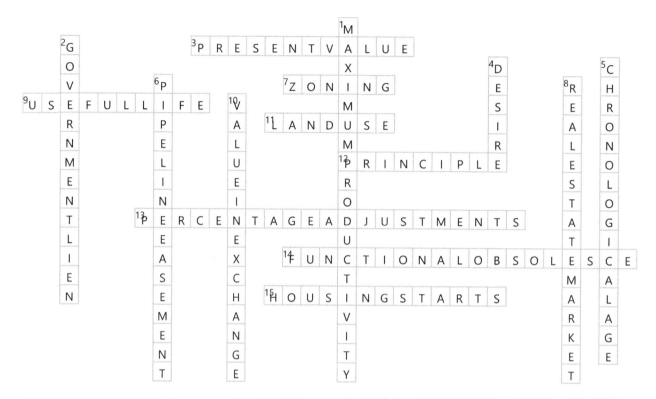

ACROSS

3. The value of a future payment or series of future payments discounted to the current date or to time period zero.
7. Public regulation of the character and extent of real estate use though police power.
9. The period of time over which a structure may reasonably be expected to perform the function for which it was designed.
11. The employment of a site or holding to produce revenue or other benefits.
12. The amount of money borrowed from lender (mortgagee).
13. Adjustments for differences between the subject and comparable properties expressed as a percentage of the sale price of the comparable property.
14. The impairment of functional capacity of a property according to market tastes and standards.
15. Newly constructed housing units; includes both single-family and multifamily domiciles.

DOWN

1. One of the four criteria the highest and best use of a property must meet; the selected land-use must yield the highest value of the possible uses.
2. Property taxes or special assessments, has priority over other liens.
4. Purchaser's wish for an item to satisfy human needs or individual wants beyond essential life-support needs.
5. The number of years since a structure or bldg. was originally built (birth).
6. The right to construct, operate, and maintain a pipeline over the lands of others within prescribed geographical limits.
8. Buyers and sellers of particular real estate and the transactions that occur among them.
10. Price an economic good will attract in the competitive market.

A. Useful life
D. Present Value
G. Maximum Productivity
J. Chronological age
M. Principle

B. Percentage Adjustments
E. Real Estate Market
H. Land Use
K. Desire
N. Pipeline Easement

C. Functional Obsolesce
F. Housing Starts
I. Zoning
L. Value in Exchange
O. Government lien

16. Using the Across and Down clues, write the correct words in the numbered grid below.

Crossword grid solution:

- 3 Across: CAPITALIZATION RATE
- 6 Across: SPECIFIC LIEN
- 7 Across: LESSOR
- 8 Across: FAIR MARKET VALUE
- 9 Across: CONSERVATION EASEMENT
- 10 Across: MASTER PLAN
- 11 Across: SYNDICATION
- 12 Across: REHABILITATION
- 13 Across: INVESTMENT VALUE
- 1 Down: REAL PROPERTY
- 2 Down: COMPETANCE (COMPETENCE)
- 3 Down: COST APPROACH
- 4 Down: ABSORPTION RATE
- 5 Down: ENCROACHMENT
- 7 Down: LOCATION

ACROSS

3. Any rate used to convert income into value.
6. Lien against a particular property owned by the debtor.
7. One who conveys the rights of occupancy and use to others under lease agreement.
8. The price at which the property would change hands between a willing buyer and a willing seller and both having reasonable knowledge of relevant facts.
9. An interest in real property restricting future land-use to preservation, conservation, wildlife habitat, or some combination of those uses.
10. A comprehensive, long-range official plan that guides the physical growth and development of the community.
11. A private or public partnership that pools funds for the acquisition and development of real estate projects or other business ventures.
12. The repair and restoration of existing improvements that are in poor condition to a state that makes the property competitive again.
13. Value to a particular individual. The present worth of anticipated future benefits.

DOWN

1. The interests, benefits, and rights inherent in ownership of real estate.
2. The state of having the requisite or adequate ability or qualities to perform the specific assignment and produce credible assignment results.
3. an estimate of replacement cost of a structure, less depreciation, plus land value.
4. Estimate of the rate at which a particular class of properties will sell in a particular geographic area.
5. Trespassing on the domain of another.
7. The relative position of the property to competitive properties and other value influences in its market area

A. Cost Approach
D. Master Plan
G. Capitalization Rate
J. Investment Value
M. Specific Lien

B. Absorption rate
E. Real Property
H. Lessor
K. Rehabilitation
N. Encroachment

C. Fair Market Value
F. Competence
I. Conservation Easement
L. Location
O. Syndication

17. Using the Across and Down clues, write the correct words in the numbered grid below.

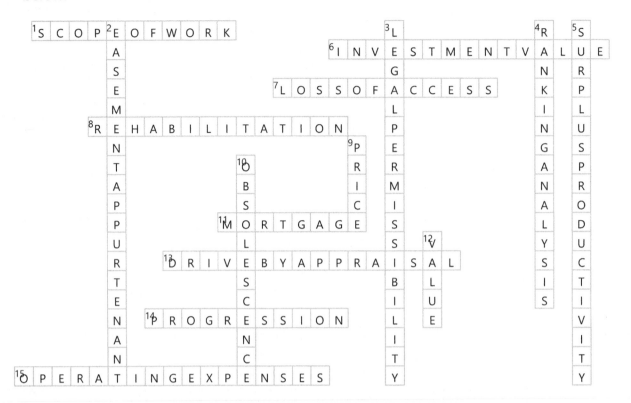

ACROSS

1. The type and extent of research and analyses in appraisal or appraisal review assignment.
6. Value to a particular individual. The present worth of anticipated future benefits.
7. Depriving an abutting owner of the inherent rights of ingress and to egress from the highway or street.
8. The repair and restoration of existing improvements that are in poor condition to a state that makes the property competitive again.
11. Pledge of a described property interest as collateral or security for the repayment of a loan under certain terms and conditions.
13. An appraisal report in which the scope of work includes an exterior-only viewing of the subject property.
14. Value of an inferior property is enhanced by its association with better properties of the same type.
15. The periodic expenditures necessary to maintain the real property and continue production of the effective gross income, assuming prudent and competent management.

DOWN

2. Easement that is attached to, benefits, and passes with the conveyance of the dominant estate. Burdens the servient estate.
3. One of the four criteria the highest and best use of a property must meet.
4. An ordinal technique for analyzing data, commonly used in the analysis of comparable sales.
5. Net income that is left after the 4 agents of production have been paid.
9. Amount a particular purchaser agrees to pay and a particular seller agrees to accept under the circumstances surrounding their transaction.
10. One cause of depreciation.
12. Monetary worth of a property, good, or service to buyers and sellers at a given time.

A. Scope of Work
D. Operating Expenses
G. Investment Value
J. Ranking Analysis
M. Progression

B. Price
E. Drive by Appraisal
H. Obsolescence
K. Easement appurtenant
N. Surplus Productivity

C. Loss of Access
F. Mortgage
I. Legal Permissibility
L. Rehabilitation
O. Value

18. Using the Across and Down clues, write the correct words in the numbered grid below.

ACROSS

1. The most probable rent the property should bring in a competitive and open market reflecting all conditions and restrictions of the lease agreement.
4. A letter or statement that serves as a notice of delivery from the appraiser to the client of a report containing an opinion or conclusion concerning real estate
5. Annual crops and plantings such as corn, wheat, and vegetables.
6. The result of the cause and effect relationship among the forces that influence real property value.
8. The legal responsibility of a plaintiff to make reasonable efforts, after an injury or breach of contract, to alleviate the effects of the injury or breach.
10. A study of the cost-benefit relationships of an economic endeavor.
11. Any claim or liability that affects our limits the title to property.
12. Two or more sales are compared to derive an indication of the size of the adjustment for a single characteristic.
13. Ability of a product to satisfy a human want, need, or desire.
14. A lease in which an intermediate, or sandwich, leaseholder is the lessee of one party and the lessor of another.

DOWN

1. Amount paid for an income producing property.
2. Complementary land uses; inhabitants, buildings, or business enterprises.
3. The rights of an owner to possess, control, enjoy, sell, lease, mortgage, and dispose of the property.
7. Land that is not needed to serve or support the existing improvement.
9. Combination of all elements that constitute proof of ownership.

A. Excess Land
D. Encumbrance
G. Paired data analysis
J. Bundle of rights
M. Market Rent

B. Utility
E. Change
H. Neighborhood
K. Mitigation of Damages
N. Sandwich lease

C. Title
F. Market Price
I. Feasibility Analysis
L. Emblements
O. Letter of Transmittal

19. Using the Across and Down clues, write the correct words in the numbered grid below.

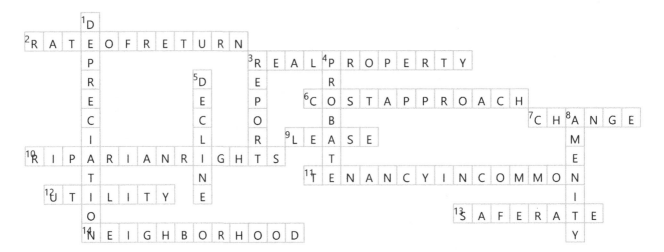

ACROSS

2. The ratio of income or yield to the original investment.
3. The interests, benefits, and rights inherent in ownership of real estate.
6. an estimate of replacement cost of a structure, less depreciation, plus land value.
7. The result of the cause and effect relationship among the forces that influence real property value.
9. A contract in which the rights to use and occupy land or structures are transferred by the owner to another for a specified period of time in return for specified rent.
10. Rights pertaining to properties touching a river or stream.
11. Estate owned by 2 or more persons, each of whom has an equal undivided interest. Unlike Joint Tenancy and Tenancy by Entirety, No right of survivorship.
12. Ability of a product to satisfy a human want, need, or desire.
13. The minimum rate of return on invested capital.
14. Complementary land uses; inhabitants, buildings, or business enterprises.

DOWN

1. In appraising, a loss in property value from any cause
3. Any communication, written or oral, of an appraisal or appraisal review that is transmitted to the client upon completion of an assignment.
4. The legal process of settling an estate after a person has died.
5. A stage of diminishing demand in a market areas life cycle.
8. A tangible or intangible benefit of real property that enhances its attractiveness or increases the satisfaction of the user.

A. Real Property
B. Riparian rights
C. Report
D. Probate
E. Cost Approach
F. Lease
G. Amenity
H. Change
I. Utility
J. Rate of return
K. Neighborhood
L. Safe Rate
M. Tenancy in Common
N. Decline
O. Depreciation

20. Using the Across and Down clues, write the correct words in the numbered grid below.

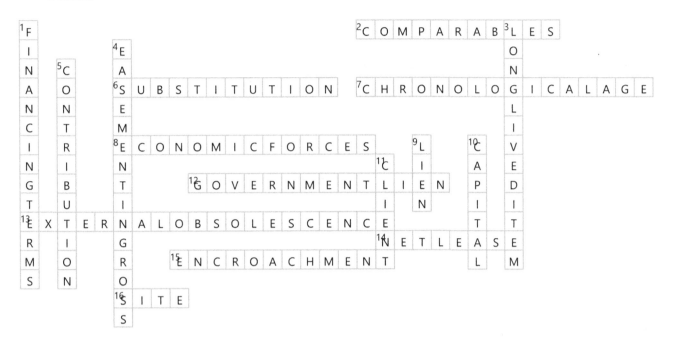

ACROSS

2. A shortened term for similar property sales, rentals, or operating expenses used for comparison in the valuation process.
6. When a property has the lowest asking price and the same utility as other properties, yet attracts the greatest demand.
7. The number of years since a structure or bldg. was originally built (birth).
8. Supply and demand for housing, economic activity.
12. Property taxes or special assessments, has priority over other liens.
13. An element of depreciation; and diminution in value caused by negative externalities and generally incurable on the part of the owner, landlord, or tenant.
14. A lease in which the landlord passes on all expenses to the tenant.
15. Trespassing on the domain of another.
16. land that is improved so that is ready to be used for a specific purpose.

DOWN

1. The manner in which a transaction was financed.
3. A building component with an expected remaining economic life that is the same as the remaining economic life of the entire structure.
4. Easement that is not attached or appurtenant to any particular estate; does not run with the land nor is it transferred through the conveyance of title.
5. The value of a particular component is measured in terms of the amount it adds to the value of the whole property.
9. Charge against property in which the property is the security for payment of the debt.
10. goods, such as equipment (machinery and tools), bldgs., and infrastructure.
11. The party of parties who engage an appraiser in a specific assignment.

A. Capital
D. Site
G. Net Lease
J. Government lien
M. Contribution
P. Economic Forces

B. Substitution
E. Financing Terms
H. Client
K. Easement in gross
N. Long Lived Item

C. Encroachment
F. Comparables
I. Lien
L. Chronological age
O. External Obsolescence

21. Using the Across and Down clues, write the correct words in the numbered grid below.

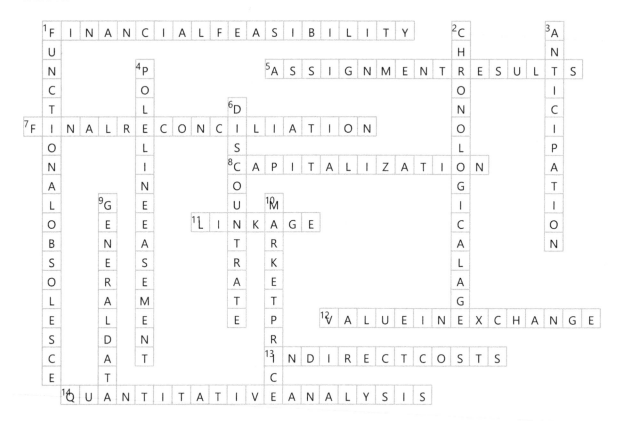

ACROSS

1. One of the four criteria the highest and best use of a property must meet.
5. An appraiser's opinions or conclusions developed specific to an assignment.
7. The last phase in the development of the value opinion in which two or more value indications derived from market data are resolved into a value opinion.
8. The conversion of income into value.
11. Time and distance relationships between a particular use and supporting facilities.
12. Price an economic good will attract in the competitive market.
13. Soft cost expenditures that are necessary components but are not typically part of the construction contract.
14. Analyzing value of a property based on numerical data.

DOWN

1. The impairment of functional capacity of a property according to market tastes and standards.
2. The number of years since a structure or bldg. was originally built (birth).
3. Value is a function of expected benefits to get from the ownership of the property.
4. An easement for the construction, maintenance, and operation of a full line, usually for the transmission of electric power.
6. The yield rate used to convert future payments or receipts into present value; usually considered to be a synonym for yield rate.
9. Items of information on value influences that derive from social, economic, governmental, and environmental forces and originate outside the property being appraised.
10. Amount paid for an income producing property.

A. Discount Rate
D. Market Price
G. Pole Line Easement
J. Value in Exchange
M. Indirect costs

B. Capitalization
E. Quantitative Analysis
H. Functional Obsolesce
K. Assignment Results
N. Financial Feasibility

C. Linkage
F. Anticipation
I. Final Reconciliation
L. Chronological age
O. General Data

22. Using the Across and Down clues, write the correct words in the numbered grid below.

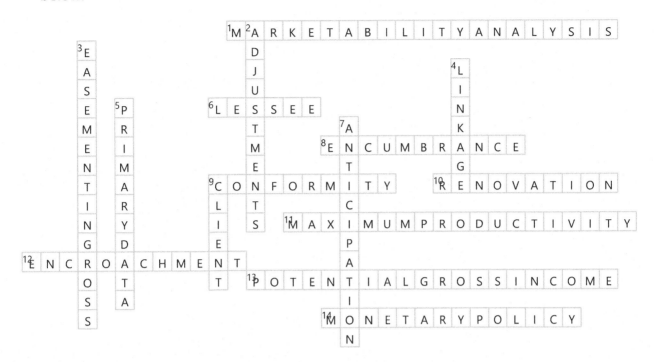

ACROSS

1. A process for examining the productive attributes of the specific property, its demand and supply, and its geographic market area.
6. One who is the right to occupancy and use of the property of another for a period of time according to a lease agreement.
8. Any claim or liability that affects our limits the title to property.
9. The more a property or its components are in harmony with the surrounding properties or components, the greater the contributory value.
10. The process in which older structures or historic buildings are modernized, remodeled, or restored.
11. One of the four criteria the highest and best use of a property must meet; the selected land-use must yield the highest value of the possible uses.
12. Trespassing on the domain of another.
13. The total income attributable to real property at full occupancy before vacancy and operating expenses are deducted.
14. Guiding control of the money supply in the economy.

DOWN

2. Changes made to basic data to facilitate comparison or understanding.
3. Easement that is not attached or appurtenant to any particular estate; does not run with the land nor is it transferred through the conveyance of title.
4. Time and distance relationships between a particular use and supporting facilities.
5. Information that is gathered in its original form by the analyst.
7. Value is a function of expected benefits to get from the ownership of the property.
9. The party of parties who engage an appraiser in a specific assignment.

A. Renovation
D. Marketability Analysis
G. Client
J. Monetary Policy
M. Lessee
B. Anticipation
E. Linkage
H. Conformity
K. Potential Gross Income
N. Encroachment
C. Adjustments
F. Encumbrance
I. Primary Data
L. Easement in gross
O. Maximum Productivity

23. Using the Across and Down clues, write the correct words in the numbered grid below.

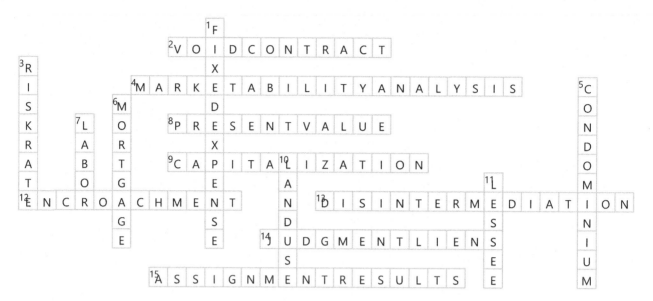

ACROSS

2. Has no legal force or binding effect and cannot be enforced in a court of law.
4. A process for examining the productive attributes of the specific property, its demand and supply, and its geographic market area.
8. The value of a future payment or series of future payments discounted to the current date or to time period zero.
9. The conversion of income into value.
12. Trespassing on the domain of another.
13. Flow of savings account money from savings and loans accounts to higher yield investments.
14. Typically result from a lawsuit in which a monetary judgment is awarded.
15. An appraiser's opinions or conclusions developed specific to an assignment.

DOWN

1. Operating expenses that generally do not vary with occupancy and that prudent management will pay whether the properties occupied or vacant.
3. The annual rate of return on capital that is commensurate with the risk assumed by the investor; the rate of interest or yield necessary to attract capital.
5. A form of ownership in which each owner possesses the exclusive right to use and occupy an allotted unit plus an undivided interest in common areas.
6. Pledge of a described property interest as collateral or security for the repayment of a loan under certain terms and conditions.
7. comprises of all costs required to construct and market the product as land alone or with improvements.
10. The employment of a site or holding to produce revenue or other benefits.
11. One who is the right to occupancy and use of the property of another for a period of time according to a lease agreement.

A. Assignment Results
B. Void contract
C. Disintermediation
D. Marketability Analysis
E. Risk Rate
F. Capitalization
G. Labor
H. Fixed Expense
I. Judgment liens
J. Condominium
K. Present Value
L. Mortgage
M. Lessee
N. Land Use
O. Encroachment

24. Using the Across and Down clues, write the correct words in the numbered grid below.

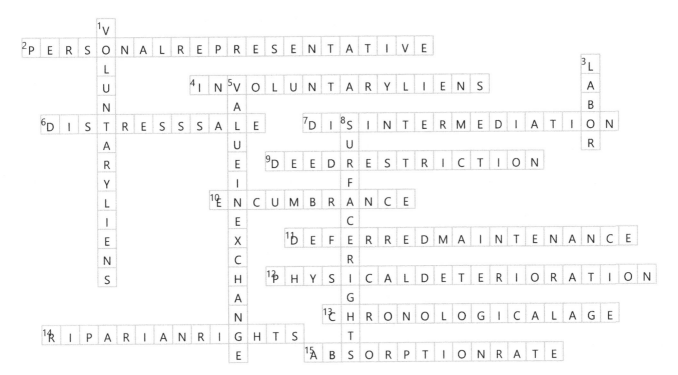

ACROSS

2. An individual or other legal person designated in a will to settle the estate of a deceased person.
4. Created by law, rather than by choice. i.e. property tax lien.
6. A sale involving a seller acting under undue distress.
7. Flow of savings account money from savings and loans accounts to higher yield investments.
9. A limitation that passes with the land regardless of the owner.
10. Any claim or liability that affects our limits the title to property.
11. Needed repairs or replacement of items that should have taken place during the course of normal maintenance.
12. The wear and tear that begins with the building is completed and placed into service.
13. The number of years since a structure or bldg. was originally built (birth).
14. Rights pertaining to properties touching a river or stream.
15. Estimate of the rate at which a particular class of properties will sell in a particular geographic area.

DOWN

1. Created intentionally by property owner's actions. i.e. mortgage
3. comprises of all costs required to construct and market the product as land alone or with improvements.
5. Price an economic good will attract in the competitive market.
8. Land, water, and anything attached to the land-either naturally or placed by human hands.

A. Deferred Maintenance
B. Value in Exchange
C. Distress Sale
D. Personal Representative
E. Encumbrance
F. Labor
G. Riparian rights
H. Surface rights
I. Voluntary liens
J. Involuntary liens
K. Absorption rate
L. Deed restriction
M. Physical Deterioration
N. Chronological age
O. Disintermediation

25. Using the Across and Down clues, write the correct words in the numbered grid below.

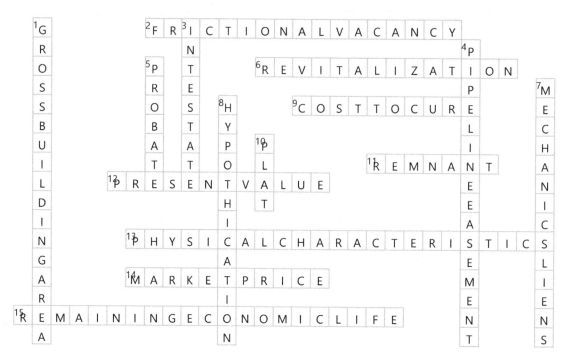

ACROSS

2. The amount of vacant space needed in a market for its orderly operation.
6. A stage in a market area's life cycle characterized by renewal, redevelopment, modernization, and increasing demand.
9. The cost to restore an item of deferred maintenance to new or reasonably new condition.
11. A remainder that has negligible economic utility or value due to its size, shape, or other detrimental characteristics.
12. The value of a future payment or series of future payments discounted to the current date or to time period zero.
13. A category of elements of comparison in the sales comparison approach
14. Amount paid for an income producing property.
15. The estimated period during which improvements will continue to represent the highest and best use of the property.

DOWN

1. Total floor area of a building, excluding unenclosed area, measured from the exterior of the walls of the above-grade area.
3. The condition of dying without a will.
4. The right to construct, operate, and maintain a pipeline over the lands of others within prescribed geographical limits.
5. The legal process of settling an estate after a person has died.
7. arise from construction and other improvements to real estate.
8. A borrower has possession of the property.
10. A plan, map, or chart of a city, town, section, or subdivision indicating the location and boundaries of individual properties.

A. Present Value
B. Remaining Economic Life
C. Remnant
D. Probate
E. Revitalization
F. Frictional Vacancy
G. Market Price
H. Mechanics liens
I. Physical Characteristics
J. Gross Building Area
K. Hypothication
L. Pipeline Easement
M. Intestate
N. Cost to Cure
O. Plat

26. Using the Across and Down clues, write the correct words in the numbered grid below.

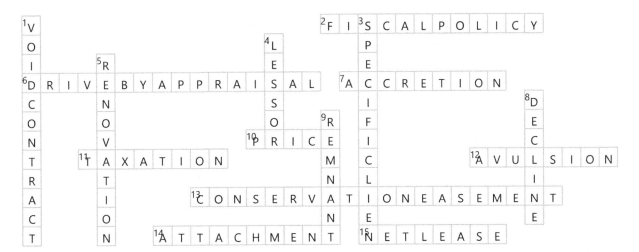

ACROSS

2. Management of government receipts and expenditures.
6. An appraisal report in which the scope of work includes an exterior-only viewing of the subject property.
7. An increase in dry land created by the gradual accumulation of waterborne solid material over formerly riparian land.
10. Amount a particular purchaser agrees to pay and a particular seller agrees to accept under the circumstances surrounding their transaction.
11. Right of government to raise revenue through assessments on valuable goods, products, and rights.
12. The sudden removal of land from the property of one owner to that of another, e.g., change in the course of a river.
13. An interest in real property restricting future land-use to preservation, conservation, wildlife habitat, or some combination of those uses.
14. Seizure of property by court order.
15. A lease in which the landlord passes on all expenses to the tenant.

DOWN

1. Has no legal force or binding effect and cannot be enforced in a court of law.
3. Lien against a particular property owned by the debtor.
4. One who conveys the rights of occupancy and use to others under lease agreement.
5. The process in which older structures or historic buildings are modernized, remodeled, or restored.
8. A stage of diminishing demand in a market areas life cycle.
9. A remainder that has negligible economic utility or value due to its size, shape, or other detrimental characteristics.

A. Net Lease	B. Conservation Easement	C. Remnant
D. Accretion	E. Lessor	F. Specific Lien
G. Decline	H. Drive by Appraisal	I. Void contract
J. Price	K. Attachment	L. Taxation
M. Renovation	N. Avulsion	O. Fiscal Policy

27. Using the Across and Down clues, write the correct words in the numbered grid below.

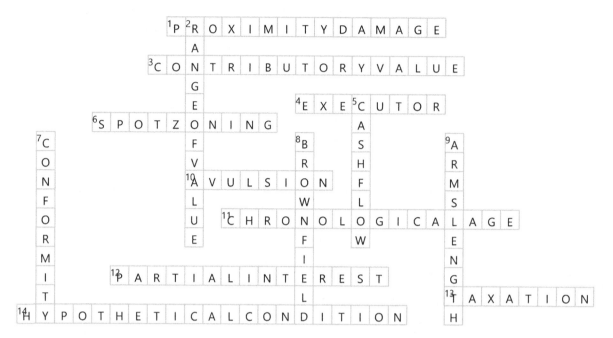

ACROSS

1. Damages that is caused by the remainder's proximity to the improvement being constructed.
3. The change in the value of a property as a whole, resulting from the addition or deletion of a property component.
4. An individual or other legal person designated in a will to settle the estate of the deceased person.
6. An exception to the general zoning regulations; permits specific, usually small, parcels of land to be zone for a use that is not permitted in the surrounding area.
10. The sudden removal of land from the property of one owner to that of another, e.g., change in the course of a river.
11. The number of years since a structure or bldg. was originally built (birth).
12. Divided or undivided rights in real estate that represent less than the whole.
13. Right of government to raise revenue through assessments on valuable goods, products, and rights.
14. A condition which is contrary to what is known by the appraiser to exist on the effective date of the assignment results, but is used for the purpose of analysis.

DOWN

2. In final reconciliation, the range in which the final market value opinion of a property may fall; usually stated as the interval between a high and low value limit.
5. The periodic income attributable to the interests in real property.
7. The more a property or its components are in harmony with the surrounding properties or components, the greater the contributory value.
8. Industrial or commercial site that is abandoned or underused because it suffers from real or perceived continuing contamination.
9. A transaction in which the buyers and sellers of a product act independently and have no relationship to each other.

A. Spot Zoning
D. Avulsion
G. Cash Flow
J. Brownfield
M. Chronological age

B. Hypothetical Condition
E. Executor
H. Proximity Damage
K. Arms Length
N. Range of Value

C. Partial Interest
F. Taxation
I. Conformity
L. Contributory Value

28. Using the Across and Down clues, write the correct words in the numbered grid below.

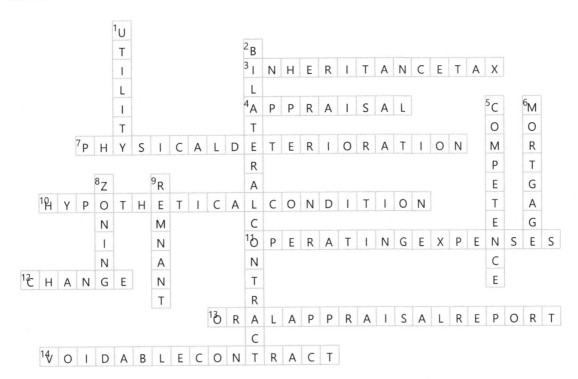

ACROSS

3. A tax on the right to receive property by inheritance; as distinguished from estate tax.
4. The act or process of developing an opinion of value.
7. The wear and tear that begins with the building is completed and placed into service.
10. A condition which is contrary to what is known by the appraiser to exist on the effective date of the assignment results, but is used for the purpose of analysis.
11. The periodic expenditures necessary to maintain the real property and continue production of the effective gross income, assuming prudent and competent management.
12. The result of the cause and effect relationship among the forces that influence real property value.
13. A report that is transmitted orally.
14. Technically valid but gives one or more parties the power to legally void the agreement and thus cancel performance.

DOWN

1. Ability of a product to satisfy a human want, need, or desire.
2. A promise made in exchange for another promise.
5. The state of having the requisite or adequate ability or qualities to perform the specific assignment and produce credible assignment results.
6. Pledge of a described property interest as collateral or security for the repayment of a loan under certain terms and conditions.
8. Public regulation of the character and extent of real estate use though police power.
9. A remainder that has negligible economic utility or value due to its size, shape, or other detrimental characteristics.

A. Bilateral contract
D. Zoning
G. Appraisal
J. Hypothetical Condition
M. Voidable contract

B. Mortgage
E. Competence
H. Physical Deterioration
K. Operating Expenses
N. Utility

C. Change
F. Remnant
I. Inheritance Tax
L. Oral Appraisal Report

29. Using the Across and Down clues, write the correct words in the numbered grid below.

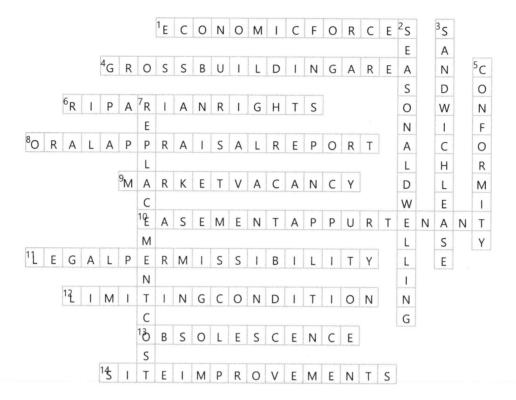

ACROSS

1. Supply and demand for housing, economic activity.
4. Total floor area of a building, excluding unenclosed area, measured from the exterior of the walls of the above-grade area.
6. Rights pertaining to properties touching a river or stream.
8. A report that is transmitted orally.
9. The overall vacancy rate that occurs as a result of the interaction of supply and demand of a particular property type in a particular region or market.
10. Easement that is attached to, benefits, and passes with the conveyance of the dominant estate. Burdens the servient estate.
11. One of the four criteria the highest and best use of a property must meet.
12. A condition that limits the use of a report.
13. One cause of depreciation.
14. Improvements on and off the site that make it suitable for its intended use or development.

DOWN

2. A dwelling not intended for year-round use, e.g., a vacation home.
3. A lease in which an intermediate, or sandwich, leaseholder is the lessee of one party and the lessor of another.
5. The more a property or its components are in harmony with the surrounding properties or components, the greater the contributory value.
7. Dollar amount required to reconstruct a bldg. or other improvement, which have the same or equivalent utility as the original.

A. Easement appurtenant
D. Seasonal Dwelling
G. Sandwich lease
J. Limiting Condition
M. Legal Permissibility

B. Market Vacancy
E. Site Improvements
H. Conformity
K. Economic Forces
N. Obsolescence

C. Replacement Cost
F. Oral Appraisal Report
I. Gross Building Area
L. Riparian rights

30. Using the Across and Down clues, write the correct words in the numbered grid below.

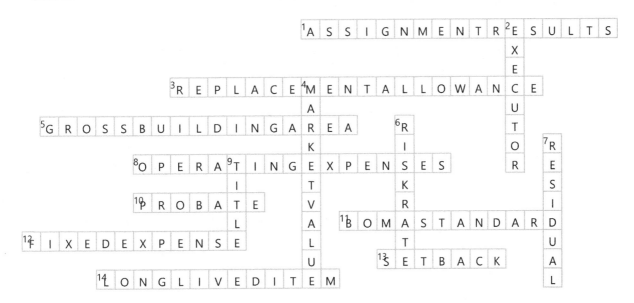

ACROSS

1. An appraiser's opinions or conclusions developed specific to an assignment.
3. An allowance that provides for the periodic replacement of building components that wear out more rapidly than the building itself.
5. Total floor area of a building, excluding unenclosed area, measured from the exterior of the walls of the above-grade area.
8. The periodic expenditures necessary to maintain the real property and continue production of the effective gross income, assuming prudent and competent management.
10. The legal process of settling an estate after a person has died.
11. The standard method of measurement for office buildings as defined by the Building Owners and Managers Association.
12. Operating expenses that generally do not vary with occupancy and that prudent management will pay whether the properties occupied or vacant.
13. Zoning regulations that designate the distance a building must be set back from the front, rear, and sides of the property lines.
14. A building component with an expected remaining economic life that is the same as the remaining economic life of the entire structure.

DOWN

2. An individual or other legal person designated in a will to settle the estate of the deceased person.
4. The most probable price at which real estate would sell.
6. The annual rate of return on capital that is commensurate with the risk assumed by the investor; the rate of interest or yield necessary to attract capital.
7. The quantity left over.
9. Combination of all elements that constitute proof of ownership.

A. Fixed Expense
B. Long Lived Item
C. Assignment Results
D. Operating Expenses
E. Gross Building Area
F. Replacement Allowance
G. Residual
H. Title
I. BOMA Standard
J. Risk Rate
K. Market Value
L. Setback
M. Probate
N. Executor

31. Using the Across and Down clues, write the correct words in the numbered grid below.

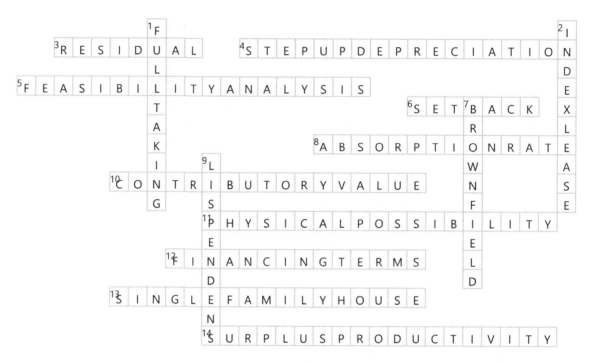

ACROSS

3. The quantity left over.
4. The readjustment of the value of an appreciated asset for tax purposes upon inheritance.
5. A study of the cost-benefit relationships of an economic endeavor.
6. Zoning regulations that designate the distance a building must be set back from the front, rear, and sides of the property lines.
8. Estimate of the rate at which a particular class of properties will sell in a particular geographic area.
10. The change in the value of a property as a whole, resulting from the addition or deletion of a property component.
11. One of the criteria for highest and best use of a property must meet.
12. The manner in which a transaction was financed.
13. The dwelling that is designated for occupancy by one family.
14. Net income that is left after the 4 agents of production have been paid.

DOWN

1. The entire taking of the full real property interest of a parcel for public use under the power of eminent domain; requires the payment of compensation.
2. The rental is based on a common index (i.e. Consumer Price Index or the Wholesale Price Index.
7. Industrial or commercial site that is abandoned or underused because it suffers from real or perceived continuing contamination.
9. Legal term signifying pending litigation that can affect ownership title to real estate.

A. Lis Pendens
D. Residual
G. Physical Possibility
J. Surplus Productivity
M. Step Up Depreciation

B. Financing Terms
E. Brownfield
H. Single Family House
K. Setback
N. Contributory Value

C. Full Taking
F. Absorption rate
I. Feasibility Analysis
L. Index lease

32. Using the Across and Down clues, write the correct words in the numbered grid below.

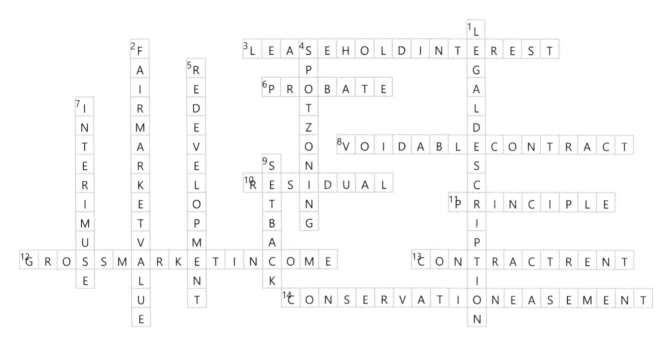

ACROSS

3. The tenant's possessory interest created by a lease.
6. The legal process of settling an estate after a person has died.
8. Technically valid but gives one or more parties the power to legally void the agreement and thus cancel performance.
10. The quantity left over.
11. The amount of money borrowed from lender (mortgagee).
12. Annual amount of total revenue that a property would generate if it were occupied all throughout the year.
13. The actual rental income specified in a lease.
14. An interest in real property restricting future land-use to preservation, conservation, wildlife habitat, or some combination of those uses.

DOWN

1. A description of land that identifies the real estate according to a system established or approved by law.
2. The price at which the property would change hands between a willing buyer and a willing seller and both having reasonable knowledge of relevant facts.
4. An exception to the general zoning regulations; permits specific, usually small, parcels of land to be zone for a use that is not permitted in the surrounding area.
5. The development or improvement of cleared or undeveloped land in an urban renewal area.
7. Temporary use to which a site or improved property is put until it is ready to be put to its future highest and best use.
9. Zoning regulations that designate the distance a building must be set back from the front, rear, and sides of the property lines.

A. Spot Zoning
D. Residual
G. Redevelopment
J. Conservation Easement
M. Legal Description

B. Probate
E. Gross Market Income
H. Setback
K. Fair Market Value
N. Interim use

C. Voidable contract
F. Leasehold Interest
I. Principle
L. Contract rent

33. Using the Across and Down clues, write the correct words in the numbered grid below.

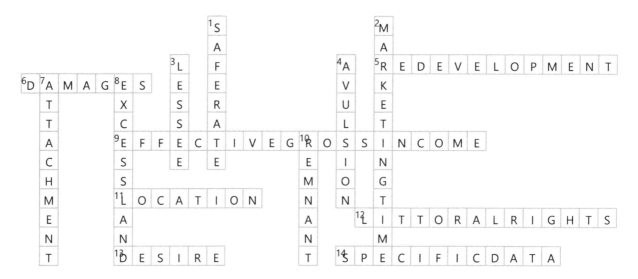

ACROSS

5. The development or improvement of cleared or undeveloped land in an urban renewal area.
6. In condemnation, the loss in value to the remainder in a partial taking of property.
9. The total annual income the rental property produces after subtracting vacancy losses and adding miscellaneous income.
11. The relative position of the property to competitive properties and other value influences in its market area
12. Rights pertaining to properties abutting a lake or pond.
13. Purchaser's wish for an item to satisfy human needs or individual wants beyond essential life-support needs.
14. Data that is analyzed through the process of comparison.

DOWN

1. The minimum rate of return on invested capital.
2. Time it takes an interest in real property to sell on the market subsequent to the date of an appraisal.
3. One who is the right to occupancy and use of the property of another for a period of time according to a lease agreement.
4. The sudden removal of land from the property of one owner to that of another, e.g., change in the course of a river.
7. Seizure of property by court order.
8. Land that is not needed to serve or support the existing improvement.
10. A remainder that has negligible economic utility or value due to its size, shape, or other detrimental characteristics.

A. Damages
D. Desire
G. Littoral rights
J. Avulsion
M. Excess Land

B. Attachment
E. Location
H. Safe Rate
K. Lessee
N. Specific Data

C. Redevelopment
F. Marketing time
I. Remnant
L. Effective Gross Income

34. Using the Across and Down clues, write the correct words in the numbered grid below.

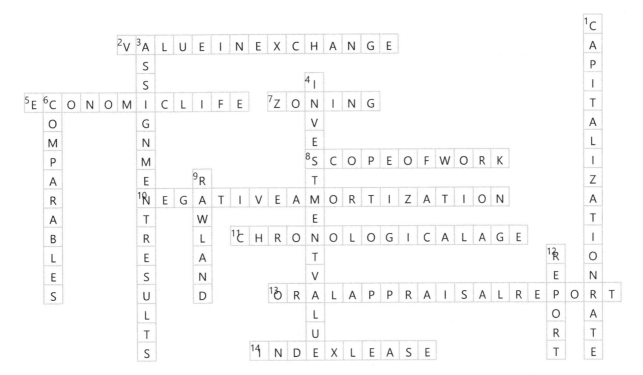

ACROSS

2. Price an economic good will attract in the competitive market.
5. The period over time which a structure may be competitive in the market.
7. Public regulation of the character and extent of real estate use though police power.
8. The type and extent of research and analyses in appraisal or appraisal review assignment.
10. Total payment is insufficient to pay interest due.
11. The number of years since a structure or bldg. was originally built (birth).
13. A report that is transmitted orally.
14. The rental is based on a common index (i.e. Consumer Price Index or the Wholesale Price Index.

DOWN

1. Any rate used to convert income into value.
3. An appraiser's opinions or conclusions developed specific to an assignment.
4. Value to a particular individual. The present worth of anticipated future benefits.
6. A shortened term for similar property sales, rentals, or operating expenses used for comparison in the valuation process.
9. Land on which no improvements have been made
12. Any communication, written or oral, of an appraisal or appraisal review that is transmitted to the client upon completion of an assignment.

A. Oral Appraisal Report
D. Negative Amortization
G. Chronological age
J. Raw Land
M. Scope of Work

B. Zoning
E. Comparables
H. Economic life
K. Investment Value
N. Value in Exchange

C. Capitalization Rate
F. Index lease
I. Report
L. Assignment Results

35. Using the Across and Down clues, write the correct words in the numbered grid below.

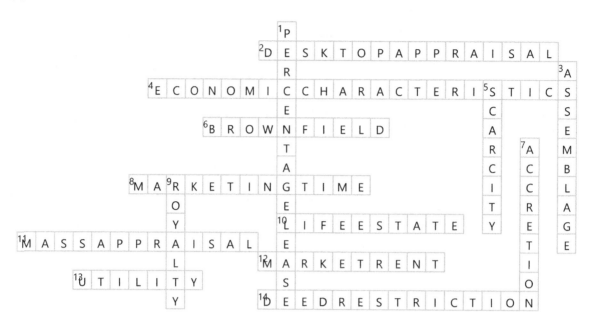

ACROSS

2. An appraisal report in which the appraiser's scope of work does not include an inspection of the subject property or comparables.
4. An element of comparison in the sales comparison approach.
6. Industrial or commercial site that is abandoned or underused because it suffers from real or perceived continuing contamination.
8. Time it takes an interest in real property to sell on the market subsequent to the date of an appraisal.
10. Total rights of use, occupancy and control, limited to the lifetime of the designated party, i.e. life tenant.
11. The process of valuing a universe of properties as of a given date using standard methodology, employing common data, and allowing for statistical testing.
12. The most probable rent the property should bring in a competitive and open market reflecting all conditions and restrictions of the lease agreement.
13. Ability of a product to satisfy a human want, need, or desire.
14. A limitation that passes with the land regardless of the owner.

DOWN

1. Most commonly found in retail business. This lease has a base rent which is fixed and an excess rent, this is most commonly based on the percentage of the sales.
3. The combining of 2 or more parcels into one ownership (tract).
5. The present or anticipated undersupply of an item relative to the demand for it. Conditions of scarcity contribute to value.
7. An increase in dry land created by the gradual accumulation of waterborne solid material over formerly riparian land.
9. Money paid to an owner of real property or mineral rights for the right to deplete natural resource.

A. Marketing time
D. Accretion
G. Scarcity
J. Market Rent
M. Mass Appraisal

B. Economic Characteristics
E. Percentage lease
H. Deed restriction
K. Royalty
N. Assemblage

C. Brownfield
F. Utility
I. Life estate
L. Desktop Appraisal

36. Using the Across and Down clues, write the correct words in the numbered grid below.

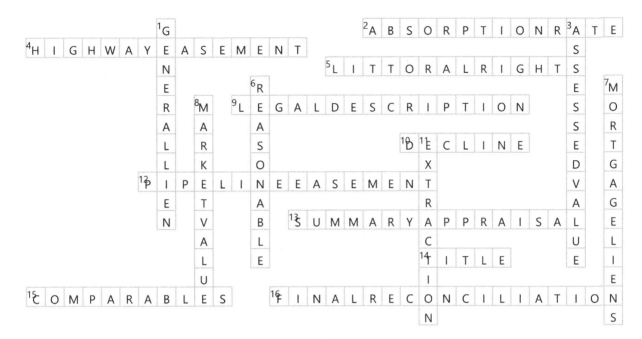

ACROSS

2. Estimate of the rate at which a particular class of properties will sell in a particular geographic area.
4. A right granted or taken for the construction, maintenance, and operation of the highway.
5. Rights pertaining to properties abutting a lake or pond.
9. A description of land that identifies the real estate according to a system established or approved by law.
10. A stage of diminishing demand in a market areas life cycle.
12. The right to construct, operate, and maintain a pipeline over the lands of others within prescribed geographical limits.
13. Data and analyses used in the assignment are summarized (i.e. less detail).
14. Combination of all elements that constitute proof of ownership.
15. A shortened term for similar property sales, rentals, or operating expenses used for comparison in the valuation process.
16. The last phase in the development of the value opinion in which two or more value indications derived from market data are resolved into a value opinion.

DOWN

1. A lien against all of the property owned by the debtor.
3. The value of a property according to the tax rolls in ad valorem taxation.
6. In law, just, rational, appropriate, ordinary, or usual in the circumstances.
7. Voluntary and one of the most common types of liens.
8. The most probable price at which real estate would sell.
11. A method of estimating value in which the depreciated cost of the improvements on the improved property is calculated and deducted from the total sale price

A. Decline
E. Absorption rate
I. Mortgage liens
M. Title

B. Market Value
F. General Lien
J. Comparables

C. Summary appraisal
G. Reasonable
K. Littoral rights
O. Highway Easement

D. Assessed Value
H. Final Reconciliation
L. Extraction
P. Pipeline Easement

37. Using the Across and Down clues, write the correct words in the numbered grid below.

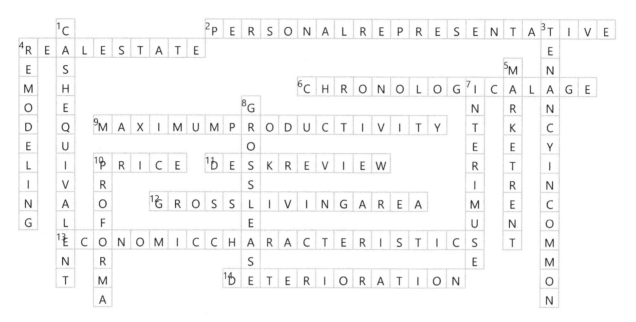

ACROSS

2. An individual or other legal person designated in a will to settle the estate of a deceased person.
4. An identified parcel or tract of land, including improvements.
6. The number of years since a structure or bldg. was originally built (birth).
9. One of the four criteria the highest and best use of a property must meet; the selected land-use must yield the highest value of the possible uses.
10. Amount a particular purchaser agrees to pay and a particular seller agrees to accept under the circumstances surrounding their transaction.
11. An appraisal review in which the reviewer's scope of work does not include an inspection of the subject property.
12. Total area of finished above-grade residential space
13. An element of comparison in the sales comparison approach.
14. Impairment of condition; because of depreciation that reflects the loss in value due to wear and tear, disintegration, use in service, and the action of the elements.

DOWN

1. The price of a property with above- or below-market financing expressed in terms of the price that would have been paid in an all-cash sale.
3. Estate owned by 2 or more persons, each of whom has an equal undivided interest. Unlike Joint Tenancy and Tenancy by Entirety, No right of survivorship.
4. A type of renovation that involves modification or updating of existing improvements.
5. The most probable rent the property should bring in a competitive and open market reflecting all conditions and restrictions of the lease agreement.
7. Temporary use to which a site or improved property is put until it is ready to be put to its future highest and best use.
8. When the lessee (tenant) does not pay any costs of ownership and pays a given amount of rent per period.
10. A projected income and expense statement for proposed development.

A. Price
D. Remodeling
G. Maximum Productivity
J. Cash Equivalent
M. Economic Characteristics
P. Deterioration

B. Market Rent
E. Gross Living Area
H. Real Estate
K. Chronological age
N. Gross lease

C. Interim use
F. Personal Representative
I. Pro Forma
L. Desk Review
O. Tenancy in Common

38. Using the Across and Down clues, write the correct words in the numbered grid below.

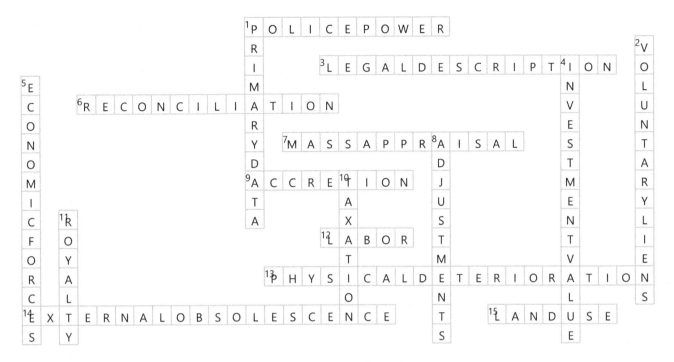

ACROSS

1. When the government regulates the land use for the good of the public.
3. A description of land that identifies the real estate according to a system established or approved by law.
6. The process of reducing a range of value indications into an appropriate conclusion for that analysis.
7. The process of valuing a universe of properties as of a given date using standard methodology, employing common data, and allowing for statistical testing.
9. An increase in dry land created by the gradual accumulation of waterborne solid material over formerly riparian land.
12. comprises of all costs required to construct and market the product as land alone or with improvements.
13. The wear and tear that begins with the building is completed and placed into service.
14. An element of depreciation; and diminution in value caused by negative externalities and generally incurable on the part of the owner, landlord, or tenant.
15. The employment of a site or holding to produce revenue or other benefits.

DOWN

1. Information that is gathered in its original form by the analyst.
2. Created intentionally by property owner's actions. i.e. mortgage
4. Value to a particular individual. The present worth of anticipated future benefits.
5. Supply and demand for housing, economic activity.
8. Changes made to basic data to facilitate comparison or understanding.
10. Right of government to raise revenue through assessments on valuable goods, products, and rights.
11. Money paid to an owner of real property or mineral rights for the right to deplete natural resource.

A. Adjustments
D. Voluntary liens
G. Police power
J. Physical Deterioration
M. Mass Appraisal
P. Labor

B. Land Use
E. Taxation
H. External Obsolescence
K. Reconciliation
N. Royalty

C. Investment Value
F. Accretion
I. Legal Description
L. Primary Data
O. Economic Forces

39. Using the Across and Down clues, write the correct words in the numbered grid below.

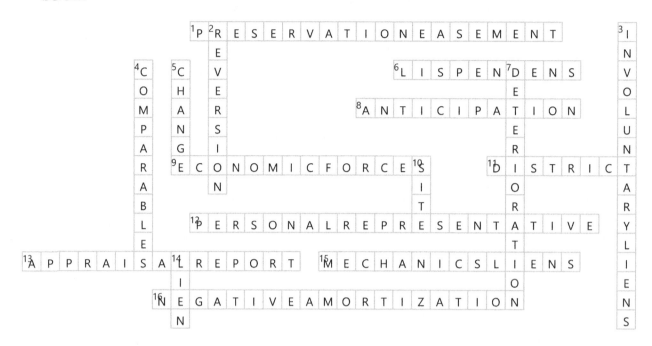

ACROSS

1. A voluntary legal agreement that becomes part of the chain of title thereby protecting a historic, archaeological, or cultural resource.
6. Legal term signifying pending litigation that can affect ownership title to real estate.
8. Value is a function of expected benefits to get from the ownership of the property.
9. Supply and demand for housing, economic activity.
11. Type of market are characterized by homogeneous land use. e.g., apt., commercial, industrial, agricultural
12. An individual or other legal person designated in a will to settle the estate of a deceased person.
13. The written or oral communication of an appraisal.
15. arise from construction and other improvements to real estate.
16. Total payment is insufficient to pay interest due.

DOWN

2. A lump sum benefit that an investor receives or expects to receive upon the termination of an investment; also called reversionary benefit.
3. Created by law, rather than by choice. i.e. property tax lien.
4. A shortened term for similar property sales, rentals, or operating expenses used for comparison in the valuation process.
5. The result of the cause and effect relationship among the forces that influence real property value.
7. Impairment of condition; because of depreciation that reflects the loss in value due to wear and tear, disintegration, use in service, and the action of the elements.
10. land that is improved so that is ready to be used for a specific purpose.
14. Charge against property in which the property is the security for payment of the debt.

A. Comparables
D. Deterioration
G. Economic Forces
J. Mechanics liens
M. Lis Pendens
P. Preservation Easement

B. Personal Representative
E. Involuntary liens
H. Negative Amortization
K. Site
N. Appraisal Report

C. District
F. Anticipation
I. Change
L. Lien
O. Reversion

40. Using the Across and Down clues, write the correct words in the numbered grid below.

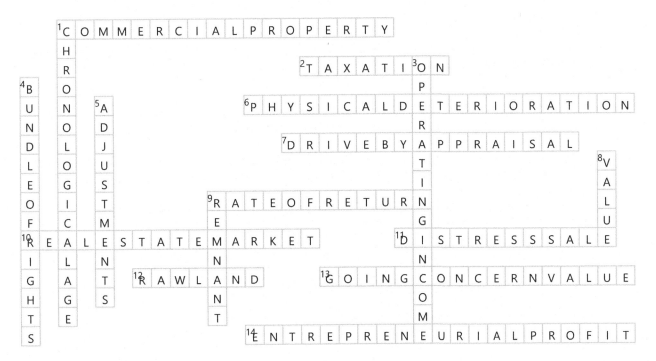

ACROSS

1. Income-producing property such as office and retail buildings.
2. Right of government to raise revenue through assessments on valuable goods, products, and rights.
6. The wear and tear that begins with the building is completed and placed into service.
7. An appraisal report in which the scope of work includes an exterior-only viewing of the subject property.
9. The ratio of income or yield to the original investment.
10. Buyers and sellers of particular real estate and the transactions that occur among them.
11. A sale involving a seller acting under undue distress.
12. Land on which no improvements have been made
13. When the value of a business plus the amount of real property is sought.
14. A market-derived figure that represents the amount an entrepreneur receives for their contribution.

DOWN

1. The number of years since a structure or bldg. was originally built (birth).
3. Income derived from the operation of a business or real property
4. The rights of an owner to possess, control, enjoy, sell, lease, mortgage, and dispose of the property.
5. Changes made to basic data to facilitate comparison or understanding.
8. Monetary worth of a property, good, or service to buyers and sellers at a given time.
9. A remainder that has negligible economic utility or value due to its size, shape, or other detrimental characteristics.

A. Remnant
D. Commercial Property
G. Entrepreneurial profit
J. Adjustments
M. Taxation
P. Chronological age

B. Physical Deterioration
E. Real Estate Market
H. Drive by Appraisal
K. Operating Income
N. Going concern value

C. Raw Land
F. Distress Sale
I. Bundle of rights
L. Rate of return
O. Value

Multiple Choice

A. From the words provided for each clue, provide the letter of the word which best matches the clue.

1. _____ Going to the State. The process that should a property be abandoned, it reverts back to the state.
   A. Neighborhood B. Overall rate C. Expert Testimony D. Escheat

2. _____ A statistical measure that attempts to determine the strength of the relationship between one dependent variable and a series of other changing variables.
   A. Estate B. Desktop Appraisal C. Regression Analysis D. Supra surface rights

3. _____ A lease in which an intermediate, or sandwich, leaseholder is the lessee of one party and the lessor of another.
   A. Eminent Domain B. Average Daily Traffic C. Sandwich lease D. Summary appraisal

4. _____ The employment of a site or holding to produce revenue or other benefits.
   A. Investment Value B. Operating Expenses C. Partial Taking D. Land Use

5. _____ comprises of all costs required to construct and market the product as land alone or with improvements.
   A. Labor B. Pole Line Easement C. Highway Easement D. Littoral rights

6. _____ The taking of part of any real property interest for public use under the power of eminent domain; requires the payment of compensation.
   A. Reproduction Cost B. Maximum Productivity C. Interim use D. Partial Taking

7. _____ Legal term signifying pending litigation that can affect ownership title to real estate.
   A. Entrepreneurial profit B. Functional Classification C. Multifamily Dwelling D. Lis Pendens

8. _____ Total dollar expenditure to develop an improvement.
   A. Maximum Productivity B. Cost C. Client D. Absorption rate

9. _____ A building component with an expected remaining economic life that is the same as the remaining economic life of the entire structure.
   A. Government lien B. Mortgage C. Long Lived Item D. Capitalization Rate

10. _____ Two or more sales are compared to derive an indication of the size of the adjustment for a single characteristic.
    A. Cost Approach B. Price C. Risk Rate D. Paired data analysis

11. _____ The number of years since a structure or bldg. was originally built (birth).
    A. Qualitative analysis B. Chronological age C. Constant D. Tenancy in Common

12. _____ The overall vacancy rate that occurs as a result of the interaction of supply and demand of a particular property type in a particular region or market.
    A. Economic Characteristics B. Market Vacancy C. Title D. Scope of Work

13. _____ Annual crops and plantings such as corn, wheat, and vegetables.
    A. Emblements B. Entrepreneurial profit C. Comparables D. Market Value

14. _____ An appraiser's opinions or conclusions developed specific to an assignment.
    A. Assignment Results B. Market Analysis C. Land Use D. Long Lived Item

15. _____ In appraising, a loss in property value from any cause
    A. Depreciation B. Regression C. Scarcity D. Partial Taking

16. _____ The repair and restoration of existing improvements that are in poor condition to a state that makes the property competitive again.
    A. Paired data analysis B. Estate Tax C. Client D. Rehabilitation

17. _____ A private or public partnership that pools funds for the acquisition and development of real estate projects or other business ventures.
    A. Syndication B. Market Value C. Client D. Estate in land

18. _____ The actual rental income specified in a lease.
A. Functional Obsolesce   B. Negative Amortization   C. Contract rent   D. Operating Income

19. _____ Method by which government can take private property.
A. Remodeling   B. Commercial Property   C. Economic life   D. Condemnation

20. _____ One of the four criteria the highest and best use of a property must meet.
A. Financial Feasibility   B. Market Rent   C. Reproduction Cost   D. Master Plan

21. _____ The minimum rate of return on invested capital.
A. Fair Market Value   B. Accretion   C. Safe Rate   D. Surface rights

22. _____ Testimony of persons who are presumed to have special knowledge of, or skill in, a particular field due to education, experience, or study.
A. Expert Testimony   B. Cost   C. Certification   D. Going concern value

23. _____ An easement for the construction, maintenance, and operation of a full line, usually for the transmission of electric power.
A. Mortgage   B. Encumbrance   C. Deferred Maintenance   D. Pole Line Easement

24. _____ The present or anticipated undersupply of an item relative to the demand for it. Conditions of scarcity contribute to value.
A. Accretion   B. Risk Rate   C. Scarcity   D. Cost

25. _____ Any rate used to convert income into value.
A. Units of comparison   B. Spot Zoning   C. Capitalization Rate   D. Quotent

26. _____ A systematic set of procedures an appraiser follows to provide answers to a client's questions about real property value.
A. Decline   B. Valuation process   C. Adjustments   D. Stability

27. _____ Analyzing value of a property based on numerical data.
A. Renovation   B. Quantitative Analysis   C. Void contract   D. Reserve

28. _____ The period of time over which a structure may reasonably be expected to perform the function for which it was designed.
A. Useful life   B. Exposure Time   C. Reproduction Cost   D. Safe Rate

29. _____ Property taxes or special assessments, has priority over other liens.
A. Amenity   B. Raw Land   C. Avulsion   D. Government lien

30. _____ When a series of different "multiplicands" are multiplied by the same multiplier it is known as.
A. Raw Land   B. Legal Permissibility   C. Constant   D. Capitalization

31. _____ The relative desirability of a property in comparison with similar or competing properties in the area.
A. Amenity   B. Capitalization   C. Marketability   D. Assessed Value

32. _____ The right to construct, operate, and maintain a pipeline over the lands of others within prescribed geographical limits.
A. Reclamation   B. Pipeline Easement   C. Range of Value   D. Competition

33. _____ An increase in value when extra utility is created by combining smaller parcels under single ownership.
A. Competition   B. Plottage   C. Physical life   D. Adjustments

34. _____ The process by which all roads are grouped into classes or systems according to the character of service they are intended to provide.
A. Functional Classification   B. Land Use   C. Mitigation of Damages   D. Entrepreneurial profit

35. _____ The process in which older structures or historic buildings are modernized, remodeled, or restored.
A. Renovation   B. Cost Approach   C. Capitalization   D. Subsurface rights

36. _____ Sum of all fixed and variable operating expenses and reserve for replacement.
A. Total Operating Expenses   B. Market Value   C. Stability   D. Scarcity

37. ___ An element of comparison in the sales comparison approach.
A. Fixed Expense   B. Erosion   C. Effective Date   D. Economic Characteristics

38. ___ Net income that is left after the 4 agents of production have been paid.
A. Intestate   B. Revitalization   C. Surplus Productivity   D. Negative Amortization

39. ___ Income-producing property such as office and retail buildings.
A. Commercial Property   B. Market Vacancy   C. Index lease   D. Voidable contract

40. ___ An individual or other legal person designated in a will to settle the estate of a deceased person.
A. Personal Representative   B. Value in use   C. Arms Length   D. Legal Permissibility

41. ___ Pledge of a described property interest as collateral or security for the repayment of a loan under certain terms and conditions.
A. Raw Land   B. Mortgage   C. Leased Fee Interest   D. Real Estate Market

42. ___ Land on which no improvements have been made
A. Avulsion   B. Raw Land   C. Condemnation   D. Encumbrance

43. ___ an estimate of replacement cost of a structure, less depreciation, plus land value.
A. Competition   B. Spot Zoning   C. Cost Approach   D. Operating Statement

44. ___ The value of a future payment or series of future payments discounted to the current date or to time period zero.
A. Constant   B. Surplus Productivity   C. Paired data analysis   D. Present Value

45. ___ Operating expenses that generally do not vary with occupancy and that prudent management will pay whether the properties occupied or vacant.
A. Estate in land   B. Potential Gross Income   C. Anticipation   D. Fixed Expense

46. ___ Trespassing on the domain of another.
A. Functional Classification   B. Voidable contract   C. Encroachment   D. Desk Review

47. ___ An exception to the general zoning regulations; permits specific, usually small, parcels of land to be zone for a use that is not permitted in the surrounding area.
A. Spot Zoning   B. Capitalization Rate   C. Attachment   D. Master Plan

48. ___ Value a specific property has to a specific person or firm for a specific use.
A. Going concern value   B. Value in use   C. Operating Expense Ratio   D. Reproduction Cost

49. ___ An increase in dry land created by the gradual accumulation of waterborne solid material over formerly riparian land.
A. Market Vacancy   B. Pole Line Easement   C. Implied contract   D. Accretion

50. ___ The most probable price at which real estate would sell.
A. Escheat   B. Market Value   C. Reproduction Cost   D. Quantitative Analysis

51. ___ Improvements on and off the site that make it suitable for its intended use or development.
A. Land   B. Deferred Maintenance   C. Site Improvements   D. Potential Gross Income

52. ___ A lease in which the landlord passes on all expenses to the tenant.
A. Mitigation of Damages   B. Financial Feasibility   C. Decline   D. Net Lease

53. ___ The ratio of total operating expenses to effective gross income
A. Legal Description   B. Indirect costs   C. Operating Expense Ratio   D. Summary appraisal

54. ___ A transaction in which the buyers and sellers of a product act independently and have no relationship to each other.
A. Assignment Results   B. Percentage lease   C. Long Lived Item   D. Arms Length

55. _____ A method of estimating value in which the depreciated cost of the improvements on the improved property is calculated and deducted from the total sale price
A. Economic Characteristics   B. Direct costs   C. Long Lived Item   D. Extraction

56. _____ The annual rate of return on capital that is commensurate with the risk assumed by the investor; the rate of interest or yield necessary to attract capital.
A. Preservation Easement   B. Frictional Vacancy   C. Risk Rate   D. Economic life

57. _____ An appropriation from surplus funds that is allocated to deferred or anticipated contingencies.
A. Market Analysis   B. Summary appraisal   C. Reserve   D. Fair Market Value

58. _____ Rights pertaining to properties abutting a lake or pond.
A. Leased Fee Interest   B. Absorption rate   C. Condemnation   D. Littoral rights

59. _____ When a property has the lowest asking price and the same utility as other properties, yet attracts the greatest demand.
A. Substitution   B. Total Operating Expenses   C. Executor   D. Rehabilitation

60. _____ A condition which is contrary to what is known by the appraiser to exist on the effective date of the assignment results, but is used for the purpose of analysis.
A. Multifamily Dwelling   B. Hypothetical Condition   C. Remnant   D. Depreciation

61. _____ arise from construction and other improvements to real estate.
A. Market Participants   B. Mechanics liens   C. Market Vacancy   D. Syndication

62. _____ A voluntary legal agreement that becomes part of the chain of title thereby protecting a historic, archaeological, or cultural resource.
A. Market Analysis   B. Cost Approach   C. Regression   D. Preservation Easement

63. _____ An individual or other legal person designated in a will to settle the estate of the deceased person.
A. Regression   B. Condemnation   C. Highway Easement   D. Executor

64. _____ Is used for elements that cannot be given a numerical value.
A. Qualitative analysis   B. Mechanics liens   C. Attachment   D. Client

65. _____ Any tax on ownership or possession of property and is measured by the number of units or value of such property.
A. Market Analysis   B. Supra surface rights   C. Property Tax   D. Gross Building Area

66. _____ The period over time which a structure may be competitive in the market.
A. Risk Rate   B. Economic life   C. Unilateral contract   D. Client

67. _____ The value of a particular component is measured in terms of the amount it adds to the value of the whole property.
A. Elements of comparison   B. Effective Date   C. Contribution   D. Certification

68. _____ Study of real estate market conditions for specific types of property.
A. Client   B. Lis Pendens   C. Market Analysis   D. Capitalization

69. _____ Stage in market area's life cycle. The market area experiences equilibrium without market gains or losses.
A. Desktop Appraisal   B. Renovation   C. Cash Equivalent   D. Stability

70. _____ Monetary worth of a property, good, or service to buyers and sellers at a given time.
A. Mass Appraisal   B. Property Class   C. Value   D. Mortgage

71. _____ Most commonly found in retail business. This lease has a base rent which is fixed and an excess rent, this is most commonly based on the percentage of the sales.
A. Drive by Appraisal   B. Highway Easement   C. Percentage lease   D. Net Lease

72. _____ An allowance that provides for the periodic replacement of building components that wear out more rapidly than the building itself.
A. Restricted use appraisal   B. Eminent Domain   C. Replacement Allowance   D. Valuation process

73. ___ The state of having the requisite or adequate ability or qualities to perform the specific assignment and produce credible assignment results.
A. Maximum Productivity   B. Competence   C. Value in use   D. Quotent

74. ___ Relevant characteristics used to compare and adjust the property prices.
A. Subsurface rights   B. Negative Amortization   C. Elements of comparison   D. Capitalization Rate

75. ___ Annual amount of total revenue that a property would generate if it were occupied all throughout the year.
A. Void contract   B. Attachment   C. Gross Market Income   D. Mechanics liens

76. ___ Value is a function of expected benefits to get from the ownership of the property.
A. Financial Feasibility   B. Anticipation   C. Labor   D. Revitalization

77. ___ When the government regulates the land use for the good of the public.
A. Police power   B. Negative Amortization   C. Entrepreneurial profit   D. Encumbrance

78. ___ The more a property or its components are in harmony with the surrounding properties or components, the greater the contributory value.
A. Chronological age   B. Cash Equivalent   C. Useful life   D. Conformity

79. ___ Total payment is insufficient to pay interest due.
A. Qualitative analysis   B. Encumbrance   C. Adjustments   D. Negative Amortization

80. ___ The effect on value produced by a property's location at or near the intersection of two streets.
A. Life tenant   B. Legal Permissibility   C. Market Value   D. Corner influence

81. ___ Conclusions of the appraisal are stated, but the data or analyses used in the appraisal to develop these conclusions do not need to be included in the report.
A. Physical Possibility   B. Restricted use appraisal   C. Going concern value   D. Final Reconciliation

82. ___ Technically valid but gives one or more parties the power to legally void the agreement and thus cancel performance.
A. Master Plan   B. Surface rights   C. Gross Market Income   D. Voidable contract

83. ___ The type and extent of research and analyses in appraisal or appraisal review assignment.
A. Tenancy in Common   B. Scope of Work   C. Competition   D. Reclamation

84. ___ Price per cubic foot, front foot, and per apartment.
A. Commercial Property   B. Net Lease   C. Units of comparison   D. Client

85. ___ An ownership interest for the possessory interest has been granted to another by creation of a contractual landlord-tenant relationship.
A. Setback   B. Operating Statement   C. Leased Fee Interest   D. Maximum Productivity

86. ___ The degree, nature, or extent of interest that a person has in land.
A. Labor   B. Average Daily Traffic   C. Voidable contract   D. Estate in land

87. ___ A tangible or intangible benefit of real property that enhances its attractiveness or increases the satisfaction of the user.
A. Amenity   B. Pole Line Easement   C. Executor   D. Avulsion

88. ___ Zoning regulations that designate the distance a building must be set back from the front, rear, and sides of the property lines.
A. Renovation   B. Setback   C. Corner influence   D. Cost Approach

89. ___ The conversion of income into value.
A. Attachment   B. Capitalization   C. Legal Permissibility   D. Operating Expenses

90. ___ Any method of bringing wasted natural resources into productive use.
A. Operating Income   B. Anticipation   C. Reclamation   D. Utility

91. _____ A stage in a market area's life cycle characterized by renewal, redevelopment, modernization, and increasing demand.
A. Comparables   B. Market Vacancy   C. Revitalization   D. Gross Building Area

92. _____ A building containing two or more dwelling units.
A. Fair Market Value   B. Ranking Analysis   C. Multifamily Dwelling   D. Conservation Easement

93. _____ Soft cost expenditures that are necessary components but are not typically part of the construction contract.
A. Fixed Expense   B. Location   C. Drive by Appraisal   D. Indirect costs

94. _____ The estimated period during which improvements will continue to provide utility.
A. Riparian rights   B. Appraisal   C. Physical life   D. Remaining Useful Life

95. _____ In accounting, a category for property under the modified accelerated cost recovery system.
A. Legal Permissibility   B. Risk Rate   C. Involuntary liens   D. Property Class

96. _____ An appraisal report in which the appraiser's scope of work does not include an inspection of the subject property or comparables.
A. Executor   B. Voidable contract   C. Physical life   D. Desktop Appraisal

97. _____ In law, just, rational, appropriate, ordinary, or usual in the circumstances.
A. Desk Review   B. Average Daily Traffic   C. Highway Easement   D. Reasonable

98. _____ Combination of all elements that constitute proof of ownership.
A. Units of comparison   B. Principle   C. Title   D. Reasonable

99. _____ Right to undisturbed use and control of designated air space above a specific land area within stated elevations.
A. Supra surface rights   B. Qualitative analysis   C. Market Value   D. Setback

100. _____ Easement that is not attached or appurtenant to any particular estate; does not run with the land nor is it transferred through the conveyance of title.
A. Easement in gross   B. Deed   C. Gross Market Income   D. Deferred Maintenance

B. From the words provided for each clue, provide the letter of the word which best matches the clue.

1. _____ The present or anticipated undersupply of an item relative to the demand for it. Conditions of scarcity contribute to value.
A. Cost Approach   B. Capitalization Rate   C. Taxation   D. Scarcity

2. _____ A form of ownership in which each owner possesses the exclusive right to use and occupy an allotted unit plus an undivided interest in common areas.
A. Desk Review   B. Site   C. Condominium   D. Lease

3. _____ An agreement put into words (written or spoken).
A. Estate in land   B. General Data   C. Express contract   D. Physical Characteristics

4. _____ Something that has been added or appended to a property and has since become an inherent part of the property.
A. Economic Characteristics   B. Total Operating Expenses   C. Remnant   D. Appurtenance

5. _____ A series of related changes brought about by a chain of causes and effects.
A. Land Use   B. Brownfield   C. Contribution   D. Trends

6. _____ Improvements on and off the site that make it suitable for its intended use or development.
A. Accretion   B. Fiscal Policy   C. Progression   D. Site Improvements

7. _____ Is used for elements that cannot be given a numerical value.
A. Capital   B. Risk Rate   C. Qualitative analysis   D. Preservation Easement

8. _____ first thing a developer considers in developing a property is the cost of land.
A. Restricted use appraisal   B. Land   C. Financial Feasibility   D. Safe Rate

9. _____ The tenant's possessory interest created by a lease.
A. Contribution   B. Littoral rights   C. Neighborhood   D. Leasehold Interest

10. _____ Created intentionally by property owner's actions. i.e. mortgage
A. Physical Possibility   B. Brownfield   C. Voluntary liens   D. Deterioration

11. _____ The process by which all roads are grouped into classes or systems according to the character of service they are intended to provide.
A. Price   B. Express contract   C. Functional Classification   D. Pole Line Easement

12. _____ Stage in market area's life cycle. The market area experiences equilibrium without market gains or losses.
A. Exposure Time   B. Personal Representative   C. Stability   D. Seasonal Dwelling

13. _____ A contract in which the rights to use and occupy land or structures are transferred by the owner to another for a specified period of time in return for specified rent.
A. Market Price   B. Cash Flow   C. Taxation   D. Lease

14. _____ Easement that is not attached or appurtenant to any particular estate; does not run with the land nor is it transferred through the conveyance of title.
A. Exposure Time   B. Gross lease   C. Easement in gross   D. Cost

15. _____ Guiding control of the money supply in the economy.
A. Labor   B. Economic Characteristics   C. Monetary Policy   D. Site Improvements

16. _____ In final reconciliation, the range in which the final market value opinion of a property may fall; usually stated as the interval between a high and low value limit.
A. Range of Value   B. Deed restriction   C. Seasonal Dwelling   D. Easement

17. _____ Right of government to raise revenue through assessments on valuable goods, products, and rights.
A. Taxation   B. Principle   C. Hypothication   D. Personal Representative

18. _____ Absolute ownership unencumbered by any other interest or estate.
A. Fee Simple Estate   B. Cost to Cure   C. Commercial Property   D. Intestate

19. _____ Total dollar expenditure to develop an improvement.
A. Proximity Damage   B. Economic Characteristics   C. Cost   D. Executor

20. _____ Data that is analyzed through the process of comparison.
A. Price   B. Specific Data   C. Contribution   D. Deed restriction

21. _____ One of the four criteria the highest and best use of a property must meet.
A. Royalty   B. Redevelopment   C. Financial Feasibility   D. Value in use

22. _____ Pledge of a described property interest as collateral or security for the repayment of a loan under certain terms and conditions.
A. Mortgage   B. Scarcity   C. Hypothetical Condition   D. Real Estate Market

23. _____ The result of the cause and effect relationship among the forces that influence real property value.
A. Personal Representative   B. Change   C. Percentage Adjustments   D. Pole Line Easement

24. _____ One cause of depreciation.
A. Site   B. Obsolescence   C. Negative Amortization   D. Remainder

25. _____ The opinion of value derived from the reconciliation of value indications and stated in the appraisal report
A. Final Opinion of Value   B. Value in use   C. Quantitative Analysis   D. Lease

26. _____ The condition of dying with a valid will.
A. Conformity   B. Testate   C. Expert Testimony   D. Operating Expense Ratio

27. _____ Annual crops and plantings such as corn, wheat, and vegetables.
A. Emblements   B. Rail Easement   C. Direct Capitalization   D. Remnant

28. _____ A condition which is contrary to what is known by the appraiser to exist on the effective date of the assignment results, but is used for the purpose of analysis.
A. Desire   B. Hypothetical Condition   C. Lis Pendens   D. Real Estate Market

29. _____ The annual rate of return on capital that is commensurate with the risk assumed by the investor; the rate of interest or yield necessary to attract capital.
A. Property Class   B. Risk Rate   C. Long Lived Item   D. Fair Market Value

30. _____ The amount of money borrowed from lender (mortgagee).
A. Intestate   B. Constant   C. Principle   D. Pipeline Easement

31. _____ The right to construct, operate, and maintain a pipeline over the lands of others within prescribed geographical limits.
A. Pipeline Easement   B. Unilateral contract   C. Market Price   D. Property Class

32. _____ Only one party makes a promise
A. Commercial Property   B. Unilateral contract   C. Reasonable   D. Range of Value

33. _____ In condemnation, the loss in value to the remainder in a partial taking of property.
A. Location   B. Life tenant   C. Damages   D. Government lien

34. _____ The more a property or its components are in harmony with the surrounding properties or components, the greater the contributory value.
A. Conformity   B. Change   C. Total Operating Expenses   D. Percentage Adjustments

35. _____ Amount a particular purchaser agrees to pay and a particular seller agrees to accept under the circumstances surrounding their transaction.
A. Marketing time   B. Price   C. Risk Rate   D. Range of Value

36. _____ Value a specific property has to a specific person or firm for a specific use.
A. Value in use   B. Operating Expense Ratio   C. Erosion   D. Assessed Value

37. _____ Information that is not gathered in its original form by the analyst.
A. Principle   B. Change   C. Secondary Data   D. Consequential Damages

38. _____ Land that is not needed to serve or support the existing improvement.
A. Negative Amortization   B. Master Plan   C. Arms Length   D. Excess Land

39. _____ The taking of part of any real property interest for public use under the power of eminent domain; requires the payment of compensation.
A. Labor   B. Subsurface rights   C. Operating Expenses   D. Partial Taking

40. _____ In accounting, a category for property under the modified accelerated cost recovery system.
A. Mechanics liens   B. Property Class   C. Cash Flow   D. Entrepreneurial Incentive

41. _____ The process of reducing a range of value indications into an appropriate conclusion for that analysis.
A. Value in use   B. Adjustments   C. Reconciliation   D. Reasonable

42. _____ A lease in which the landlord passes on all expenses to the tenant.
A. Physical Characteristics   B. Net Lease   C. Encroachment   D. Cost Approach

43. _____ Testimony of persons who are presumed to have special knowledge of, or skill in, a particular field due to education, experience, or study.
A. Earnest money   B. Cost Approach   C. Raw Land   D. Expert Testimony

44. One who owns an interest in real property for his or her own lifetime.
A. Proximity Damage   B. Quantitative Analysis   C. Arms Length   D. Life tenant

45. Damage to property arising as a consequence of a taking over and above direct damages.
A. Consequential Damages   B. Present Value   C. Average Daily Traffic   D. Land Use

46. A market-derived figure that represents the amount an entrepreneur receives for their contribution.
A. Entrepreneurial profit   B. Site   C. Loss of Access   D. Estate in land

47. Temporary use to which a site or improved property is put until it is ready to be put to its future highest and best use.
A. Entrepreneurial Incentive   B. Chronological age   C. Interim use   D. Highway Easement

48. Any rate used to convert income into value.
A. Land Use   B. Percentage lease   C. Constant   D. Capitalization Rate

49. Two or more sales are compared to derive an indication of the size of the adjustment for a single characteristic.
A. Internal Rate of Return   B. Paired data analysis   C. Partial Taking   D. Mitigation of Damages

50. A method used to convert an estimate of a single year's income expectancy into an indication of value in one direct step
A. Rail Easement   B. Direct Capitalization   C. Final Reconciliation   D. Index lease

51. The employment of a site or holding to produce revenue or other benefits.
A. Financial Feasibility   B. Land Use   C. Exposure Time   D. Assignment Results

52. Going to the State. The process that should a property be abandoned, it reverts back to the state.
A. Escheat   B. Competition   C. Capital   D. Fiscal Policy

53. A report that is transmitted orally.
A. Investment Value   B. Total Operating Expenses   C. Market Price   D. Oral Appraisal Report

54. An appraisal review in which the reviewer's scope of work does not include an inspection of the subject property.
A. Desk Review   B. Units of comparison   C. Decline   D. Physical Characteristics

55. Needed repairs or replacement of items that should have taken place during the course of normal maintenance.
A. Assemblage   B. Deferred Maintenance   C. Assignment Results   D. Ranking Analysis

56. Dollar amount required to reconstruct a bldg. or other improvement, which have the same or equivalent utility as the original.
A. Intestate   B. Specific Data   C. Replacement Cost   D. Operating Expenses

57. The most probable price at which real estate would sell.
A. Easement   B. Hypothetical Condition   C. Market Value   D. Real Estate Market

58. The cost to restore an item of deferred maintenance to new or reasonably new condition.
A. Cost to Cure   B. Accretion   C. Remainder interest   D. Redevelopment

59. A plan, map, or chart of a city, town, section, or subdivision indicating the location and boundaries of individual properties.
A. Plat   B. Mass Appraisal   C. Substitution   D. Easement in gross

60. goods, such as equipment (machinery and tools), bldgs., and infrastructure.
A. Chronological age   B. Capital   C. Cost   D. Risk Rate

61. Purchaser's wish for an item to satisfy human needs or individual wants beyond essential life-support needs.
A. Desire   B. Frictional Vacancy   C. Escheat   D. Emblements

62. The total period a building lasts or is expected to last as opposed to its economic life.
A. Present Value   B. Chronological age   C. Physical life   D. Change

63. ____ Conclusions of the appraisal are stated, but the data or analyses used in the appraisal to develop these conclusions do not need to be included in the report.
A. Financing Terms   B. Restricted use appraisal   C. Specific Data   D. Internal Rate of Return

64. ____ A right granted or taken for the construction, maintenance, and operation of the highway.
A. Littoral rights   B. Highway Easement   C. Fair Market Value   D. Estate Tax

65. ____ The value of a particular component is measured in terms of the amount it adds to the value of the whole property.
A. Contribution   B. Setback   C. Voluntary liens   D. Lease

66. ____ Value is a function of expected benefits to get from the ownership of the property.
A. Mechanics liens   B. Anticipation   C. Neighborhood   D. Site

67. ____ Right to undisturbed use and control of designated air space above a specific land area within stated elevations.
A. Encroachment   B. Supra surface rights   C. Deed   D. Hypothetical Condition

68. ____ Complementary land uses; inhabitants, buildings, or business enterprises.
A. Average Daily Traffic   B. Constant   C. Neighborhood   D. Leasehold Interest

69. ____ Total payment is insufficient to pay interest due.
A. Royalty   B. Preservation Easement   C. Title   D. Negative Amortization

70. ____ A letter or statement that serves as a notice of delivery from the appraiser to the client of a report containing an opinion or conclusion concerning real estate
A. Remaining Useful Life   B. Bundle of rights   C. Oral Appraisal Report   D. Letter of Transmittal

71. ____ The actual rental income specified in a lease.
A. Loss of Access   B. Contract rent   C. Government lien   D. Marketability

72. ____ Management of government receipts and expenditures.
A. Marketability   B. Operating Expenses   C. Fiscal Policy   D. Pipeline Easement

73. ____ A future possessor read interest in real estate that is given to a third-party and matures upon the termination of a limited or determinable be.
A. Risk Rate   B. Voluntary liens   C. Remainder   D. Net Lease

74. ____ Monetary worth of a property, good, or service to buyers and sellers at a given time.
A. Expert Testimony   B. Leasehold Interest   C. Value   D. Market Price

75. ____ The number of years since a structure or bldg. was originally built (birth).
A. Lease   B. Direct Capitalization   C. Rail Easement   D. Chronological age

76. ____ The time of property remains on the market.
A. Risk Rate   B. Police power   C. Gross Living Area   D. Exposure Time

77. ____ The right to use another's land for a stated purpose.
A. Commercial Property   B. Pole Line Easement   C. Easement   D. Assignment Results

78. ____ A statistical measure that attempts to determine the strength of the relationship between one dependent variable and a series of other changing variables.
A. Highway Easement   B. Marketing time   C. Trends   D. Regression Analysis

79. ____ The periodic expenditures necessary to maintain the real property and continue production of the effective gross income, assuming prudent and competent management.
A. Substitution   B. Gross lease   C. Operating Expenses   D. Financing Terms

80. ____ The period of time over which a structure may reasonably be expected to perform the function for which it was designed.
A. Scarcity   B. Useful life   C. Mitigation of Damages   D. Cost Approach

81. ____ The last phase in the development of the value opinion in which two or more value indications derived from market data are resolved into a value opinion.
A. Final Reconciliation   B. Property Class   C. Estate Tax   D. Letter of Transmittal

82. ____ Annual amount of total revenue that a property would generate if it were occupied all throughout the year.
A. Erosion   B. Trends   C. Voluntary liens   D. Gross Market Income

83. ____ Rights to the use and profits of the underground portion of a designated property.
A. Regression   B. Subsurface rights   C. Physical Possibility   D. Fair Market Value

84. ____ Land on which no improvements have been made
A. Raw Land   B. Anticipation   C. Location   D. Total Operating Expenses

85. ____ The impairment of functional capacity of a property according to market tastes and standards.
A. Capitalization   B. Functional Obsolesce   C. Long Lived Item   D. Obsolescence

86. ____ Sum of all fixed and variable operating expenses and reserve for replacement.
A. Total Operating Expenses   B. Final Opinion of Value   C. Restricted use appraisal   D. Police power

87. ____ The right for the construction, maintenance, and operation of a rail line on a property.
A. Testate   B. Rail Easement   C. Cash Flow   D. Encroachment

88. ____ The yield rate used to convert future payments or receipts into present value; usually considered to be a synonym for yield rate.
A. Proximity Damage   B. Discount Rate   C. Effective Gross Income   D. Decline

89. ____ When a series of different "multiplicands" are multiplied by the same multiplier it is known as.
A. Constant   B. Real Estate   C. Easement in gross   D. Trends

90. ____ Seizure of property by court order.
A. Financing Terms   B. Qualitative analysis   C. Deferred Maintenance   D. Attachment

91. ____ Most commonly found in retail business. This lease has a base rent which is fixed and an excess rent, this is most commonly based on the percentage of the sales.
A. Price   B. Percentage lease   C. Risk Rate   D. Utility

92. ____ The minimum rate of return on invested capital.
A. Mechanics liens   B. Safe Rate   C. Executor   D. Appraisal

93. ____ The development or improvement of cleared or undeveloped land in an urban renewal area.
A. Quantitative Analysis   B. Safe Rate   C. Just Compensation   D. Redevelopment

94. ____ An element of comparison in the sales comparison approach.
A. Investment Value   B. Economic Characteristics   C. Negative Amortization   D. Average Daily Traffic

95. ____ In condemnation, the amount of loss for which a property owner is compensated when his or her property is taken.
A. Land   B. Brownfield   C. Just Compensation   D. Chronological age

96. ____ The relative position of the property to competitive properties and other value influences in its market area
A. Valuation process   B. Location   C. Subsurface rights   D. Supra surface rights

97. ____ land that is improved so that is ready to be used for a specific purpose.
A. Site   B. Remainder   C. Desk Review   D. Zoning

98. ____ Legal term signifying pending litigation that can affect ownership title to real estate.
A. Lis Pendens   B. Market Value   C. Unilateral contract   D. Bilateral contract

99. ____ An individual or other legal person designated in a will to settle the estate of a deceased person.
A. Personal Representative   B. Percentage Adjustments   C. Physical life   D. Anticipation

100. ____ Money paid to an owner of real property or mineral rights for the right to deplete natural resource.
A. Conformity B. Desk Review C. Royalty D. Deed

C. From the words provided for each clue, provide the letter of the word which best matches the clue.

1. ____ Divided or undivided rights in real estate that represent less than the whole.
A. Internal Rate of Return B. Partial Interest C. Market Value D. Accretion

2. ____ An exception to the general zoning regulations; permits specific, usually small, parcels of land to be zone for a use that is not permitted in the surrounding area.
A. Mechanics liens B. Regression Analysis C. Spot Zoning D. Valuation process

3. ____ A tax on the estate or wealth of the deceased person that is usually computed as a percentage of the market value of the assets of the estate.
A. Pro Forma B. Capitalization C. Estate Tax D. Lease

4. ____ An element of comparison in the sales comparison approach.
A. Intestate B. Cash Flow C. Economic Characteristics D. Multifamily Dwelling

5. ____ A limitation that passes with the land regardless of the owner.
A. Setback B. Master Plan C. Deed restriction D. Discount Rate

6. ____ Adjustments for differences between the subject and comparable properties expressed as a percentage of the sale price of the comparable property.
A. Percentage Adjustments B. Qualitative analysis C. Attachment D. Capitalization Rate

7. ____ A study of the cost-benefit relationships of an economic endeavor.
A. Feasibility Analysis B. Total Operating Expenses C. Estate in land D. Valid contract

8. ____ Stage in market area's life cycle. The market area experiences equilibrium without market gains or losses.
A. Growth B. Lease C. Stability D. Specific Lien

9. ____ Value of a superior property is adversely affected by its association with an inferior property of the same type.
A. Change B. Regression C. Revitalization D. Physical life

10. ____ The condition of dying without a will.
A. Intestate B. Regression C. Bundle of rights D. Frictional Vacancy

11. ____ A stage in a market areas life cycle in which the market area gains public favor and acceptance.
A. Reclamation B. Progression C. Growth D. Rehabilitation

12. ____ An increase in value when extra utility is created by combining smaller parcels under single ownership.
A. Plottage B. Revitalization C. Discount Rate D. Royalty

13. ____ Time and distance relationships between a particular use and supporting facilities.
A. Discount Rate B. Interim use C. Linkage D. Economic Characteristics

14. ____ The conversion of income into value.
A. Certification B. Scope of Work C. Capitalization D. Estate in land

15. ____ One who conveys the rights of occupancy and use to others under lease agreement.
A. Lessor B. Growth C. Limiting Condition D. Proximity Damage

16. ____ One of the four criteria the highest and best use of a property must meet.
A. Primary Data B. Disintermediation C. Residential Property D. Legal Permissibility

17. ___ A condition which is contrary to what is known by the appraiser to exist on the effective date of the assignment results, but is used for the purpose of analysis.
A. Financial Feasibility   B. Debt coverage ratio   C. Fee Simple Estate   D. Hypothetical Condition

18. ___ Monetary worth of a property, good, or service to buyers and sellers at a given time.
A. Rate of return   B. Value   C. Property Class   D. Desktop Appraisal

19. ___ Total floor area of a building, excluding unenclosed area, measured from the exterior of the walls of the above-grade area.
A. Gross Building Area   B. Rehabilitation   C. Unilateral contract   D. Taxation

20. ___ The wear and tear that begins with the building is completed and placed into service.
A. Utility   B. Leasehold Interest   C. Physical Deterioration   D. Unilateral contract

21. ___ Damages that is caused by the remainder's proximity to the improvement being constructed.
A. Reconciliation   B. Proximity Damage   C. Distress Sale   D. Negative Amortization

22. ___ The written or oral communication of an appraisal.
A. Partial Interest   B. Appraisal Report   C. Expert Testimony   D. Supra surface rights

23. ___ In final reconciliation, the range in which the final market value opinion of a property may fall; usually stated as the interval between a high and low value limit.
A. Range of Value   B. Personal Representative   C. Location   D. Legal Permissibility

24. ___ The ratio of total operating expenses to effective gross income
A. Reserve   B. Desk Review   C. Operating Expense Ratio   D. Quotent

25. ___ An appropriation from surplus funds that is allocated to deferred or anticipated contingencies.
A. Probate   B. Reserve   C. Physical Possibility   D. Pole Line Easement

26. ___ The tenant's possessory interest created by a lease.
A. Market Price   B. Attachment   C. Lessor   D. Leasehold Interest

27. ___ The change in the value of a property as a whole, resulting from the addition or deletion of a property component.
A. Contributory Value   B. Consequential Damages   C. Investment Value   D. Elements of comparison

28. ___ Ann agreement that is presumed to exist because of the parties' actions.
A. Land   B. Implied contract   C. Deferred Maintenance   D. Distress Sale

29. ___ The right for the construction, maintenance, and operation of a rail line on a property.
A. Rail Easement   B. Certification   C. Index lease   D. Remaining Economic Life

30. ___ A market-derived figure that represents the amount an entrepreneur receives for their contribution.
A. Restricted use appraisal   B. Plat   C. Entrepreneurial profit   D. Property Tax

31. ___ The ratio of income or yield to the original investment.
A. Rate of return   B. Specific Lien   C. Restricted use appraisal   D. Maximum Productivity

32. ___ The combining of 2 or more parcels into one ownership (tract).
A. Market Value   B. Assemblage   C. Implied contract   D. Property Class

33. ___ Easement that is attached to, benefits, and passes with the conveyance of the dominant estate. Burdens the servient estate.
A. Life estate   B. Easement appurtenant   C. Sandwich lease   D. Market Vacancy

34. ___ Any tax on ownership or possession of property and is measured by the number of units or value of such property.
A. Encroachment   B. Probate   C. Property Tax   D. Interim use

35. ____ A part of an appraisal report in which the appraiser certifies that the work was completed according to the applicable standards.
A. Cash Flow   B. Certification   C. Summary appraisal   D. Lease

36. ____ A financial statement that reflects the gross revenues, expenses, and net operating profit or loss of an investment over a fixed period.
A. Going concern value   B. Master Plan   C. Operating Statement   D. Cost Approach

37. ____ A projected income and expense statement for proposed development.
A. Scope of Work   B. Pole Line Easement   C. Pro Forma   D. Unilateral contract

38. ____ One cause of depreciation.
A. Value in use   B. Obsolescence   C. Certification   D. Title

39. ____ The estimated period during which improvements will continue to provide utility.
A. Going concern value   B. Remaining Useful Life   C. Functional Classification   D. Attachment

40. ____ An appraisal report in which the scope of work includes an exterior-only viewing of the subject property.
A. Escheat   B. Emblements   C. Drive by Appraisal   D. Earnest money

41. ____ An identified parcel or tract of land, including improvements.
A. Real Estate   B. Present Value   C. Estate Tax   D. Fiscal Policy

42. ____ An increase in dry land created by the gradual accumulation of waterborne solid material over formerly riparian land.
A. Attachment   B. Easement in gross   C. Accretion   D. Cost to Cure

43. ____ The interests, benefits, and rights inherent in ownership of real estate.
A. Rehabilitation   B. Consequential Damages   C. Real Property   D. Primary Data

44. ____ Two or more sales are compared to derive an indication of the size of the adjustment for a single characteristic.
A. Cost   B. Utility   C. Inheritance Tax   D. Paired data analysis

45. ____ Any communication, written or oral, of an appraisal or appraisal review that is transmitted to the client upon completion of an assignment.
A. Value in use   B. Earnest money   C. Comparables   D. Report

46. ____ Management of government receipts and expenditures.
A. Regression   B. Units of comparison   C. Accretion   D. Fiscal Policy

47. ____ A stage in a market area's life cycle characterized by renewal, redevelopment, modernization, and increasing demand.
A. Revitalization   B. Lease   C. Reserve   D. Taxation

48. ____ Right to undisturbed use and control of designated air space above a specific land area within stated elevations.
A. Revitalization   B. Tenancy in Common   C. Supra surface rights   D. Police power

49. ____ Value to a particular individual. The present worth of anticipated future benefits.
A. Investment Value   B. Entrepreneurial profit   C. Linkage   D. Escheat

50. ____ A type of renovation that involves modification or updating of existing improvements.
A. Remodeling   B. Principle   C. Spot Zoning   D. Surface rights

51. ____ A future possessor read interest in real estate that is given to a third-party and matures upon the termination of a limited or determinable be.
A. Market Participants   B. Market Price   C. Remainder   D. Primary Data

52. ____ Is used for elements that cannot be given a numerical value.
A. Operating Expense Ratio   B. Entrepreneurial profit   C. Contributory Value   D. Qualitative analysis

53. _____ A vacant or in proof parcel of land devoted to or available for use as a residence.
A. Residential Property   B. Qualitative analysis   C. Sandwich lease   D. Direct costs

54. _____ Method by which government can take private property.
A. Corner influence   B. Growth   C. Condemnation   D. Contributory Value

55. _____ Depriving an abutting owner of the inherent rights of ingress and to egress from the highway or street.
A. Loss of Access   B. Total Operating Expenses   C. Physical Possibility   D. Escheat

56. _____ One of the criteria for highest and best use of a property must meet.
A. Remainder interest   B. Land Use   C. Physical Possibility   D. Probate

57. _____ An appraisal report in which the appraiser's scope of work does not include an inspection of the subject property or comparables.
A. Restricted use appraisal   B. Market Participants   C. Desktop Appraisal   D. Utility

58. _____ The process by which all roads are grouped into classes or systems according to the character of service they are intended to provide.
A. Decline   B. Property Tax   C. Functional Classification   D. Appraisal Report

59. _____ A rate derived from a single year's NOI and the total property value.
A. Overall rate   B. Economic Characteristics   C. Frictional Vacancy   D. Land Use

60. _____ Person who is entitled to an estate after a prior estate or interest has expired
A. Contributory Value   B. Remainder interest   C. Investment Value   D. Reserve

61. _____ The legal responsibility of a plaintiff to make reasonable efforts, after an injury or breach of contract, to alleviate the effects of the injury or breach.
A. Mitigation of Damages   B. Assemblage   C. Pipeline Easement   D. Preservation Easement

62. _____ Items of information on value influences that derive from social, economic, governmental, and environmental forces and originate outside the property being appraised.
A. Pole Line Easement   B. Bundle of rights   C. Subsurface rights   D. General Data

63. _____ Annual amount of total revenue that a property would generate if it were occupied all throughout the year.
A. Paired data analysis   B. Land Use   C. Reproduction Cost   D. Gross Market Income

64. _____ Only one party makes a promise
A. Pipeline Easement   B. Unilateral contract   C. Raw Land   D. Total Operating Expenses

65. _____ Value a specific property has to a specific person or firm for a specific use.
A. Real Estate   B. Feasibility Analysis   C. Value in use   D. Assemblage

66. _____ A shortened term for similar property sales, rentals, or operating expenses used for comparison in the valuation process.
A. Comparables   B. Unilateral contract   C. Assignment Results   D. Paired data analysis

67. _____ The period over time which a structure may be competitive in the market.
A. Physical life   B. Bundle of rights   C. Drive by Appraisal   D. Economic life

68. _____ Seizure of property by court order.
A. Preservation Easement   B. Brownfield   C. Subsurface rights   D. Attachment

69. _____ Damage to property arising as a consequence of a taking over and above direct damages.
A. Drive by Appraisal   B. Consequential Damages   C. Encroachment   D. Cash Flow

70. _____ Right of government to raise revenue through assessments on valuable goods, products, and rights.
A. Taxation   B. Encroachment   C. Range of Value   D. Personal Representative

71. ____ In accounting, a category for property under the modified accelerated cost recovery system.
A. Property Class   B. Gentrification   C. Financial Feasibility   D. Contract rent

72. ____ Combination of all elements that constitute proof of ownership.
A. Pro Forma   B. Title   C. Land Use   D. Partial Interest

73. ____ Any method of bringing wasted natural resources into productive use.
A. Police power   B. Gross Market Income   C. Reclamation   D. Percentage Adjustments

74. ____ When the government regulates the land use for the good of the public.
A. Excess Land   B. Partial Interest   C. Police power   D. Negative Amortization

75. ____ Annual crops and plantings such as corn, wheat, and vegetables.
A. Emblements   B. Valuation process   C. Functional Classification   D. Capitalization Rate

76. ____ A stage of diminishing demand in a market areas life cycle.
A. Property Tax   B. Decline   C. Emblements   D. Replacement Cost

77. ____ The amount entrepreneur expects to receive for his or her contribution to the project.
A. Entrepreneurial Incentive   B. Implied contract   C. Present Value   D. Remainder

78. ____ A tax on the right to receive property by inheritance; as distinguished from estate tax.
A. Mechanics liens   B. Market Analysis   C. Implied contract   D. Inheritance Tax

79. ____ The period of time over which a structure may reasonably be expected to perform the function for which it was designed.
A. Gross lease   B. Primary Data   C. Useful life   D. Remainder interest

80. ____ When the lessee (tenant) does not pay any costs of ownership and pays a given amount of rent per period.
A. Gross lease   B. Total Operating Expenses   C. Gross Market Income   D. Summary appraisal

81. ____ Created by law, rather than by choice. i.e. property tax lien.
A. Full Taking   B. Hypothetical Condition   C. Taxation   D. Involuntary liens

82. ____ A comprehensive, long-range official plan that guides the physical growth and development of the community.
A. Master Plan   B. Debt coverage ratio   C. Hypothetical Condition   D. Regression

83. ____ The estimated period during which improvements will continue to represent the highest and best use of the property.
A. Remaining Economic Life   B. Site   C. General Data   D. Estate Tax

84. ____ An easement for the construction, maintenance, and operation of a full line, usually for the transmission of electric power.
A. Pole Line Easement   B. Reproduction Cost   C. Certification   D. Inheritance Tax

85. ____ One of the four criteria the highest and best use of a property must meet.
A. Financial Feasibility   B. Obsolescence   C. Voidable contract   D. Feasibility Analysis

86. ____ A lump sum benefit that an investor receives or expects to receive upon the termination of an investment; also called reversionary benefit.
A. Step Up Depreciation   B. Reversion   C. Percentage Adjustments   D. Entrepreneurial Incentive

87. ____ The right to use another's land for a stated purpose.
A. Financial Feasibility   B. Remaining Economic Life   C. Easement   D. Spot Zoning

88. ____ The most probable price at which real estate would sell.
A. Entrepreneurial profit   B. Spot Zoning   C. Final Reconciliation   D. Market Value

89. ____ Principle that real property value is created and sustained when contrasting, opposing, or interacting elements are in a state of equilibrium.
A. Balance   B. Value in use   C. Desktop Appraisal   D. Reserve

90. ____ Land that is not needed to serve or support the existing improvement.
A. Excess Land   B. Market Vacancy   C. Quotent   D. Mitigation of Damages

91. ____ Money paid to an owner of real property or mineral rights for the right to deplete natural resource.
A. Marketing time   B. Paired data analysis   C. Royalty   D. Reclamation

92. ____ Trespassing on the domain of another.
A. Direct costs   B. Reclamation   C. Encroachment   D. Living trust

93. ____ An agreement in which all the elements of a contract are present and, therefore, legally enforceable.
A. Distress Sale   B. Valid contract   C. Financial Feasibility   D. Lis Pendens

94. ____ Neighborhood phenomenon in which middle- and upper-income persons purchase neighborhood properties and renovate or rehabilitate them.
A. Gentrification   B. Comparables   C. District   D. Encroachment

95. ____ Dollar amount required to reconstruct a bldg. or other improvement, which have the same or equivalent utility as the original.
A. Operating Expense Ratio   B. Residential Property   C. Replacement Cost   D. Percentage Adjustments

96. ____ The degree, nature, or extent of interest that a person has in land.
A. Estate in land   B. Real Estate   C. Hypothetical Condition   D. Brownfield

97. ____ A report that is prepared regularly, usually each month, and indicates the rent-paying status of each tenant.
A. Voidable contract   B. Rent Roll   C. Remainder   D. Mitigation of Damages

98. ____ Needed repairs or replacement of items that should have taken place during the course of normal maintenance.
A. Lis Pendens   B. Utility   C. Easement appurtenant   D. Deferred Maintenance

99. ____ The amount of vacant space needed in a market for its orderly operation.
A. Potential Gross Income   B. Frictional Vacancy   C. Sandwich lease   D. Encroachment

100. ____ Study of real estate market conditions for specific types of property.
A. Property Tax   B. Market Analysis   C. Leasehold Interest   D. Property Class

D. From the words provided for each clue, provide the letter of the word which best matches the clue.

1. ____ An element of depreciation; and diminution in value caused by negative externalities and generally incurable on the part of the owner, landlord, or tenant.
A. Housing Starts   B. Contract rent   C. Zoning   D. External Obsolescence

2. ____ An appraiser's opinions or conclusions developed specific to an assignment.
A. Assignment Results   B. Involuntary liens   C. Functional Classification   D. Average Daily Traffic

3. ____ Study of real estate market conditions for specific types of property.
A. Personal Representative   B. Property Class   C. Market Analysis   D. Restricted use appraisal

4. ____ Guiding control of the money supply in the economy.
A. Monetary Policy   B. Property Class   C. Change   D. Assignment Results

5. ____ When the value of a business plus the amount of real property is sought.
A. Effective age   B. Fixed Expense   C. Going concern value   D. Condominium

6. ____ Zoning regulations that designate the distance a building must be set back from the front, rear, and sides of the property lines.
A. Setback   B. Site   C. Cash Equivalent   D. Hypothetical Condition

7. ___ Method by which government can take private property.
A. Quotent B. Safe Rate C. Condemnation D. Net Lease

8. ___ Total payment is insufficient to pay interest due.
A. Present Value B. Competition C. Net Lease D. Negative Amortization

9. ___ The periodic expenditures necessary to maintain the real property and continue production of the effective gross income, assuming prudent and competent management.
A. Mechanics liens B. Operating Expenses C. Single Family House D. Marketing time

10. ___ Any claim or liability that affects our limits the title to property.
A. Encumbrance B. Restricted use appraisal C. Summary appraisal D. Condemnation

11. ___ Buyers and sellers of particular real estate and the transactions that occur among them.
A. Stability B. Seasonal Dwelling C. Lease D. Real Estate Market

12. ___ Price an economic good will attract in the competitive market.
A. BOMA Standard B. Value in Exchange C. Lien D. Partial Interest

13. ___ Damages that is caused by the remainder's proximity to the improvement being constructed.
A. Extraction B. Proximity Damage C. Leased Fee Interest D. Condemnation

14. ___ Estate owned by 2 or more persons, each of whom has an equal undivided interest. Unlike Joint Tenancy and Tenancy by Entirety, No right of survivorship.
A. Void contract B. Tenancy in Common C. Price D. Present Value

15. ___ A lease in which the landlord passes on all expenses to the tenant.
A. Elements of comparison B. Net Lease C. General Lien D. Voluntary liens

16. ___ The manner in which a transaction was financed.
A. Real Property B. Financing Terms C. Summary appraisal D. Principle

17. ___ An ordinal technique for analyzing data, commonly used in the analysis of comparable sales.
A. Voidable contract B. Ranking Analysis C. Property Class D. Regression

18. ___ The process of valuing a universe of properties as of a given date using standard methodology, employing common data, and allowing for statistical testing.
A. Contribution B. Labor C. Specific Data D. Mass Appraisal

19. ___ An appropriation from surplus funds that is allocated to deferred or anticipated contingencies.
A. Cost to Cure B. Mortgage liens C. Residential Property D. Reserve

20. ___ The relative desirability of a property in comparison with similar or competing properties in the area.
A. Reserve B. Marketability C. Specific Lien D. Voidable contract

21. ___ The actual rental income specified in a lease.
A. Average Daily Traffic B. Contract rent C. Revitalization D. Ranking Analysis

22. ___ The difference between an improvements total economic life and its remaining economic life.
A. Estate Tax B. Involuntary liens C. Capitalization D. Effective age

23. ___ The effect on value produced by a property's location at or near the intersection of two streets.
A. Qualitative analysis B. Going concern value C. Stability D. Corner influence

24. ___ arise from construction and other improvements to real estate.
A. Extraction B. General Lien C. Mechanics liens D. Potential Gross Income

25. ____ The entire taking of the full real property interest of a parcel for public use under the power of eminent domain; requires the payment of compensation.
A. Feasibility Analysis   B. Full Taking   C. Physical Deterioration   D. Lis Pendens

26. ____ Value to a particular individual. The present worth of anticipated future benefits.
A. Zoning   B. Useful life   C. Progression   D. Investment Value

27. ____ Technically valid but gives one or more parties the power to legally void the agreement and thus cancel performance.
A. Final Reconciliation   B. Effective Gross Income   C. Voidable contract   D. Physical Possibility

28. ____ A condition which is contrary to what is known by the appraiser to exist on the effective date of the assignment results, but is used for the purpose of analysis.
A. Hypothetical Condition   B. Rail Easement   C. General Data   D. Market Analysis

29. ____ A category of elements of comparison in the sales comparison approach
A. Physical Characteristics   B. Cash Equivalent   C. Neighborhood   D. Fiscal Policy

30. ____ Dollar amount required to reconstruct a bldg. or other improvement, which have the same or equivalent utility as the original.
A. Residential Property   B. Adverse possession   C. Replacement Cost   D. Regression

31. ____ Value of an inferior property is enhanced by its association with better properties of the same type.
A. Scarcity   B. Extraction   C. Restricted use appraisal   D. Progression

32. ____ A lease in which an intermediate, or sandwich, leaseholder is the lessee of one party and the lessor of another.
A. Functional Classification   B. Price   C. Sandwich lease   D. Value in use

33. ____ comprises of all costs required to construct and market the product as land alone or with improvements.
A. Personal Representative   B. Rate of return   C. Pipeline Easement   D. Labor

34. ____ Amount a particular purchaser agrees to pay and a particular seller agrees to accept under the circumstances surrounding their transaction.
A. Change   B. Specific Lien   C. Price   D. Internal Rate of Return

35. ____ Part of the purchase price given to bind a bargain.
A. Certification   B. Corner influence   C. Remnant   D. Earnest money

36. ____ Testimony of persons who are presumed to have special knowledge of, or skill in, a particular field due to education, experience, or study.
A. BOMA Standard   B. Expert Testimony   C. Useful life   D. Units of comparison

37. ____ The wear and tear that begins with the building is completed and placed into service.
A. Ranking Analysis   B. Physical Deterioration   C. Going concern value   D. Valuation process

38. ____ An agreement put into words (written or spoken).
A. Economic Characteristics   B. Potential Gross Income   C. Accretion   D. Express contract

39. ____ The cost to restore an item of deferred maintenance to new or reasonably new condition.
A. Cost to Cure   B. Rate of return   C. Assessed Value   D. Condominium

40. ____ A rate derived from a single year's NOI and the total property value.
A. Market Participants   B. Drive by Appraisal   C. Pro Forma   D. Overall rate

41. ____ Purchaser's wish for an item to satisfy human needs or individual wants beyond essential life-support needs.
A. Voidable contract   B. Functional Classification   C. Desire   D. Regression Analysis

42. ____ The value of a future payment or series of future payments discounted to the current date or to time period zero.
A. Lessor   B. Syndication   C. Physical Deterioration   D. Present Value

43. _____ The taking of part of any real property interest for public use under the power of eminent domain; requires the payment of compensation.
A. Partial Taking   B. Loss of Access   C. Change   D. Appurtenance

44. _____ An agreement in which all the elements of a contract are present and, therefore, legally enforceable.
A. Entrepreneurial profit   B. Involuntary liens   C. Final Opinion of Value   D. Valid contract

45. _____ A rivalry between buyers or between sellers.
A. Competition   B. Quotent   C. Condominium   D. Certification

46. _____ Person who is entitled to an estate after a prior estate or interest has expired
A. Lessee   B. Remainder interest   C. Mechanics liens   D. Voluntary liens

47. _____ The process of reducing a range of value indications into an appropriate conclusion for that analysis.
A. Reconciliation   B. Market Participants   C. Void contract   D. Growth

48. _____ Easement that is not attached or appurtenant to any particular estate; does not run with the land nor is it transferred through the conveyance of title.
A. Easement in gross   B. Littoral rights   C. Decline   D. Anticipation

49. _____ The right to use another's land for a stated purpose.
A. Contribution   B. Cost to Cure   C. Easement   D. Proximity Damage

50. _____ The opinion of value derived from the reconciliation of value indications and stated in the appraisal report
A. Present Value   B. Final Opinion of Value   C. Contract rent   D. Rail Easement

51. _____ A stage of diminishing demand in a market areas life cycle.
A. Ranking Analysis   B. Decline   C. BOMA Standard   D. Residential Property

52. _____ Amount paid for an income producing property.
A. Financing Terms   B. Loss of Access   C. Regression Analysis   D. Market Price

53. _____ A study of the cost-benefit relationships of an economic endeavor.
A. Percentage lease   B. Amenity   C. Competence   D. Feasibility Analysis

54. _____ The quantity left over.
A. Substitution   B. Residual   C. Effective age   D. Encroachment

55. _____ Monetary worth of a property, good, or service to buyers and sellers at a given time.
A. Scarcity   B. Value   C. Overall rate   D. Physical Possibility

56. _____ An increase in dry land created by the gradual accumulation of waterborne solid material over formerly riparian land.
A. Raw Land   B. Accretion   C. Physical Possibility   D. Pro Forma

57. _____ Written, legal instrument that conveys an estate or interest in real property to someone else, assuming it is executed and delivered.
A. Change   B. Restricted use appraisal   C. Deed   D. Supra surface rights

58. _____ The process by which all roads are grouped into classes or systems according to the character of service they are intended to provide.
A. Appurtenance   B. Operating Expenses   C. Functional Classification   D. Executor

59. _____ Sum of all fixed and variable operating expenses and reserve for replacement.
A. Total Operating Expenses   B. Sandwich lease   C. Master Plan   D. Proximity Damage

60. _____ The type and extent of research and analyses in appraisal or appraisal review assignment.
A. Mortgage liens   B. Market Analysis   C. Competition   D. Scope of Work

61. _____ An individual or other legal person designated in a will to settle the estate of a deceased person.
A. Personal Representative   B. Regression Analysis   C. Elements of comparison   D. Remainder interest

62. _____ One who is the right to occupancy and use of the property of another for a period of time according to a lease agreement.
A. Lessee   B. Assemblage   C. Value in use   D. Easement

63. _____ Divided or undivided rights in real estate that represent less than the whole.
A. Mortgage liens   B. Mass Appraisal   C. Rail Easement   D. Partial Interest

64. _____ A stage in a market area's life cycle characterized by renewal, redevelopment, modernization, and increasing demand.
A. Secondary Data   B. Revitalization   C. Regression Analysis   D. Value in use

65. _____ The act or process of developing an opinion of value.
A. Personal Representative   B. Express contract   C. Voluntary liens   D. Appraisal

66. _____ The price of a property with above- or below-market financing expressed in terms of the price that would have been paid in an all-cash sale.
A. Market Participants   B. Exposure Time   C. Safe Rate   D. Cash Equivalent

67. _____ Damage to property arising as a consequence of a taking over and above direct damages.
A. Market Participants   B. Housing Starts   C. Pipeline Easement   D. Consequential Damages

68. _____ Voluntary and one of the most common types of liens.
A. Adverse possession   B. Primary Data   C. Mortgage liens   D. Pipeline Easement

69. _____ When a series of different "multiplicands" are multiplied by the same multiplier it is known as.
A. Lessor   B. Constant   C. Loss of Access   D. Marketability

70. _____ Time and distance relationships between a particular use and supporting facilities.
A. Linkage   B. Specific Data   C. Change   D. Final Reconciliation

71. _____ goods, such as equipment (machinery and tools), bldgs., and infrastructure.
A. Capital   B. Risk Rate   C. Market Participants   D. Rate of return

72. _____ Flow of savings account money from savings and loans accounts to higher yield investments.
A. Disintermediation   B. Contract rent   C. Final Reconciliation   D. Oral Appraisal Report

73. _____ The yield rate used to convert future payments or receipts into present value; usually considered to be a synonym for yield rate.
A. Oral Appraisal Report   B. Discount Rate   C. Deterioration   D. Expert Testimony

74. _____ The value of a particular component is measured in terms of the amount it adds to the value of the whole property.
A. Operating Income   B. Utility   C. Effective Gross Income   D. Contribution

75. _____ These are hard cost expenditures for the labor and materials used in the construction of improvements.
A. Overall rate   B. Direct costs   C. Property Tax   D. General Data

76. _____ Data that is analyzed through the process of comparison.
A. Safe Rate   B. Fair Market Value   C. Secondary Data   D. Specific Data

77. _____ A statistical measure that attempts to determine the strength of the relationship between one dependent variable and a series of other changing variables.
A. Percentage lease   B. Risk Rate   C. Judgment liens   D. Regression Analysis

78. _____ Information that is gathered in its original form by the analyst.
A. Disintermediation   B. Pro Forma   C. Primary Data   D. Housing Starts

79. _____ Trespassing on the domain of another.
A. Hypothetical Condition   B. Encroachment   C. Oral Appraisal Report   D. Lis Pendens

80. ___ The right to construct, operate, and maintain a pipeline over the lands of others within prescribed geographical limits.
A. Pipeline Easement   B. Restricted use appraisal   C. Assemblage   D. Client

81. ___ The right for the construction, maintenance, and operation of a rail line on a property.
A. Lien   B. Scarcity   C. Bilateral contract   D. Rail Easement

82. ___ Has no legal force or binding effect and cannot be enforced in a court of law.
A. Stability   B. Accretion   C. Decline   D. Void contract

83. ___ The tenant's possessory interest created by a lease.
A. Decline   B. BOMA Standard   C. Leasehold Interest   D. Amenity

84. ___ Principle that real property value is created and sustained when contrasting, opposing, or interacting elements are in a state of equilibrium.
A. Ranking Analysis   B. Financing Terms   C. Involuntary liens   D. Balance

85. ___ The legal responsibility of a plaintiff to make reasonable efforts, after an injury or breach of contract, to alleviate the effects of the injury or breach.
A. Linkage   B. Effective Gross Income   C. Mitigation of Damages   D. Earnest money

86. ___ The relative position of the property to competitive properties and other value influences in its market area
A. Physical Characteristics   B. Mechanics liens   C. Loss of Access   D. Location

87. ___ Management of government receipts and expenditures.
A. Encumbrance   B. Ranking Analysis   C. Percentage lease   D. Fiscal Policy

88. ___ A type of renovation that involves modification or updating of existing improvements.
A. Remodeling   B. Seasonal Dwelling   C. Property Class   D. Expert Testimony

89. ___ A part of an appraisal report in which the appraiser certifies that the work was completed according to the applicable standards.
A. Physical Possibility   B. Certification   C. Assemblage   D. Conservation Easement

90. ___ A projected income and expense statement for proposed development.
A. Mechanics liens   B. Pro Forma   C. Riparian rights   D. Regression

91. ___ Created intentionally by property owner's actions. i.e. mortgage
A. Voluntary liens   B. Direct costs   C. Certification   D. Extraction

92. ___ Most commonly found in retail business. This lease has a base rent which is fixed and an excess rent, this is most commonly based on the percentage of the sales.
A. Effective age   B. Fair Market Value   C. Percentage lease   D. Oral Appraisal Report

93. ___ A lump sum benefit that an investor receives or expects to receive upon the termination of an investment; also called reversionary benefit.
A. Reversion   B. Housing Starts   C. Remainder interest   D. Estate Tax

94. ___ Public regulation of the character and extent of real estate use though police power.
A. Zoning   B. Partial Interest   C. Adverse possession   D. Quantitative Analysis

95. ___ Typically result from a lawsuit in which a monetary judgment is awarded.
A. Judgment liens   B. Constant   C. Effective age   D. Operating Income

96. ___ A voluntary legal agreement that becomes part of the chain of title thereby protecting a historic, archaeological, or cultural resource.
A. Specific Lien   B. Preservation Easement   C. Arms Length   D. Valid contract

97. ___ A vacant or in proof parcel of land devoted to or available for use as a residence.
A. Cost to Cure   B. Residential Property   C. Pipeline Easement   D. Rights in real property

98. ____ Neighborhood phenomenon in which middle- and upper-income persons purchase neighborhood properties and renovate or rehabilitate them.
A. Lis Pendens   B. Gentrification   C. Present Value   D. Partial Taking

99. ____ An identified parcel or tract of land, including improvements.
A. Valuation process   B. General Lien   C. Leasehold Interest   D. Real Estate

100. ____ An ownership interest for the possessory interest has been granted to another by creation of a contractual landlord-tenant relationship.
A. Leased Fee Interest   B. Appraisal Report   C. Capitalization Rate   D. Negative Amortization

A. From the words provided for each clue, provide the letter of the word which best matches the clue.

1. __D__ Going to the State. The process that should a property be abandoned, it reverts back to the state.
   A. Neighborhood   B. Overall rate   C. Expert Testimony   D. Escheat

2. __C__ A statistical measure that attempts to determine the strength of the relationship between one dependent variable and a series of other changing variables.
   A. Estate   B. Desktop Appraisal   C. Regression Analysis   D. Supra surface rights

3. __C__ A lease in which an intermediate, or sandwich, leaseholder is the lessee of one party and the lessor of another.
   A. Eminent Domain   B. Average Daily Traffic   C. Sandwich lease   D. Summary appraisal

4. __D__ The employment of a site or holding to produce revenue or other benefits.
   A. Investment Value   B. Operating Expenses   C. Partial Taking   D. Land Use

5. __A__ comprises of all costs required to construct and market the product as land alone or with improvements.
   A. Labor   B. Pole Line Easement   C. Highway Easement   D. Littoral rights

6. __D__ The taking of part of any real property interest for public use under the power of eminent domain; requires the payment of compensation.
   A. Reproduction Cost   B. Maximum Productivity   C. Interim use   D. Partial Taking

7. __D__ Legal term signifying pending litigation that can affect ownership title to real estate.
   A. Entrepreneurial profit   B. Functional Classification   C. Multifamily Dwelling   D. Lis Pendens

8. __B__ Total dollar expenditure to develop an improvement.
   A. Maximum Productivity   B. Cost   C. Client   D. Absorption rate

9. __C__ A building component with an expected remaining economic life that is the same as the remaining economic life of the entire structure.
   A. Government lien   B. Mortgage   C. Long Lived Item   D. Capitalization Rate

10. __D__ Two or more sales are compared to derive an indication of the size of the adjustment for a single characteristic.
    A. Cost Approach   B. Price   C. Risk Rate   D. Paired data analysis

11. __B__ The number of years since a structure or bldg. was originally built (birth).
    A. Qualitative analysis   B. Chronological age   C. Constant   D. Tenancy in Common

12. __B__ The overall vacancy rate that occurs as a result of the interaction of supply and demand of a particular property type in a particular region or market.
    A. Economic Characteristics   B. Market Vacancy   C. Title   D. Scope of Work

13. __A__ Annual crops and plantings such as corn, wheat, and vegetables.
    A. Emblements   B. Entrepreneurial profit   C. Comparables   D. Market Value

14. __A__ An appraiser's opinions or conclusions developed specific to an assignment.
    A. Assignment Results   B. Market Analysis   C. Land Use   D. Long Lived Item

15. __A__ In appraising, a loss in property value from any cause
    A. Depreciation   B. Regression   C. Scarcity   D. Partial Taking

16. __D__ The repair and restoration of existing improvements that are in poor condition to a state that makes the property competitive again.
    A. Paired data analysis   B. Estate Tax   C. Client   D. Rehabilitation

17. __A__ A private or public partnership that pools funds for the acquisition and development of real estate projects or other business ventures.
    A. Syndication   B. Market Value   C. Client   D. Estate in land

18. __C__ The actual rental income specified in a lease.
A. Functional Obsolesce B. Negative Amortization C. Contract rent D. Operating Income

19. __D__ Method by which government can take private property.
A. Remodeling B. Commercial Property C. Economic life D. Condemnation

20. __A__ One of the four criteria the highest and best use of a property must meet.
A. Financial Feasibility B. Market Rent C. Reproduction Cost D. Master Plan

21. __C__ The minimum rate of return on invested capital.
A. Fair Market Value B. Accretion C. Safe Rate D. Surface rights

22. __A__ Testimony of persons who are presumed to have special knowledge of, or skill in, a particular field due to education, experience, or study.
A. Expert Testimony B. Cost C. Certification D. Going concern value

23. __D__ An easement for the construction, maintenance, and operation of a full line, usually for the transmission of electric power.
A. Mortgage B. Encumbrance C. Deferred Maintenance D. Pole Line Easement

24. __C__ The present or anticipated undersupply of an item relative to the demand for it. Conditions of scarcity contribute to value.
A. Accretion B. Risk Rate C. Scarcity D. Cost

25. __C__ Any rate used to convert income into value.
A. Units of comparison B. Spot Zoning C. Capitalization Rate D. Quotient

26. __B__ A systematic set of procedures an appraiser follows to provide answers to a client's questions about real property value.
A. Decline B. Valuation process C. Adjustments D. Stability

27. __B__ Analyzing value of a property based on numerical data.
A. Renovation B. Quantitative Analysis C. Void contract D. Reserve

28. __A__ The period of time over which a structure may reasonably be expected to perform the function for which it was designed.
A. Useful life B. Exposure Time C. Reproduction Cost D. Safe Rate

29. __D__ Property taxes or special assessments, has priority over other liens.
A. Amenity B. Raw Land C. Avulsion D. Government lien

30. __C__ When a series of different "multiplicands" are multiplied by the same multiplier it is known as.
A. Raw Land B. Legal Permissibility C. Constant D. Capitalization

31. __C__ The relative desirability of a property in comparison with similar or competing properties in the area.
A. Amenity B. Capitalization C. Marketability D. Assessed Value

32. __B__ The right to construct, operate, and maintain a pipeline over the lands of others within prescribed geographical limits.
A. Reclamation B. Pipeline Easement C. Range of Value D. Competition

33. __B__ An increase in value when extra utility is created by combining smaller parcels under single ownership.
A. Competition B. Plottage C. Physical life D. Adjustments

34. __A__ The process by which all roads are grouped into classes or systems according to the character of service they are intended to provide.
A. Functional Classification B. Land Use C. Mitigation of Damages D. Entrepreneurial profit

35. __A__ The process in which older structures or historic buildings are modernized, remodeled, or restored.
A. Renovation B. Cost Approach C. Capitalization D. Subsurface rights

36. __A__ Sum of all fixed and variable operating expenses and reserve for replacement.
A. Total Operating Expenses B. Market Value C. Stability D. Scarcity

37. __D__ An element of comparison in the sales comparison approach.
A. Fixed Expense B. Erosion C. Effective Date D. Economic Characteristics

38. __C__ Net income that is left after the 4 agents of production have been paid.
A. Intestate B. Revitalization C. Surplus Productivity D. Negative Amortization

39. __A__ Income-producing property such as office and retail buildings.
A. Commercial Property B. Market Vacancy C. Index lease D. Voidable contract

40. __A__ An individual or other legal person designated in a will to settle the estate of a deceased person.
A. Personal Representative B. Value in use C. Arms Length D. Legal Permissibility

41. __B__ Pledge of a described property interest as collateral or security for the repayment of a loan under certain terms and conditions.
A. Raw Land B. Mortgage C. Leased Fee Interest D. Real Estate Market

42. __B__ Land on which no improvements have been made
A. Avulsion B. Raw Land C. Condemnation D. Encumbrance

43. __C__ an estimate of replacement cost of a structure, less depreciation, plus land value.
A. Competition B. Spot Zoning C. Cost Approach D. Operating Statement

44. __D__ The value of a future payment or series of future payments discounted to the current date or to time period zero.
A. Constant B. Surplus Productivity C. Paired data analysis D. Present Value

45. __D__ Operating expenses that generally do not vary with occupancy and that prudent management will pay whether the properties occupied or vacant.
A. Estate in land B. Potential Gross Income C. Anticipation D. Fixed Expense

46. __C__ Trespassing on the domain of another.
A. Functional Classification B. Voidable contract C. Encroachment D. Desk Review

47. __A__ An exception to the general zoning regulations; permits specific, usually small, parcels of land to be zone for a use that is not permitted in the surrounding area.
A. Spot Zoning B. Capitalization Rate C. Attachment D. Master Plan

48. __B__ Value a specific property has to a specific person or firm for a specific use.
A. Going concern value B. Value in use C. Operating Expense Ratio D. Reproduction Cost

49. __D__ An increase in dry land created by the gradual accumulation of waterborne solid material over formerly riparian land.
A. Market Vacancy B. Pole Line Easement C. Implied contract D. Accretion

50. __B__ The most probable price at which real estate would sell.
A. Escheat B. Market Value C. Reproduction Cost D. Quantitative Analysis

51. __C__ Improvements on and off the site that make it suitable for its intended use or development.
A. Land B. Deferred Maintenance C. Site Improvements D. Potential Gross Income

52. __D__ A lease in which the landlord passes on all expenses to the tenant.
A. Mitigation of Damages B. Financial Feasibility C. Decline D. Net Lease

53. __C__ The ratio of total operating expenses to effective gross income
A. Legal Description B. Indirect costs C. Operating Expense Ratio D. Summary appraisal

54. __D__ A transaction in which the buyers and sellers of a product act independently and have no relationship to each other.
A. Assignment Results B. Percentage lease C. Long Lived Item D. Arms Length

55. __D__ A method of estimating value in which the depreciated cost of the improvements on the improved property is calculated and deducted from the total sale price
A. Economic Characteristics B. Direct costs C. Long Lived Item D. Extraction

56. __C__ The annual rate of return on capital that is commensurate with the risk assumed by the investor; the rate of interest or yield necessary to attract capital.
A. Preservation Easement B. Frictional Vacancy C. Risk Rate D. Economic life

57. __C__ An appropriation from surplus funds that is allocated to deferred or anticipated contingencies.
A. Market Analysis B. Summary appraisal C. Reserve D. Fair Market Value

58. __D__ Rights pertaining to properties abutting a lake or pond.
A. Leased Fee Interest B. Absorption rate C. Condemnation D. Littoral rights

59. __A__ When a property has the lowest asking price and the same utility as other properties, yet attracts the greatest demand.
A. Substitution B. Total Operating Expenses C. Executor D. Rehabilitation

60. __B__ A condition which is contrary to what is known by the appraiser to exist on the effective date of the assignment results, but is used for the purpose of analysis.
A. Multifamily Dwelling B. Hypothetical Condition C. Remnant D. Depreciation

61. __B__ arise from construction and other improvements to real estate.
A. Market Participants B. Mechanics liens C. Market Vacancy D. Syndication

62. __D__ A voluntary legal agreement that becomes part of the chain of title thereby protecting a historic, archaeological, or cultural resource.
A. Market Analysis B. Cost Approach C. Regression D. Preservation Easement

63. __D__ An individual or other legal person designated in a will to settle the estate of the deceased person.
A. Regression B. Condemnation C. Highway Easement D. Executor

64. __A__ Is used for elements that cannot be given a numerical value.
A. Qualitative analysis B. Mechanics liens C. Attachment D. Client

65. __C__ Any tax on ownership or possession of property and is measured by the number of units or value of such property.
A. Market Analysis B. Supra surface rights C. Property Tax D. Gross Building Area

66. __B__ The period over time which a structure may be competitive in the market.
A. Risk Rate B. Economic life C. Unilateral contract D. Client

67. __C__ The value of a particular component is measured in terms of the amount it adds to the value of the whole property.
A. Elements of comparison B. Effective Date C. Contribution D. Certification

68. __C__ Study of real estate market conditions for specific types of property.
A. Client B. Lis Pendens C. Market Analysis D. Capitalization

69. __D__ Stage in market area's life cycle. The market area experiences equilibrium without market gains or losses.
A. Desktop Appraisal B. Renovation C. Cash Equivalent D. Stability

70. __C__ Monetary worth of a property, good, or service to buyers and sellers at a given time.
A. Mass Appraisal B. Property Class C. Value D. Mortgage

71. __C__ Most commonly found in retail business. This lease has a base rent which is fixed and an excess rent, this is most commonly based on the percentage of the sales.
A. Drive by Appraisal B. Highway Easement C. Percentage lease D. Net Lease

72. __C__ An allowance that provides for the periodic replacement of building components that wear out more rapidly than the building itself.
A. Restricted use appraisal B. Eminent Domain C. Replacement Allowance D. Valuation process

73. B The state of having the requisite or adequate ability or qualities to perform the specific assignment and produce credible assignment results.
A. Maximum Productivity   B. Competence   C. Value in use   D. Quotent

74. C Relevant characteristics used to compare and adjust the property prices.
A. Subsurface rights   B. Negative Amortization   C. Elements of comparison   D. Capitalization Rate

75. C Annual amount of total revenue that a property would generate if it were occupied all throughout the year.
A. Void contract   B. Attachment   C. Gross Market Income   D. Mechanics liens

76. B Value is a function of expected benefits to get from the ownership of the property.
A. Financial Feasibility   B. Anticipation   C. Labor   D. Revitalization

77. A When the government regulates the land use for the good of the public.
A. Police power   B. Negative Amortization   C. Entrepreneurial profit   D. Encumbrance

78. D The more a property or its components are in harmony with the surrounding properties or components, the greater the contributory value.
A. Chronological age   B. Cash Equivalent   C. Useful life   D. Conformity

79. D Total payment is insufficient to pay interest due.
A. Qualitative analysis   B. Encumbrance   C. Adjustments   D. Negative Amortization

80. D The effect on value produced by a property's location at or near the intersection of two streets.
A. Life tenant   B. Legal Permissibility   C. Market Value   D. Corner influence

81. B Conclusions of the appraisal are stated, but the data or analyses used in the appraisal to develop these conclusions do not need to be included in the report.
A. Physical Possibility   B. Restricted use appraisal   C. Going concern value   D. Final Reconciliation

82. D Technically valid but gives one or more parties the power to legally void the agreement and thus cancel performance.
A. Master Plan   B. Surface rights   C. Gross Market Income   D. Voidable contract

83. B The type and extent of research and analyses in appraisal or appraisal review assignment.
A. Tenancy in Common   B. Scope of Work   C. Competition   D. Reclamation

84. C Price per cubic foot, front foot, and per apartment.
A. Commercial Property   B. Net Lease   C. Units of comparison   D. Client

85. C An ownership interest for the possessory interest has been granted to another by creation of a contractual landlord-tenant relationship.
A. Setback   B. Operating Statement   C. Leased Fee Interest   D. Maximum Productivity

86. D The degree, nature, or extent of interest that a person has in land.
A. Labor   B. Average Daily Traffic   C. Voidable contract   D. Estate in land

87. A A tangible or intangible benefit of real property that enhances its attractiveness or increases the satisfaction of the user.
A. Amenity   B. Pole Line Easement   C. Executor   D. Avulsion

88. B Zoning regulations that designate the distance a building must be set back from the front, rear, and sides of the property lines.
A. Renovation   B. Setback   C. Corner influence   D. Cost Approach

89. B The conversion of income into value.
A. Attachment   B. Capitalization   C. Legal Permissibility   D. Operating Expenses

90. C Any method of bringing wasted natural resources into productive use.
A. Operating Income   B. Anticipation   C. Reclamation   D. Utility

91. C A stage in a market area's life cycle characterized by renewal, redevelopment, modernization, and increasing demand.
A. Comparables B. Market Vacancy C. Revitalization D. Gross Building Area

92. C A building containing two or more dwelling units.
A. Fair Market Value B. Ranking Analysis C. Multifamily Dwelling D. Conservation Easement

93. D Soft cost expenditures that are necessary components but are not typically part of the construction contract.
A. Fixed Expense B. Location C. Drive by Appraisal D. Indirect costs

94. D The estimated period during which improvements will continue to provide utility.
A. Riparian rights B. Appraisal C. Physical life D. Remaining Useful Life

95. D In accounting, a category for property under the modified accelerated cost recovery system.
A. Legal Permissibility B. Risk Rate C. Involuntary liens D. Property Class

96. D An appraisal report in which the appraiser's scope of work does not include an inspection of the subject property or comparables.
A. Executor B. Voidable contract C. Physical life D. Desktop Appraisal

97. D In law, just, rational, appropriate, ordinary, or usual in the circumstances.
A. Desk Review B. Average Daily Traffic C. Highway Easement D. Reasonable

98. C Combination of all elements that constitute proof of ownership.
A. Units of comparison B. Principle C. Title D. Reasonable

99. A Right to undisturbed use and control of designated air space above a specific land area within stated elevations.
A. Supra surface rights B. Qualitative analysis C. Market Value D. Setback

100. A Easement that is not attached or appurtenant to any particular estate; does not run with the land nor is it transferred through the conveyance of title.
A. Easement in gross B. Deed C. Gross Market Income D. Deferred Maintenance

B. From the words provided for each clue, provide the letter of the word which best matches the clue.

1. D The present or anticipated undersupply of an item relative to the demand for it. Conditions of scarcity contribute to value.
A. Cost Approach B. Capitalization Rate C. Taxation D. Scarcity

2. C A form of ownership in which each owner possesses the exclusive right to use and occupy an allotted unit plus an undivided interest in common areas.
A. Desk Review B. Site C. Condominium D. Lease

3. C An agreement put into words (written or spoken).
A. Estate in land B. General Data C. Express contract D. Physical Characteristics

4. D Something that has been added or appended to a property and has since become an inherent part of the property.
A. Economic Characteristics B. Total Operating Expenses C. Remnant D. Appurtenance

5. D A series of related changes brought about by a chain of causes and effects.
A. Land Use B. Brownfield C. Contribution D. Trends

6. D Improvements on and off the site that make it suitable for its intended use or development.
A. Accretion B. Fiscal Policy C. Progression D. Site Improvements

7. C Is used for elements that cannot be given a numerical value.
A. Capital B. Risk Rate C. Qualitative analysis D. Preservation Easement

8. __B__ first thing a developer considers in developing a property is the cost of land.
A. Restricted use appraisal   B. Land   C. Financial Feasibility   D. Safe Rate

9. __D__ The tenant's possessory interest created by a lease.
A. Contribution   B. Littoral rights   C. Neighborhood   D. Leasehold Interest

10. __C__ Created intentionally by property owner's actions. i.e. mortgage
A. Physical Possibility   B. Brownfield   C. Voluntary liens   D. Deterioration

11. __C__ The process by which all roads are grouped into classes or systems according to the character of service they are intended to provide.
A. Price   B. Express contract   C. Functional Classification   D. Pole Line Easement

12. __C__ Stage in market area's life cycle. The market area experiences equilibrium without market gains or losses.
A. Exposure Time   B. Personal Representative   C. Stability   D. Seasonal Dwelling

13. __D__ A contract in which the rights to use and occupy land or structures are transferred by the owner to another for a specified period of time in return for specified rent.
A. Market Price   B. Cash Flow   C. Taxation   D. Lease

14. __C__ Easement that is not attached or appurtenant to any particular estate; does not run with the land nor is it transferred through the conveyance of title.
A. Exposure Time   B. Gross lease   C. Easement in gross   D. Cost

15. __C__ Guiding control of the money supply in the economy.
A. Labor   B. Economic Characteristics   C. Monetary Policy   D. Site Improvements

16. __A__ In final reconciliation, the range in which the final market value opinion of a property may fall; usually stated as the interval between a high and low value limit.
A. Range of Value   B. Deed restriction   C. Seasonal Dwelling   D. Easement

17. __A__ Right of government to raise revenue through assessments on valuable goods, products, and rights.
A. Taxation   B. Principle   C. Hypothication   D. Personal Representative

18. __A__ Absolute ownership unencumbered by any other interest or estate.
A. Fee Simple Estate   B. Cost to Cure   C. Commercial Property   D. Intestate

19. __C__ Total dollar expenditure to develop an improvement.
A. Proximity Damage   B. Economic Characteristics   C. Cost   D. Executor

20. __B__ Data that is analyzed through the process of comparison.
A. Price   B. Specific Data   C. Contribution   D. Deed restriction

21. __C__ One of the four criteria the highest and best use of a property must meet.
A. Royalty   B. Redevelopment   C. Financial Feasibility   D. Value in use

22. __A__ Pledge of a described property interest as collateral or security for the repayment of a loan under certain terms and conditions.
A. Mortgage   B. Scarcity   C. Hypothetical Condition   D. Real Estate Market

23. __B__ The result of the cause and effect relationship among the forces that influence real property value.
A. Personal Representative   B. Change   C. Percentage Adjustments   D. Pole Line Easement

24. __B__ One cause of depreciation.
A. Site   B. Obsolescence   C. Negative Amortization   D. Remainder

25. __A__ The opinion of value derived from the reconciliation of value indications and stated in the appraisal report
A. Final Opinion of Value   B. Value in use   C. Quantitative Analysis   D. Lease

26. B   The condition of dying with a valid will.
    A. Conformity   B. Testate   C. Expert Testimony   D. Operating Expense Ratio

27. A   Annual crops and plantings such as corn, wheat, and vegetables.
    A. Emblements   B. Rail Easement   C. Direct Capitalization   D. Remnant

28. B   A condition which is contrary to what is known by the appraiser to exist on the effective date of the assignment results, but is used for the purpose of analysis.
    A. Desire   B. Hypothetical Condition   C. Lis Pendens   D. Real Estate Market

29. B   The annual rate of return on capital that is commensurate with the risk assumed by the investor; the rate of interest or yield necessary to attract capital.
    A. Property Class   B. Risk Rate   C. Long Lived Item   D. Fair Market Value

30. C   The amount of money borrowed from lender (mortgagee).
    A. Intestate   B. Constant   C. Principle   D. Pipeline Easement

31. A   The right to construct, operate, and maintain a pipeline over the lands of others within prescribed geographical limits.
    A. Pipeline Easement   B. Unilateral contract   C. Market Price   D. Property Class

32. B   Only one party makes a promise
    A. Commercial Property   B. Unilateral contract   C. Reasonable   D. Range of Value

33. C   In condemnation, the loss in value to the remainder in a partial taking of property.
    A. Location   B. Life tenant   C. Damages   D. Government lien

34. A   The more a property or its components are in harmony with the surrounding properties or components, the greater the contributory value.
    A. Conformity   B. Change   C. Total Operating Expenses   D. Percentage Adjustments

35. B   Amount a particular purchaser agrees to pay and a particular seller agrees to accept under the circumstances surrounding their transaction.
    A. Marketing time   B. Price   C. Risk Rate   D. Range of Value

36. A   Value a specific property has to a specific person or firm for a specific use.
    A. Value in use   B. Operating Expense Ratio   C. Erosion   D. Assessed Value

37. C   Information that is not gathered in its original form by the analyst.
    A. Principle   B. Change   C. Secondary Data   D. Consequential Damages

38. D   Land that is not needed to serve or support the existing improvement.
    A. Negative Amortization   B. Master Plan   C. Arms Length   D. Excess Land

39. D   The taking of part of any real property interest for public use under the power of eminent domain; requires the payment of compensation.
    A. Labor   B. Subsurface rights   C. Operating Expenses   D. Partial Taking

40. B   In accounting, a category for property under the modified accelerated cost recovery system.
    A. Mechanics liens   B. Property Class   C. Cash Flow   D. Entrepreneurial Incentive

41. C   The process of reducing a range of value indications into an appropriate conclusion for that analysis.
    A. Value in use   B. Adjustments   C. Reconciliation   D. Reasonable

42. B   A lease in which the landlord passes on all expenses to the tenant.
    A. Physical Characteristics   B. Net Lease   C. Encroachment   D. Cost Approach

43. D   Testimony of persons who are presumed to have special knowledge of, or skill in, a particular field due to education, experience, or study.
    A. Earnest money   B. Cost Approach   C. Raw Land   D. Expert Testimony

44. __D__ One who owns an interest in real property for his or her own lifetime.
A. Proximity Damage   B. Quantitative Analysis   C. Arms Length   D. Life tenant

45. __A__ Damage to property arising as a consequence of a taking over and above direct damages.
A. Consequential Damages   B. Present Value   C. Average Daily Traffic   D. Land Use

46. __A__ A market-derived figure that represents the amount an entrepreneur receives for their contribution.
A. Entrepreneurial profit   B. Site   C. Loss of Access   D. Estate in land

47. __C__ Temporary use to which a site or improved property is put until it is ready to be put to its future highest and best use.
A. Entrepreneurial Incentive   B. Chronological age   C. Interim use   D. Highway Easement

48. __D__ Any rate used to convert income into value.
A. Land Use   B. Percentage lease   C. Constant   D. Capitalization Rate

49. __B__ Two or more sales are compared to derive an indication of the size of the adjustment for a single characteristic.
A. Internal Rate of Return   B. Paired data analysis   C. Partial Taking   D. Mitigation of Damages

50. __B__ A method used to convert an estimate of a single year's income expectancy into an indication of value in one direct step
A. Rail Easement   B. Direct Capitalization   C. Final Reconciliation   D. Index lease

51. __B__ The employment of a site or holding to produce revenue or other benefits.
A. Financial Feasibility   B. Land Use   C. Exposure Time   D. Assignment Results

52. __A__ Going to the State. The process that should a property be abandoned, it reverts back to the state.
A. Escheat   B. Competition   C. Capital   D. Fiscal Policy

53. __D__ A report that is transmitted orally.
A. Investment Value   B. Total Operating Expenses   C. Market Price   D. Oral Appraisal Report

54. __A__ An appraisal review in which the reviewer's scope of work does not include an inspection of the subject property.
A. Desk Review   B. Units of comparison   C. Decline   D. Physical Characteristics

55. __B__ Needed repairs or replacement of items that should have taken place during the course of normal maintenance.
A. Assemblage   B. Deferred Maintenance   C. Assignment Results   D. Ranking Analysis

56. __C__ Dollar amount required to reconstruct a bldg. or other improvement, which have the same or equivalent utility as the original.
A. Intestate   B. Specific Data   C. Replacement Cost   D. Operating Expenses

57. __C__ The most probable price at which real estate would sell.
A. Easement   B. Hypothetical Condition   C. Market Value   D. Real Estate Market

58. __A__ The cost to restore an item of deferred maintenance to new or reasonably new condition.
A. Cost to Cure   B. Accretion   C. Remainder interest   D. Redevelopment

59. __A__ A plan, map, or chart of a city, town, section, or subdivision indicating the location and boundaries of individual properties.
A. plat   B. Mass Appraisal   C. Substitution   D. Easement in gross

60. __B__ goods, such as equipment (machinery and tools), bldgs., and infrastructure.
A. Chronological age   B. Capital   C. Cost   D. Risk Rate

61. __A__ Purchaser's wish for an item to satisfy human needs or individual wants beyond essential life-support needs.
A. Desire   B. Frictional Vacancy   C. Escheat   D. Emblements

62. __C__ The total period a building lasts or is expected to last as opposed to its economic life.
A. Present Value   B. Chronological age   C. Physical life   D. Change

63. B Conclusions of the appraisal are stated, but the data or analyses used in the appraisal to develop these conclusions do not need to be included in the report.
A. Financing Terms B. Restricted use appraisal C. Specific Data D. Internal Rate of Return

64. B A right granted or taken for the construction, maintenance, and operation of the highway.
A. Littoral rights B. Highway Easement C. Fair Market Value D. Estate Tax

65. A The value of a particular component is measured in terms of the amount it adds to the value of the whole property.
A. Contribution B. Setback C. Voluntary liens D. Lease

66. B Value is a function of expected benefits to get from the ownership of the property.
A. Mechanics liens B. Anticipation C. Neighborhood D. Site

67. B Right to undisturbed use and control of designated air space above a specific land area within stated elevations.
A. Encroachment B. Supra surface rights C. Deed D. Hypothetical Condition

68. C Complementary land uses; inhabitants, buildings, or business enterprises.
A. Average Daily Traffic B. Constant C. Neighborhood D. Leasehold Interest

69. D Total payment is insufficient to pay interest due.
A. Royalty B. Preservation Easement C. Title D. Negative Amortization

70. D A letter or statement that serves as a notice of delivery from the appraiser to the client of a report containing an opinion or conclusion concerning real estate
A. Remaining Useful Life B. Bundle of rights C. Oral Appraisal Report D. Letter of Transmittal

71. B The actual rental income specified in a lease.
A. Loss of Access B. Contract rent C. Government lien D. Marketability

72. C Management of government receipts and expenditures.
A. Marketability B. Operating Expenses C. Fiscal Policy D. Pipeline Easement

73. C A future possessor read interest in real estate that is given to a third-party and matures upon the termination of a limited or determinable be.
A. Risk Rate B. Voluntary liens C. Remainder D. Net Lease

74. C Monetary worth of a property, good, or service to buyers and sellers at a given time.
A. Expert Testimony B. Leasehold Interest C. Value D. Market Price

75. D The number of years since a structure or bldg. was originally built (birth).
A. Lease B. Direct Capitalization C. Rail Easement D. Chronological age

76. D The time of property remains on the market.
A. Risk Rate B. Police power C. Gross Living Area D. Exposure Time

77. C The right to use another's land for a stated purpose.
A. Commercial Property B. Pole Line Easement C. Easement D. Assignment Results

78. D A statistical measure that attempts to determine the strength of the relationship between one dependent variable and a series of other changing variables.
A. Highway Easement B. Marketing time C. Trends D. Regression Analysis

79. C The periodic expenditures necessary to maintain the real property and continue production of the effective gross income, assuming prudent and competent management.
A. Substitution B. Gross lease C. Operating Expenses D. Financing Terms

80. B The period of time over which a structure may reasonably be expected to perform the function for which it was designed.
A. Scarcity B. Useful life C. Mitigation of Damages D. Cost Approach

81. A   The last phase in the development of the value opinion in which two or more value indications derived from market data are resolved into a value opinion.
A. Final Reconciliation B. Property Class C. Estate Tax D. Letter of Transmittal

82. D   Annual amount of total revenue that a property would generate if it were occupied all throughout the year.
A. Erosion B. Trends C. Voluntary liens D. Gross Market Income

83. B   Rights to the use and profits of the underground portion of a designated property.
A. Regression B. Subsurface rights C. Physical Possibility D. Fair Market Value

84. A   Land on which no improvements have been made
A. Raw Land B. Anticipation C. Location D. Total Operating Expenses

85. B   The impairment of functional capacity of a property according to market tastes and standards.
A. Capitalization B. Functional Obsolesce C. Long Lived Item D. Obsolescence

86. A   Sum of all fixed and variable operating expenses and reserve for replacement.
A. Total Operating Expenses B. Final Opinion of Value C. Restricted use appraisal D. Police power

87. B   The right for the construction, maintenance, and operation of a rail line on a property.
A. Testate B. Rail Easement C. Cash Flow D. Encroachment

88. B   The yield rate used to convert future payments or receipts into present value; usually considered to be a synonym for yield rate.
A. Proximity Damage B. Discount Rate C. Effective Gross Income D. Decline

89. A   When a series of different "multiplicands" are multiplied by the same multiplier it is known as.
A. Constant B. Real Estate C. Easement in gross D. Trends

90. D   Seizure of property by court order.
A. Financing Terms B. Qualitative analysis C. Deferred Maintenance D. Attachment

91. B   Most commonly found in retail business. This lease has a base rent which is fixed and an excess rent, this is most commonly based on the percentage of the sales.
A. Price B. Percentage lease C. Risk Rate D. Utility

92. B   The minimum rate of return on invested capital.
A. Mechanics liens B. Safe Rate C. Executor D. Appraisal

93. D   The development or improvement of cleared or undeveloped land in an urban renewal area.
A. Quantitative Analysis B. Safe Rate C. Just Compensation D. Redevelopment

94. B   An element of comparison in the sales comparison approach.
A. Investment Value B. Economic Characteristics C. Negative Amortization D. Average Daily Traffic

95. C   In condemnation, the amount of loss for which a property owner is compensated when his or her property is taken.
A. Land B. Brownfield C. Just Compensation D. Chronological age

96. B   The relative position of the property to competitive properties and other value influences in its market area
A. Valuation process B. Location C. Subsurface rights D. Supra surface rights

97. A   land that is improved so that is ready to be used for a specific purpose.
A. Site B. Remainder C. Desk Review D. Zoning

98. A   Legal term signifying pending litigation that can affect ownership title to real estate.
A. Lis Pendens B. Market Value C. Unilateral contract D. Bilateral contract

99. A   An individual or other legal person designated in a will to settle the estate of a deceased person.
A. Personal Representative B. Percentage Adjustments C. Physical life D. Anticipation

100. C Money paid to an owner of real property or mineral rights for the right to deplete natural resource.
A. Conformity   B. Desk Review   C. Royalty   D. Deed

C. From the words provided for each clue, provide the letter of the word which best matches the clue.

1. B Divided or undivided rights in real estate that represent less than the whole.
A. Internal Rate of Return   B. Partial Interest   C. Market Value   D. Accretion

2. C An exception to the general zoning regulations; permits specific, usually small, parcels of land to be zone for a use that is not permitted in the surrounding area.
A. Mechanics liens   B. Regression Analysis   C. Spot Zoning   D. Valuation process

3. C A tax on the estate or wealth of the deceased person that is usually computed as a percentage of the market value of the assets of the estate.
A. Pro Forma   B. Capitalization   C. Estate Tax   D. Lease

4. C An element of comparison in the sales comparison approach.
A. Intestate   B. Cash Flow   C. Economic Characteristics   D. Multifamily Dwelling

5. C A limitation that passes with the land regardless of the owner.
A. Setback   B. Master Plan   C. Deed restriction   D. Discount Rate

6. A Adjustments for differences between the subject and comparable properties expressed as a percentage of the sale price of the comparable property.
A. Percentage Adjustments   B. Qualitative analysis   C. Attachment   D. Capitalization Rate

7. A A study of the cost-benefit relationships of an economic endeavor.
A. Feasibility Analysis   B. Total Operating Expenses   C. Estate in land   D. Valid contract

8. C Stage in market area's life cycle. The market area experiences equilibrium without market gains or losses.
A. Growth   B. Lease   C. Stability   D. Specific Lien

9. B Value of a superior property is adversely affected by its association with an inferior property of the same type.
A. Change   B. Regression   C. Revitalization   D. Physical life

10. A The condition of dying without a will.
A. Intestate   B. Regression   C. Bundle of rights   D. Frictional Vacancy

11. C A stage in a market areas life cycle in which the market area gains public favor and acceptance.
A. Reclamation   B. Progression   C. Growth   D. Rehabilitation

12. A An increase in value when extra utility is created by combining smaller parcels under single ownership.
A. Plottage   B. Revitalization   C. Discount Rate   D. Royalty

13. C Time and distance relationships between a particular use and supporting facilities.
A. Discount Rate   B. Interim use   C. Linkage   D. Economic Characteristics

14. C The conversion of income into value.
A. Certification   B. Scope of Work   C. Capitalization   D. Estate in land

15. A One who conveys the rights of occupancy and use to others under lease agreement.
A. Lessor   B. Growth   C. Limiting Condition   D. Proximity Damage

16. D One of the four criteria the highest and best use of a property must meet.
A. Primary Data   B. Disintermediation   C. Residential Property   D. Legal Permissibility

17. D   A condition which is contrary to what is known by the appraiser to exist on the effective date of the assignment results, but is used for the purpose of analysis.
A. Financial Feasibility   B. Debt coverage ratio   C. Fee Simple Estate   D. Hypothetical Condition

18. B   Monetary worth of a property, good, or service to buyers and sellers at a given time.
A. Rate of return   B. Value   C. Property Class   D. Desktop Appraisal

19. A   Total floor area of a building, excluding unenclosed area, measured from the exterior of the walls of the above-grade area.
A. Gross Building Area   B. Rehabilitation   C. Unilateral contract   D. Taxation

20. C   The wear and tear that begins with the building is completed and placed into service.
A. Utility   B. Leasehold Interest   C. Physical Deterioration   D. Unilateral contract

21. B   Damages that is caused by the remainder's proximity to the improvement being constructed.
A. Reconciliation   B. Proximity Damage   C. Distress Sale   D. Negative Amortization

22. B   The written or oral communication of an appraisal.
A. Partial Interest   B. Appraisal Report   C. Expert Testimony   D. Supra surface rights

23. A   In final reconciliation, the range in which the final market value opinion of a property may fall; usually stated as the interval between a high and low value limit.
A. Range of Value   B. Personal Representative   C. Location   D. Legal Permissibility

24. C   The ratio of total operating expenses to effective gross income
A. Reserve   B. Desk Review   C. Operating Expense Ratio   D. Quotient

25. B   An appropriation from surplus funds that is allocated to deferred or anticipated contingencies.
A. Probate   B. Reserve   C. Physical Possibility   D. Pole Line Easement

26. D   The tenant's possessory interest created by a lease.
A. Market Price   B. Attachment   C. Lessor   D. Leasehold Interest

27. A   The change in the value of a property as a whole, resulting from the addition or deletion of a property component.
A. Contributory Value   B. Consequential Damages   C. Investment Value   D. Elements of comparison

28. B   Ann agreement that is presumed to exist because of the parties' actions.
A. Land   B. Implied contract   C. Deferred Maintenance   D. Distress Sale

29. A   The right for the construction, maintenance, and operation of a rail line on a property.
A. Rail Easement   B. Certification   C. Index lease   D. Remaining Economic Life

30. C   A market-derived figure that represents the amount an entrepreneur receives for their contribution.
A. Restricted use appraisal   B. Plat   C. Entrepreneurial profit   D. Property Tax

31. A   The ratio of income or yield to the original investment.
A. Rate of return   B. Specific Lien   C. Restricted use appraisal   D. Maximum Productivity

32. B   The combining of 2 or more parcels into one ownership (tract).
A. Market Value   B. Assemblage   C. Implied contract   D. Property Class

33. B   Easement that is attached to, benefits, and passes with the conveyance of the dominant estate. Burdens the servient estate.
A. Life estate   B. Easement appurtenant   C. Sandwich lease   D. Market Vacancy

34. C   Any tax on ownership or possession of property and is measured by the number of units or value of such property.
A. Encroachment   B. Probate   C. Property Tax   D. Interim use

35. B A part of an appraisal report in which the appraiser certifies that the work was completed according to the applicable standards.
A. Cash Flow   B. Certification   C. Summary appraisal   D. Lease

36. C A financial statement that reflects the gross revenues, expenses, and net operating profit or loss of an investment over a fixed period.
A. Going concern value   B. Master Plan   C. Operating Statement   D. Cost Approach

37. C A projected income and expense statement for proposed development.
A. Scope of Work   B. Pole Line Easement   C. Pro Forma   D. Unilateral contract

38. B One cause of depreciation.
A. Value in use   B. Obsolescence   C. Certification   D. Title

39. B The estimated period during which improvements will continue to provide utility.
A. Going concern value   B. Remaining Useful Life   C. Functional Classification   D. Attachment

40. C An appraisal report in which the scope of work includes an exterior-only viewing of the subject property.
A. Escheat   B. Emblements   C. Drive by Appraisal   D. Earnest money

41. A An identified parcel or tract of land, including improvements.
A. Real Estate   B. Present Value   C. Estate Tax   D. Fiscal Policy

42. C An increase in dry land created by the gradual accumulation of waterborne solid material over formerly riparian land.
A. Attachment   B. Easement in gross   C. Accretion   D. Cost to Cure

43. C The interests, benefits, and rights inherent in ownership of real estate.
A. Rehabilitation   B. Consequential Damages   C. Real Property   D. Primary Data

44. D Two or more sales are compared to derive an indication of the size of the adjustment for a single characteristic.
A. Cost   B. Utility   C. Inheritance Tax   D. Paired data analysis

45. D Any communication, written or oral, of an appraisal or appraisal review that is transmitted to the client upon completion of an assignment.
A. Value in use   B. Earnest money   C. Comparables   D. Report

46. D Management of government receipts and expenditures.
A. Regression   B. Units of comparison   C. Accretion   D. Fiscal Policy

47. A A stage in a market area's life cycle characterized by renewal, redevelopment, modernization, and increasing demand.
A. Revitalization   B. Lease   C. Reserve   D. Taxation

48. C Right to undisturbed use and control of designated air space above a specific land area within stated elevations.
A. Revitalization   B. Tenancy in Common   C. Supra surface rights   D. Police power

49. A Value to a particular individual. The present worth of anticipated future benefits.
A. Investment Value   B. Entrepreneurial profit   C. Linkage   D. Escheat

50. A A type of renovation that involves modification or updating of existing improvements.
A. Remodeling   B. Principle   C. Spot Zoning   D. Surface rights

51. C A future possessor read interest in real estate that is given to a third-party and matures upon the termination of a limited or determinable be.
A. Market Participants   B. Market Price   C. Remainder   D. Primary Data

52. D Is used for elements that cannot be given a numerical value.
A. Operating Expense Ratio   B. Entrepreneurial profit   C. Contributory Value   D. Qualitative analysis

53. __A__ A vacant or in proof parcel of land devoted to or available for use as a residence.
A. Residential Property   B. Qualitative analysis   C. Sandwich lease   D. Direct costs

54. __C__ Method by which government can take private property.
A. Corner influence   B. Growth   C. Condemnation   D. Contributory Value

55. __A__ Depriving an abutting owner of the inherent rights of ingress and to egress from the highway or street.
A. Loss of Access   B. Total Operating Expenses   C. Physical Possibility   D. Escheat

56. __C__ One of the criteria for highest and best use of a property must meet.
A. Remainder interest   B. Land Use   C. Physical Possibility   D. Probate

57. __C__ An appraisal report in which the appraiser's scope of work does not include an inspection of the subject property or comparables.
A. Restricted use appraisal   B. Market Participants   C. Desktop Appraisal   D. Utility

58. __C__ The process by which all roads are grouped into classes or systems according to the character of service they are intended to provide.
A. Decline   B. Property Tax   C. Functional Classification   D. Appraisal Report

59. __A__ A rate derived from a single year's NOI and the total property value.
A. Overall rate   B. Economic Characteristics   C. Frictional Vacancy   D. Land Use

60. __B__ Person who is entitled to an estate after a prior estate or interest has expired
A. Contributory Value   B. Remainder interest   C. Investment Value   D. Reserve

61. __A__ The legal responsibility of a plaintiff to make reasonable efforts, after an injury or breach of contract, to alleviate the effects of the injury or breach.
A. Mitigation of Damages   B. Assemblage   C. Pipeline Easement   D. Preservation Easement

62. __D__ Items of information on value influences that derive from social, economic, governmental, and environmental forces and originate outside the property being appraised.
A. Pole Line Easement   B. Bundle of rights   C. Subsurface rights   D. General Data

63. __D__ Annual amount of total revenue that a property would generate if it were occupied all throughout the year.
A. Paired data analysis   B. Land Use   C. Reproduction Cost   D. Gross Market Income

64. __B__ Only one party makes a promise
A. Pipeline Easement   B. Unilateral contract   C. Raw Land   D. Total Operating Expenses

65. __C__ Value a specific property has to a specific person or firm for a specific use.
A. Real Estate   B. Feasibility Analysis   C. Value in use   D. Assemblage

66. __A__ A shortened term for similar property sales, rentals, or operating expenses used for comparison in the valuation process.
A. Comparables   B. Unilateral contract   C. Assignment Results   D. Paired data analysis

67. __D__ The period over time which a structure may be competitive in the market.
A. Physical life   B. Bundle of rights   C. Drive by Appraisal   D. Economic life

68. __D__ Seizure of property by court order.
A. Preservation Easement   B. Brownfield   C. Subsurface rights   D. Attachment

69. __B__ Damage to property arising as a consequence of a taking over and above direct damages.
A. Drive by Appraisal   B. Consequential Damages   C. Encroachment   D. Cash Flow

70. __A__ Right of government to raise revenue through assessments on valuable goods, products, and rights.
A. Taxation   B. Encroachment   C. Range of Value   D. Personal Representative

71. A In accounting, a category for property under the modified accelerated cost recovery system.
A. Property Class   B. Gentrification   C. Financial Feasibility   D. Contract rent

72. B Combination of all elements that constitute proof of ownership.
A. Pro Forma   B. Title   C. Land Use   D. Partial Interest

73. C Any method of bringing wasted natural resources into productive use.
A. Police power   B. Gross Market Income   C. Reclamation   D. Percentage Adjustments

74. C When the government regulates the land use for the good of the public.
A. Excess Land   B. Partial Interest   C. Police power   D. Negative Amortization

75. A Annual crops and plantings such as corn, wheat, and vegetables.
A. Emblements   B. Valuation process   C. Functional Classification   D. Capitalization Rate

76. B A stage of diminishing demand in a market areas life cycle.
A. Property Tax   B. Decline   C. Emblements   D. Replacement Cost

77. A The amount entrepreneur expects to receive for his or her contribution to the project.
A. Entrepreneurial Incentive   B. Implied contract   C. Present Value   D. Remainder

78. D A tax on the right to receive property by inheritance; as distinguished from estate tax.
A. Mechanics liens   B. Market Analysis   C. Implied contract   D. Inheritance Tax

79. C The period of time over which a structure may reasonably be expected to perform the function for which it was designed.
A. Gross lease   B. Primary Data   C. Useful life   D. Remainder interest

80. A When the lessee (tenant) does not pay any costs of ownership and pays a given amount of rent per period.
A. Gross lease   B. Total Operating Expenses   C. Gross Market Income   D. Summary appraisal

81. D Created by law, rather than by choice. i.e. property tax lien.
A. Full Taking   B. Hypothetical Condition   C. Taxation   D. Involuntary liens

82. A A comprehensive, long-range official plan that guides the physical growth and development of the community.
A. Master Plan   B. Debt coverage ratio   C. Hypothetical Condition   D. Regression

83. A The estimated period during which improvements will continue to represent the highest and best use of the property.
A. Remaining Economic Life   B. Site   C. General Data   D. Estate Tax

84. A An easement for the construction, maintenance, and operation of a full line, usually for the transmission of electric power.
A. Pole Line Easement   B. Reproduction Cost   C. Certification   D. Inheritance Tax

85. A One of the four criteria the highest and best use of a property must meet.
A. Financial Feasibility   B. Obsolescence   C. Voidable contract   D. Feasibility Analysis

86. B A lump sum benefit that an investor receives or expects to receive upon the termination of an investment; also called reversionary benefit.
A. Step Up Depreciation   B. Reversion   C. Percentage Adjustments   D. Entrepreneurial Incentive

87. C The right to use another's land for a stated purpose.
A. Financial Feasibility   B. Remaining Economic Life   C. Easement   D. Spot Zoning

88. D The most probable price at which real estate would sell.
A. Entrepreneurial profit   B. Spot Zoning   C. Final Reconciliation   D. Market Value

89. A Principle that real property value is created and sustained when contrasting, opposing, or interacting elements are in a state of equilibrium.
A. Balance   B. Value in use   C. Desktop Appraisal   D. Reserve

90. __A__ Land that is not needed to serve or support the existing improvement.
A. Excess Land   B. Market Vacancy   C. Quotent   D. Mitigation of Damages

91. __C__ Money paid to an owner of real property or mineral rights for the right to deplete natural resource.
A. Marketing time   B. Paired data analysis   C. Royalty   D. Reclamation

92. __C__ Trespassing on the domain of another.
A. Direct costs   B. Reclamation   C. Encroachment   D. Living trust

93. __B__ An agreement in which all the elements of a contract are present and, therefore, legally enforceable.
A. Distress Sale   B. Valid contract   C. Financial Feasibility   D. Lis Pendens

94. __A__ Neighborhood phenomenon in which middle- and upper-income persons purchase neighborhood properties and renovate or rehabilitate them.
A. Gentrification   B. Comparables   C. District   D. Encroachment

95. __C__ Dollar amount required to reconstruct a bldg. or other improvement, which have the same or equivalent utility as the original.
A. Operating Expense Ratio   B. Residential Property   C. Replacement Cost   D. Percentage Adjustments

96. __A__ The degree, nature, or extent of interest that a person has in land.
A. Estate in land   B. Real Estate   C. Hypothetical Condition   D. Brownfield

97. __B__ A report that is prepared regularly, usually each month, and indicates the rent-paying status of each tenant.
A. Voidable contract   B. Rent Roll   C. Remainder   D. Mitigation of Damages

98. __D__ Needed repairs or replacement of items that should have taken place during the course of normal maintenance.
A. Lis Pendens   B. Utility   C. Easement appurtenant   D. Deferred Maintenance

99. __B__ The amount of vacant space needed in a market for its orderly operation.
A. Potential Gross Income   B. Frictional Vacancy   C. Sandwich lease   D. Encroachment

100. __B__ Study of real estate market conditions for specific types of property.
A. Property Tax   B. Market Analysis   C. Leasehold Interest   D. Property Class

D. From the words provided for each clue, provide the letter of the word which best matches the clue.

1. __D__ An element of depreciation; and diminution in value caused by negative externalities and generally incurable on the part of the owner, landlord, or tenant.
A. Housing Starts   B. Contract rent   C. Zoning   D. External Obsolescence

2. __A__ An appraiser's opinions or conclusions developed specific to an assignment.
A. Assignment Results   B. Involuntary liens   C. Functional Classification   D. Average Daily Traffic

3. __C__ Study of real estate market conditions for specific types of property.
A. Personal Representative   B. Property Class   C. Market Analysis   D. Restricted use appraisal

4. __A__ Guiding control of the money supply in the economy.
A. Monetary Policy   B. Property Class   C. Change   D. Assignment Results

5. __C__ When the value of a business plus the amount of real property is sought.
A. Effective age   B. Fixed Expense   C. Going concern value   D. Condominium

6. __A__ Zoning regulations that designate the distance a building must be set back from the front, rear, and sides of the property lines.
A. Setback   B. Site   C. Cash Equivalent   D. Hypothetical Condition

7. __C__ Method by which government can take private property.
A. Quotent B. Safe Rate C. Condemnation D. Net Lease

8. __D__ Total payment is insufficient to pay interest due.
A. Present Value B. Competition C. Net Lease D. Negative Amortization

9. __B__ The periodic expenditures necessary to maintain the real property and continue production of the effective gross income, assuming prudent and competent management.
A. Mechanics liens B. Operating Expenses C. Single Family House D. Marketing time

10. __A__ Any claim or liability that affects our limits the title to property.
A. Encumbrance B. Restricted use appraisal C. Summary appraisal D. Condemnation

11. __D__ Buyers and sellers of particular real estate and the transactions that occur among them.
A. Stability B. Seasonal Dwelling C. Lease D. Real Estate Market

12. __B__ Price an economic good will attract in the competitive market.
A. BOMA Standard B. Value in Exchange C. Lien D. Partial Interest

13. __B__ Damages that is caused by the remainder's proximity to the improvement being constructed.
A. Extraction B. Proximity Damage C. Leased Fee Interest D. Condemnation

14. __B__ Estate owned by 2 or more persons, each of whom has an equal undivided interest. Unlike Joint Tenancy and Tenancy by Entirety, No right of survivorship.
A. Void contract B. Tenancy in Common C. Price D. Present Value

15. __B__ A lease in which the landlord passes on all expenses to the tenant.
A. Elements of comparison B. Net Lease C. General Lien D. Voluntary liens

16. __B__ The manner in which a transaction was financed.
A. Real Property B. Financing Terms C. Summary appraisal D. Principle

17. __B__ An ordinal technique for analyzing data, commonly used in the analysis of comparable sales.
A. Voidable contract B. Ranking Analysis C. Property Class D. Regression

18. __D__ The process of valuing a universe of properties as of a given date using standard methodology, employing common data, and allowing for statistical testing.
A. Contribution B. Labor C. Specific Data D. Mass Appraisal

19. __D__ An appropriation from surplus funds that is allocated to deferred or anticipated contingencies.
A. Cost to Cure B. Mortgage liens C. Residential Property D. Reserve

20. __B__ The relative desirability of a property in comparison with similar or competing properties in the area.
A. Reserve B. Marketability C. Specific Lien D. Voidable contract

21. __B__ The actual rental income specified in a lease.
A. Average Daily Traffic B. Contract rent C. Revitalization D. Ranking Analysis

22. __D__ The difference between an improvements total economic life and its remaining economic life.
A. Estate Tax B. Involuntary liens C. Capitalization D. Effective age

23. __D__ The effect on value produced by a property's location at or near the intersection of two streets.
A. Qualitative analysis B. Going concern value C. Stability D. Corner influence

24. __C__ arise from construction and other improvements to real estate.
A. Extraction B. General Lien C. Mechanics liens D. Potential Gross Income

25. __B__ The entire taking of the full real property interest of a parcel for public use under the power of eminent domain; requires the payment of compensation.
A. Feasibility Analysis   B. Full Taking   C. Physical Deterioration   D. Lis Pendens

26. __D__ Value to a particular individual. The present worth of anticipated future benefits.
A. Zoning   B. Useful life   C. Progression   D. Investment Value

27. __C__ Technically valid but gives one or more parties the power to legally void the agreement and thus cancel performance.
A. Final Reconciliation   B. Effective Gross Income   C. Voidable contract   D. Physical Possibility

28. __A__ A condition which is contrary to what is known by the appraiser to exist on the effective date of the assignment results, but is used for the purpose of analysis.
A. Hypothetical Condition   B. Rail Easement   C. General Data   D. Market Analysis

29. __A__ A category of elements of comparison in the sales comparison approach
A. Physical Characteristics   B. Cash Equivalent   C. Neighborhood   D. Fiscal Policy

30. __C__ Dollar amount required to reconstruct a bldg. or other improvement, which have the same or equivalent utility as the original.
A. Residential Property   B. Adverse possession   C. Replacement Cost   D. Regression

31. __D__ Value of an inferior property is enhanced by its association with better properties of the same type.
A. Scarcity   B. Extraction   C. Restricted use appraisal   D. Progression

32. __C__ A lease in which an intermediate, or sandwich, leaseholder is the lessee of one party and the lessor of another.
A. Functional Classification   B. Price   C. Sandwich lease   D. Value in use

33. __D__ comprises of all costs required to construct and market the product as land alone or with improvements.
A. Personal Representative   B. Rate of return   C. Pipeline Easement   D. Labor

34. __C__ Amount a particular purchaser agrees to pay and a particular seller agrees to accept under the circumstances surrounding their transaction.
A. Change   B. Specific Lien   C. Price   D. Internal Rate of Return

35. __D__ Part of the purchase price given to bind a bargain.
A. Certification   B. Corner influence   C. Remnant   D. Earnest money

36. __B__ Testimony of persons who are presumed to have special knowledge of, or skill in, a particular field due to education, experience, or study.
A. BOMA Standard   B. Expert Testimony   C. Useful life   D. Units of comparison

37. __B__ The wear and tear that begins with the building is completed and placed into service.
A. Ranking Analysis   B. Physical Deterioration   C. Going concern value   D. Valuation process

38. __D__ An agreement put into words (written or spoken).
A. Economic Characteristics   B. Potential Gross Income   C. Accretion   D. Express contract

39. __A__ The cost to restore an item of deferred maintenance to new or reasonably new condition.
A. Cost to Cure   B. Rate of return   C. Assessed Value   D. Condominium

40. __D__ A rate derived from a single year's NOI and the total property value.
A. Market Participants   B. Drive by Appraisal   C. Pro Forma   D. Overall rate

41. __C__ Purchaser's wish for an item to satisfy human needs or individual wants beyond essential life-support needs.
A. Voidable contract   B. Functional Classification   C. Desire   D. Regression Analysis

42. __D__ The value of a future payment or series of future payments discounted to the current date or to time period zero.
A. Lessor   B. Syndication   C. Physical Deterioration   D. Present Value

43. __A__ The taking of part of any real property interest for public use under the power of eminent domain; requires the payment of compensation.
A. Partial Taking   B. Loss of Access   C. Change   D. Appurtenance

44. __D__ An agreement in which all the elements of a contract are present and, therefore, legally enforceable.
A. Entrepreneurial profit   B. Involuntary liens   C. Final Opinion of Value   D. Valid contract

45. __A__ A rivalry between buyers or between sellers.
A. Competition   B. Quotent   C. Condominium   D. Certification

46. __B__ Person who is entitled to an estate after a prior estate or interest has expired
A. Lessee   B. Remainder interest   C. Mechanics liens   D. Voluntary liens

47. __A__ The process of reducing a range of value indications into an appropriate conclusion for that analysis.
A. Reconciliation   B. Market Participants   C. Void contract   D. Growth

48. __A__ Easement that is not attached or appurtenant to any particular estate; does not run with the land nor is it transferred through the conveyance of title.
A. Easement in gross   B. Littoral rights   C. Decline   D. Anticipation

49. __C__ The right to use another's land for a stated purpose.
A. Contribution   B. Cost to Cure   C. Easement   D. Proximity Damage

50. __B__ The opinion of value derived from the reconciliation of value indications and stated in the appraisal report
A. Present Value   B. Final Opinion of Value   C. Contract rent   D. Rail Easement

51. __B__ A stage of diminishing demand in a market areas life cycle.
A. Ranking Analysis   B. Decline   C. BOMA Standard   D. Residential Property

52. __D__ Amount paid for an income producing property.
A. Financing Terms   B. Loss of Access   C. Regression Analysis   D. Market Price

53. __D__ A study of the cost-benefit relationships of an economic endeavor.
A. Percentage lease   B. Amenity   C. Competence   D. Feasibility Analysis

54. __B__ The quantity left over.
A. Substitution   B. Residual   C. Effective age   D. Encroachment

55. __B__ Monetary worth of a property, good, or service to buyers and sellers at a given time.
A. Scarcity   B. Value   C. Overall rate   D. Physical Possibility

56. __B__ An increase in dry land created by the gradual accumulation of waterborne solid material over formerly riparian land.
A. Raw Land   B. Accretion   C. Physical Possibility   D. Pro Forma

57. __C__ Written, legal instrument that conveys an estate or interest in real property to someone else, assuming it is executed and delivered.
A. Change   B. Restricted use appraisal   C. Deed   D. Supra surface rights

58. __C__ The process by which all roads are grouped into classes or systems according to the character of service they are intended to provide.
A. Appurtenance   B. Operating Expenses   C. Functional Classification   D. Executor

59. __A__ Sum of all fixed and variable operating expenses and reserve for replacement.
A. Total Operating Expenses   B. Sandwich lease   C. Master Plan   D. Proximity Damage

60. __D__ The type and extent of research and analyses in appraisal or appraisal review assignment.
A. Mortgage liens   B. Market Analysis   C. Competition   D. Scope of Work

61. A An individual or other legal person designated in a will to settle the estate of a deceased person.
A. Personal Representative   B. Regression Analysis   C. Elements of comparison   D. Remainder interest

62. A One who is the right to occupancy and use of the property of another for a period of time according to a lease agreement.

A. Lessee   B. Assemblage   C. Value in use   D. Easement

63. D Divided or undivided rights in real estate that represent less than the whole.
A. Mortgage liens   B. Mass Appraisal   C. Rail Easement   D. Partial Interest

64. B A stage in a market area's life cycle characterized by renewal, redevelopment, modernization, and increasing demand.
A. Secondary Data   B. Revitalization   C. Regression Analysis   D. Value in use

65. D The act or process of developing an opinion of value.
A. Personal Representative   B. Express contract   C. Voluntary liens   D. Appraisal

66. D The price of a property with above- or below-market financing expressed in terms of the price that would have been paid in an all-cash sale.
A. Market Participants   B. Exposure Time   C. Safe Rate   D. Cash Equivalent

67. D Damage to property arising as a consequence of a taking over and above direct damages.
A. Market Participants   B. Housing Starts   C. Pipeline Easement   D. Consequential Damages

68. C Voluntary and one of the most common types of liens.
A. Adverse possession   B. Primary Data   C. Mortgage liens   D. Pipeline Easement

69. B When a series of different "multiplicands" are multiplied by the same multiplier it is known as.
A. Lessor   B. Constant   C. Loss of Access   D. Marketability

70. A Time and distance relationships between a particular use and supporting facilities.
A. Linkage   B. Specific Data   C. Change   D. Final Reconciliation

71. A goods, such as equipment (machinery and tools), bldgs., and infrastructure.
A. Capital   B. Risk Rate   C. Market Participants   D. Rate of return

72. A Flow of savings account money from savings and loans accounts to higher yield investments.
A. Disintermediation   B. Contract rent   C. Final Reconciliation   D. Oral Appraisal Report

73. B The yield rate used to convert future payments or receipts into present value; usually considered to be a synonym for yield rate.
A. Oral Appraisal Report   B. Discount Rate   C. Deterioration   D. Expert Testimony

74. D The value of a particular component is measured in terms of the amount it adds to the value of the whole property.
A. Operating Income   B. Utility   C. Effective Gross Income   D. Contribution

75. B These are hard cost expenditures for the labor and materials used in the construction of improvements.
A. Overall rate   B. Direct costs   C. Property Tax   D. General Data

76. D Data that is analyzed through the process of comparison.
A. Safe Rate   B. Fair Market Value   C. Secondary Data   D. Specific Data

77. D A statistical measure that attempts to determine the strength of the relationship between one dependent variable and a series of other changing variables.
A. Percentage lease   B. Risk Rate   C. Judgment liens   D. Regression Analysis

78. C Information that is gathered in its original form by the analyst.
A. Disintermediation   B. Pro Forma   C. Primary Data   D. Housing Starts

79. B Trespassing on the domain of another.
A. Hypothetical Condition   B. Encroachment   C. Oral Appraisal Report   D. Lis Pendens

80. __A__ The right to construct, operate, and maintain a pipeline over the lands of others within prescribed geographical limits.
A. Pipeline Easement   B. Restricted use appraisal   C. Assemblage   D. Client

81. __D__ The right for the construction, maintenance, and operation of a rail line on a property.
A. Lien   B. Scarcity   C. Bilateral contract   D. Rail Easement

82. __D__ Has no legal force or binding effect and cannot be enforced in a court of law.
A. Stability   B. Accretion   C. Decline   D. Void contract

83. __C__ The tenant's possessory interest created by a lease.
A. Decline   B. BOMA Standard   C. Leasehold Interest   D. Amenity

84. __D__ Principle that real property value is created and sustained when contrasting, opposing, or interacting elements are in a state of equilibrium.
A. Ranking Analysis   B. Financing Terms   C. Involuntary liens   D. Balance

85. __C__ The legal responsibility of a plaintiff to make reasonable efforts, after an injury or breach of contract, to alleviate the effects of the injury or breach.
A. Linkage   B. Effective Gross Income   C. Mitigation of Damages   D. Earnest money

86. __D__ The relative position of the property to competitive properties and other value influences in its market area
A. Physical Characteristics   B. Mechanics liens   C. Loss of Access   D. Location

87. __D__ Management of government receipts and expenditures.
A. Encumbrance   B. Ranking Analysis   C. Percentage lease   D. Fiscal Policy

88. __A__ A type of renovation that involves modification or updating of existing improvements.
A. Remodeling   B. Seasonal Dwelling   C. Property Class   D. Expert Testimony

89. __B__ A part of an appraisal report in which the appraiser certifies that the work was completed according to the applicable standards.
A. Physical Possibility   B. Certification   C. Assemblage   D. Conservation Easement

90. __B__ A projected income and expense statement for proposed development.
A. Mechanics liens   B. Pro Forma   C. Riparian rights   D. Regression

91. __A__ Created intentionally by property owner's actions. i.e. mortgage
A. Voluntary liens   B. Direct costs   C. Certification   D. Extraction

92. __C__ Most commonly found in retail business. This lease has a base rent which is fixed and an excess rent, this is most commonly based on the percentage of the sales.
A. Effective age   B. Fair Market Value   C. Percentage lease   D. Oral Appraisal Report

93. __A__ A lump sum benefit that an investor receives or expects to receive upon the termination of an investment; also called reversionary benefit.
A. Reversion   B. Housing Starts   C. Remainder interest   D. Estate Tax

94. __A__ Public regulation of the character and extent of real estate use though police power.
A. Zoning   B. Partial Interest   C. Adverse possession   D. Quantitative Analysis

95. __A__ Typically result from a lawsuit in which a monetary judgment is awarded.
A. Judgment liens   B. Constant   C. Effective age   D. Operating Income

96. __B__ A voluntary legal agreement that becomes part of the chain of title thereby protecting a historic, archaeological, or cultural resource.
A. Specific Lien   B. Preservation Easement   C. Arms Length   D. Valid contract

97. __B__ A vacant or in proof parcel of land devoted to or available for use as a residence.
A. Cost to Cure   B. Residential Property   C. Pipeline Easement   D. Rights in real property

98. __B__ Neighborhood phenomenon in which middle- and upper-income persons purchase neighborhood properties and renovate or rehabilitate them.
A. Lis Pendens   B. Gentrification   C. Present Value   D. Partial Taking

99. __D__ An identified parcel or tract of land, including improvements.
A. Valuation process   B. General Lien   C. Leasehold Interest   D. Real Estate

100. __A__ An ownership interest for the possessory interest has been granted to another by creation of a contractual landlord-tenant relationship.
A. Leased Fee Interest   B. Appraisal Report   C. Capitalization Rate   D. Negative Amortization

Matching

A. Provide the word that best matches each clue.

1. _____ Temporary use to which a site or improved property is put until it is ready to be put to its future highest and best use.

2. _____ The standard method of measurement for office buildings as defined by the Building Owners and Managers Association.

3. _____ When the government regulates the land use for the good of the public.

4. _____ Annual crops and plantings such as corn, wheat, and vegetables.

5. _____ A rate derived from a single year's NOI and the total property value.

6. _____ Value of an inferior property is enhanced by its association with better properties of the same type.

7. _____ Data that is analyzed through the process of comparison.

8. _____ an estimate of replacement cost of a structure, less depreciation, plus land value.

9. _____ Depriving an abutting owner of the inherent rights of ingress and to egress from the highway or street.

10. _____ Process of dividing one number (dividend) by another number (divisor) produces this result.

11. _____ Principle that real property value is created and sustained when contrasting, opposing, or interacting elements are in a state of equilibrium.

12. _____ An identified parcel or tract of land, including improvements.

13. _____ A report that is transmitted orally.

14. _____ The right for the construction, maintenance, and operation of a rail line on a property.

15. _____ An element of depreciation; and diminution in value caused by negative externalities and generally incurable on the part of the owner, landlord, or tenant.

16. _____ The value of a future payment or series of future payments discounted to the current date or to time period zero.

17. _____ Public regulation of the character and extent of real estate use though police power.

18. _____ In appraising, a loss in property value from any cause

19. _____ Damages that is caused by the remainder's proximity to the improvement being constructed.

20. _____ The employment of a site or holding to produce revenue or other benefits.

21. _____ The state of having the requisite or adequate ability or qualities to perform the specific assignment and produce credible assignment results.

22. _____ Seizure of property by court order.

23. _____ The number of years since a structure or bldg. was originally built (birth).

24. _____ Created by agreement during the property owner's lifetime

25. _____ Dollar amount required to construct an exact duplicate of the subject improvements, at current prices.

A. Real Estate
D. Cost Approach
G. Proximity Damage
J. Loss of Access
M. Land Use
P. Reproduction Cost
S. Zoning
V. External Obsolescence
Y. Progression

B. Balance
E. Police power
H. Living trust
K. Quotent
N. BOMA Standard
Q. Attachment
T. Chronological age
W. Emblements

C. Interim use
F. Competence
I. Oral Appraisal Report
L. Specific Data
O. Present Value
R. Depreciation
U. Overall rate
X. Rail Easement

B. Provide the word that best matches each clue.

1. _____ One who conveys the rights of occupancy and use to others under lease agreement.

2. _____ A dwelling not intended for year-round use, e.g., a vacation home.

3. _____ Legal term signifying pending litigation that can affect ownership title to real estate.

4. _____ Impairment of condition; because of depreciation that reflects the loss in value due to wear and tear, disintegration, use in service, and the action of the elements.

5. _____ Conclusions of the appraisal are stated, but the data or analyses used in the appraisal to develop these conclusions do not need to be included in the report.

6. _____ Guiding control of the money supply in the economy.

7. _____ A report that is transmitted orally.

8. _____ A rivalry between buyers or between sellers.

9. _____ The degree, nature, or extent of interest that a person has in land.

10. _____ Principle that real property value is created and sustained when contrasting, opposing, or interacting elements are in a state of equilibrium.

11. _____ The amount of vacant space needed in a market for its orderly operation.

12. _____ The total annual income the rental property produces after subtracting vacancy losses and adding miscellaneous income.

13. _____ Combination of all elements that constitute proof of ownership.

14. _____ A letter or statement that serves as a notice of delivery from the appraiser to the client of a report containing an opinion or conclusion concerning real estate

15. _____ Study of real estate market conditions for specific types of property.

16. _____ A lien against all of the property owned by the debtor.

17. _____ The process in which older structures or historic buildings are modernized, remodeled, or restored.

18. _____ The legal process of settling an estate after a person has died.

19. _____ The annual rate of return on capital that is commensurate with the risk assumed by the investor; the rate of interest or yield necessary to attract capital.

20. _____ When a series of different "multiplicands" are multiplied by the same multiplier it is known as.

21. _____ The right to use another's land for a stated purpose.

22. _____ Divided or undivided rights in real estate that represent less than the whole.

23. _____ The amount of money borrowed from lender (mortgagee).

24. _____ Total payment is insufficient to pay interest due.

25. _____ The cost to restore an item of deferred maintenance to new or reasonably new condition.

A. Market Analysis
D. Letter of Transmittal
G. Frictional Vacancy
J. Principle
M. Easement
P. Effective Gross Income
S. Balance
V. Probate

B. Oral Appraisal Report
E. Estate in land
H. Lis Pendens
K. Restricted use appraisal
N. Title
Q. Lessor
T. Negative Amortization
W. General Lien

C. Renovation
F. Seasonal Dwelling
I. Partial Interest
L. Risk Rate
O. Monetary Policy
R. Deterioration
U. Cost to Cure
X. Competition

C. Provide the word that best matches each clue.

1. _____ Purchaser's wish for an item to satisfy human needs or individual wants beyond essential life-support needs.

2. _____ Time it takes an interest in real property to sell on the market subsequent to the date of an appraisal.

3. _____ A borrower has possession of the property.

4. _____ The act or process of developing an opinion of value.

5. _____ Land that is not needed to serve or support the existing improvement.

6. _____ A condition which is contrary to what is known by the appraiser to exist on the effective date of the assignment results, but is used for the purpose of analysis.

7. _____ The entire taking of the full real property interest of a parcel for public use under the power of eminent domain; requires the payment of compensation.

8. _____ When the value of a business plus the amount of real property is sought.

9. _____ The parties involved in the transfer of property rights. Includes buyers, sellers, lessors, lessees, and brokers and their agents.

10. _____ An appraisal review in which the reviewer's scope of work does not include an inspection of the subject property.

11. _____ Rights pertaining to properties abutting a lake or pond.

12. _____ The yield rate used to convert future payments or receipts into present value; usually considered to be a synonym for yield rate.

13. _____ A right granted or taken for the construction, maintenance, and operation of the highway.

14. _____ One of the four criteria the highest and best use of a property must meet.

15. _____ The change in the value of a property as a whole, resulting from the addition or deletion of a property component.

16. _____ land that is improved so that is ready to be used for a specific purpose.

17. _____ Method by which government can take private property.

18. _____ Industrial or commercial site that is abandoned or underused because it suffers from real or perceived continuing contamination.

19. _____ Estate owned by 2 or more persons, each of whom has an equal undivided interest. Unlike Joint Tenancy and Tenancy by Entirety, No right of survivorship.

20. _____ goods, such as equipment (machinery and tools), bldgs., and infrastructure.

21. _____ A future possessor read interest in real estate that is given to a third-party and matures upon the termination of a limited or determinable be.

22. _____ Is used for elements that cannot be given a numerical value.

23. _____ Lien against a particular property owned by the debtor.

24. _____ An increase in value when extra utility is created by combining smaller parcels under single ownership.

25. _____ Damages that is caused by the remainder's proximity to the improvement being constructed.

A. Going concern value   B. Specific Lien   C. Littoral rights
D. Market Participants   E. Plottage   F. Capital
G. Site   H. Hypothetical Condition   I. Remainder
J. Qualitative analysis   K. Legal Permissibility   L. Tenancy in Common
M. Proximity Damage   N. Discount Rate   O. Excess Land
P. Marketing time   Q. Hypothication   R. Appraisal
S. Condemnation   T. Desk Review   U. Contributory Value
V. Desire   W. Highway Easement   X. Brownfield
Y. Full Taking

D. Provide the word that best matches each clue.

1. _____ A stage in a market area's life cycle characterized by renewal, redevelopment, modernization, and increasing demand.

2. _____ In condemnation, the amount of loss for which a property owner is compensated when his or her property is taken.

3. _____ An individual or other legal person designated in a will to settle the estate of a deceased person.

4. _____ A contract in which the rights to use and occupy land or structures are transferred by the owner to another for a specified period of time in return for specified rent.

5. _____ The legal process of settling an estate after a person has died.

6. _____ A condition that limits the use of a report.

7. _____ The periodic income attributable to the interests in real property.

8. _____ Easement that is not attached or appurtenant to any particular estate; does not run with the land nor is it transferred through the conveyance of title.

9. _____ The interests, benefits, and rights inherent in ownership of real estate.

10. _____ An appraisal report in which the scope of work includes an exterior-only viewing of the subject property.

11. _____ A private or public partnership that pools funds for the acquisition and development of real estate projects or other business ventures.

12. _____ Method by which government can take private property.

13. _____ A tax on the estate or wealth of the deceased person that is usually computed as a percentage of the market value of the assets of the estate.

14. _____ The condition of dying with a valid will.

15. _____ The condition of dying without a will.

16. _____ Charge against property in which the property is the security for payment of the debt.

17. _____ Price an economic good will attract in the competitive market.

18. _____ An appraisal review in which the reviewer's scope of work does not include an inspection of the subject property.

19. _____ Temporary use to which a site or improved property is put until it is ready to be put to its future highest and best use.

20. _____ Rights to the use and profits of the underground portion of a designated property.

21. _____ The estimated period during which improvements will continue to provide utility.

22. _____ Seizure of property by court order.

23. _____ Combination of all elements that constitute proof of ownership.

24. _____ The process of valuing a universe of properties as of a given date using standard methodology, employing common data, and allowing for statistical testing.

25. _____ An identified parcel or tract of land, including improvements.

A. Drive by Appraisal   B. Mass Appraisal   C. Revitalization
D. Desk Review   E. Cash Flow   F. Just Compensation
G. Estate Tax   H. Subsurface rights   I. Easement in gross
J. Probate   K. Interim use   L. Syndication

M. Attachment   N. Personal Representative   O. Limiting Condition
P. Real Estate   Q. Lien   R. Condemnation
S. Intestate   T. Value in Exchange   U. Title
V. Remaining Useful Life   W. Lease   X. Testate
Y. Real Property

E. Provide the word that best matches each clue.

1. _____ Estimate of the rate at which a particular class of properties will sell in a particular geographic area.

2. _____ The condition of dying with a valid will.

3. _____ The period of time over which a structure may reasonably be expected to perform the function for which it was designed.

4. _____ Amount paid for an income producing property.

5. _____ comprises of all costs required to construct and market the product as land alone or with improvements.

6. _____ In condemnation, the amount of loss for which a property owner is compensated when his or her property is taken.

7. _____ Any tax on ownership or possession of property and is measured by the number of units or value of such property.

8. _____ Is used for elements that cannot be given a numerical value.

9. _____ Data and analyses used in the assignment are summarized (i.e. less detail).

10. _____ Total rights of use, occupancy and control, limited to the lifetime of the designated party, i.e. life tenant.

11. _____ An allowance that provides for the periodic replacement of building components that wear out more rapidly than the building itself.

12. _____ Analyzing value of a property based on numerical data.

13. _____ Annual amount of total revenue that a property would generate if it were occupied all throughout the year.

14. _____ The actual rental income specified in a lease.

15. _____ When a series of different "multiplicands" are multiplied by the same multiplier it is known as.

16. _____ The opinion of value derived from the reconciliation of value indications and stated in the appraisal report

17. _____ Most commonly found in retail business. This lease has a base rent which is fixed and an excess rent, this is most commonly based on the percentage of the sales.

18. _____ The wear and tear that begins with the building is completed and placed into service.

19. _____ Going to the State. The process that should a property be abandoned, it reverts back to the state.

20. _____ Depriving an abutting owner of the inherent rights of ingress and to egress from the highway or street.

21. _____ Price per cubic foot, front foot, and per apartment.

22. _____ Dollar amount required to reconstruct a bldg. or other improvement, which have the same or equivalent utility as the original.

23. _____ The employment of a site or holding to produce revenue or other benefits.

24. _____ The cost to restore an item of deferred maintenance to new or reasonably new condition.

25. _____ A future possessor read interest in real estate that is given to a third-party and matures upon the termination of a limited or determinable be.

A. Life estate
D. Qualitative analysis
G. Gross Market Income
J. Contract rent
M. Replacement Cost
P. Market Price
S. Cost to Cure
V. Quantitative Analysis
Y. Testate

B. Physical Deterioration
E. Absorption rate
H. Labor
K. Constant
N. Units of comparison
Q. Replacement Allowance
T. Escheat
W. Loss of Access

C. Just Compensation
F. Summary appraisal
I. Property Tax
L. Percentage lease
O. Land Use
R. Remainder
U. Final Opinion of Value
X. Useful life

F. Provide the word that best matches each clue.

1. _____ A lease in which an intermediate, or sandwich, leaseholder is the lessee of one party and the lessor of another.

2. _____ Annual amount of total revenue that a property would generate if it were occupied all throughout the year.

3. _____ The relative desirability of a property in comparison with similar or competing properties in the area.

4. _____ A report that is prepared regularly, usually each month, and indicates the rent-paying status of each tenant.

5. _____ A comprehensive, long-range official plan that guides the physical growth and development of the community.

6. _____ The value of a property according to the tax rolls in ad valorem taxation.

7. _____ The present or anticipated undersupply of an item relative to the demand for it. Conditions of scarcity contribute to value.

8. _____ Trespassing on the domain of another.

9. _____ A stage of diminishing demand in a market areas life cycle.

10. _____ The actual rental income specified in a lease.

11. _____ Value to a particular individual. The present worth of anticipated future benefits.

12. _____ The wearing away of surface land by natural causes.

13. _____ The ratio of income or yield to the original investment.

14. _____ A series of related changes brought about by a chain of causes and effects.

15. _____ A part of an appraisal report in which the appraiser certifies that the work was completed according to the applicable standards.

16. _____ A type of renovation that involves modification or updating of existing improvements.

17. _____ The ratio of total operating expenses to effective gross income

18. _____ A tangible or intangible benefit of real property that enhances its attractiveness or increases the satisfaction of the user.

19. _____ Value of an inferior property is enhanced by its association with better properties of the same type.

20. _____ An appraisal report in which the scope of work includes an exterior-only viewing of the subject property.

21. _____ The cost to restore an item of deferred maintenance to new or reasonably new condition.

22. _____ Property taxes or special assessments, has priority over other liens.

23. _____ One of the criteria for highest and best use of a property must meet.

24. _____ Data that is analyzed through the process of comparison.

25. _____ Any rate used to convert income into value.

A. Assessed Value	B. Government lien	C. Rent Roll
D. Erosion	E. Capitalization Rate	F. Physical Possibility
G. Master Plan	H. Contract rent	I. Encroachment
J. Decline	K. Trends	L. Cost to Cure
M. Remodeling	N. Drive by Appraisal	O. Sandwich lease
P. Rate of return	Q. Gross Market Income	R. Marketability
S. Specific Data	T. Certification	U. Progression
V. Amenity	W. Scarcity	X. Investment Value
Y. Operating Expense Ratio

G. Provide the word that best matches each clue.

1. _____ A process for examining the productive attributes of the specific property, its demand and supply, and its geographic market area.

2. _____ The value of a particular component is measured in terms of the amount it adds to the value of the whole property.

3. _____ Legal term signifying pending litigation that can affect ownership title to real estate.

4. _____ The most probable price at which real estate would sell.

5. _____ The change in the value of a property as a whole, resulting from the addition or deletion of a property component.

6. _____ Estimate of the rate at which a particular class of properties will sell in a particular geographic area.

7. _____ Operating expenses that generally do not vary with occupancy and that prudent management will pay whether the properties occupied or vacant.

8. _____ Charge against property in which the property is the security for payment of the debt.

9. _____ Total payment is insufficient to pay interest due.

10. _____ An agreement put into words (written or spoken).

11. _____ Neighborhood phenomenon in which middle- and upper-income persons purchase neighborhood properties and renovate or rehabilitate them.

12. _____ The amount entrepreneur expects to receive for his or her contribution to the project.

13. _____ One who conveys the rights of occupancy and use to others under lease agreement.

14. _____ A stage in a market areas life cycle in which the market area gains public favor and acceptance.

15. _____ The periodic expenditures necessary to maintain the real property and continue production of the effective gross income, assuming prudent and competent management.

16. _____ Annual amount of total revenue that a property would generate if it were occupied all throughout the year.

17. _____ In appraising, a loss in property value from any cause

18. _____ The entire taking of the full real property interest of a parcel for public use under the power of eminent domain; requires the payment of compensation.

19. _____ Any rate used to convert income into value.

20. _____ One who is the right to occupancy and use of the property of another for a period of time according to a lease agreement.

21. _____ A statistical measure that attempts to determine the strength of the relationship between one dependent variable and a series of other changing variables.

22. _____ The right of government to take private property for public use upon payment of just compensation.

23. _____ An appraisal report in which the appraiser's scope of work does not include an inspection of the subject property or comparables.

24. _____ The rights of possession, transfer, lease, mortgage, improve.

25. _____ Value to a particular individual. The present worth of anticipated future benefits.

A. Lis Pendens
B. Desktop Appraisal
C. Lien
D. Operating Expenses
E. Capitalization Rate
F. Investment Value
G. Absorption rate
H. Gentrification
I. Contribution
J. Express contract
K. Lessor
L. Entrepreneurial Incentive
M. Lessee
N. Marketability Analysis
O. Contributory Value
P. Rights in real property
Q. Market Value
R. Full Taking
S. Growth
T. Fixed Expense
U. Gross Market Income
V. Depreciation
W. Negative Amortization
X. Regression Analysis
Y. Eminent Domain

H. Provide the word that best matches each clue.

1. _____ Trespassing on the domain of another.

2. _____ A lump sum benefit that an investor receives or expects to receive upon the termination of an investment; also called reversionary benefit.

3. _____ Value of a superior property is adversely affected by its association with an inferior property of the same type.

4. _____ An ordinal technique for analyzing data, commonly used in the analysis of comparable sales.

5. _____ Involuntary transfer of property takes place when a party makes a property claim by taking possession over a period of years.

6. _____ A stage in a market areas life cycle in which the market area gains public favor and acceptance.

7. _____ An interest in real property restricting future land-use to preservation, conservation, wildlife habitat, or some combination of those uses.

8. _____ Amount a particular purchaser agrees to pay and a particular seller agrees to accept under the circumstances surrounding their transaction.

9. _____ Operating expenses that generally do not vary with occupancy and that prudent management will pay whether the properties occupied or vacant.

10. _____ The relative position of the property to competitive properties and other value influences in its market area

11. _____ Newly constructed housing units; includes both single-family and multifamily domiciles.

12. _____ Public regulation of the character and extent of real estate use though police power.

13. _____ The process by which all roads are grouped into classes or systems according to the character of service they are intended to provide.

14. _____ The period over time which a structure may be competitive in the market.

15. _____ Seizure of property by court order.

16. _____ Income derived from the operation of a business or real property

17. _____ Legal term signifying pending litigation that can affect ownership title to real estate.

18. _____ Data and analyses used in the assignment are summarized (i.e. less detail).

19. _____ A condition that limits the use of a report.

20. _____ Price per cubic foot, front foot, and per apartment.

21. _____ One of the criteria for highest and best use of a property must meet.

22. _____ The rights of possession, transfer, lease, mortgage, improve.

23. _____ The more a property or its components are in harmony with the surrounding properties or components, the greater the contributory value.

24. _____ The date on which the analyses, opinions, and advice in an appraisal, review, or consulting service apply.

25. _____ Damage to property arising as a consequence of a taking over and above direct damages.

A. Fixed Expense
B. Attachment
C. Growth
D. Adverse possession
E. Physical Possibility
F. Ranking Analysis
G. Encroachment
H. Zoning
I. Limiting Condition
J. Economic life
K. Rights in real property
L. Conservation Easement
M. Lis Pendens
N. Functional Classification
O. Reversion
P. Effective Date
Q. Housing Starts
R. Units of comparison
S. Price
T. Consequential Damages
U. Conformity
V. Location
W. Summary appraisal
X. Regression
Y. Operating Income

I. Provide the word that best matches each clue.

1. _____ An individual or other legal person designated in a will to settle the estate of the deceased person.

2. _____ The period of time over which a structure may reasonably be expected to perform the function for which it was designed.

3. _____ In accounting, a category for property under the modified accelerated cost recovery system.

4. _____ The amount entrepreneur expects to receive for his or her contribution to the project.

5. _____ The total annual income the rental property produces after subtracting vacancy losses and adding miscellaneous income.

6. _____ Has no legal force or binding effect and cannot be enforced in a court of law.

7. _____ Data that is analyzed through the process of comparison.

8. _____ The wearing away of surface land by natural causes.

9. _____ A rate derived from a single year's NOI and the total property value.

10. _____ The act or process of developing an opinion of value.

11. _____ Total payment is insufficient to pay interest due.

12. _____ Newly constructed housing units; includes both single-family and multifamily domiciles.

13. _____ Easement that is not attached or appurtenant to any particular estate; does not run with the land nor is it transferred through the conveyance of title.

14. _____ Seizure of property by court order.

15. _____ The repair and restoration of existing improvements that are in poor condition to a state that makes the property competitive again.

16. _____ Created intentionally by property owner's actions. i.e. mortgage

17. _____ Guiding control of the money supply in the economy.

18. _____ The periodic income attributable to the interests in real property.

19. _____ Price per cubic foot, front foot, and per apartment.

20. _____ An individual or other legal person designated in a will to settle the estate of a deceased person.

21. _____ Voluntary and one of the most common types of liens.

22. _____ One of the criteria for highest and best use of a property must meet.

23. _____ Absolute ownership unencumbered by any other interest or estate.

24. _____ An appraisal review in which the reviewer's scope of work does not include an inspection of the subject property.

25. _____ Operating expenses that generally do not vary with occupancy and that prudent management will pay whether the properties occupied or vacant.

A. Units of comparison
B. Erosion
C. Void contract
D. Personal Representative
E. Useful life
F. Cash Flow
G. Housing Starts
H. Monetary Policy
I. Mortgage liens
J. Desk Review
K. Entrepreneurial Incentive
L. Negative Amortization
M. Property Class
N. Fee Simple Estate
O. Fixed Expense
P. Executor
Q. Specific Data
R. Easement in gross
S. Rehabilitation
T. Voluntary liens
U. Physical Possibility
V. Overall rate
W. Appraisal
X. Effective Gross Income
Y. Attachment

J. Provide the word that best matches each clue.

1. _____ The parties involved in the transfer of property rights. Includes buyers, sellers, lessors, lessees, and brokers and their agents.

2. _____ Supply and demand for housing, economic activity.

3. _____ Total payment is insufficient to pay interest due.

4. _____ Income-producing property such as office and retail buildings.

5. _____ Testimony of persons who are presumed to have special knowledge of, or skill in, a particular field due to education, experience, or study.

6. _____ Ability of a product to satisfy a human want, need, or desire.

7. _____ Any method of bringing wasted natural resources into productive use.

8. _____ Sum of all fixed and variable operating expenses and reserve for replacement.

9. _____ The value of a future payment or series of future payments discounted to the current date or to time period zero.

10. _____ The time of property remains on the market.

11. _____ One who owns an interest in real property for his or her own lifetime.

12. _____ These are hard cost expenditures for the labor and materials used in the construction of improvements.

13. _____ The manner in which a transaction was financed.

14. _____ A condition which is contrary to what is known by the appraiser to exist on the effective date of the assignment results, but is used for the purpose of analysis.

15. _____ A borrower has possession of the property.

16. _____ The conversion of income into value.

17. _____ An ownership interest for the possessory interest has been granted to another by creation of a contractual landlord-tenant relationship.

18. _____ Annual amount of total revenue that a property would generate if it were occupied all throughout the year.

19. _____ Amount a particular purchaser agrees to pay and a particular seller agrees to accept under the circumstances surrounding their transaction.

20. _____ Adjustments for differences between the subject and comparable properties expressed as a percentage of the sale price of the comparable property.

21. _____ A limitation that passes with the land regardless of the owner.

22. _____ A letter or statement that serves as a notice of delivery from the appraiser to the client of a report containing an opinion or conclusion concerning real estate

23. _____ The right to use another's land for a stated purpose.

24. _____ Value of a superior property is adversely affected by its association with an inferior property of the same type.

25. _____ The repair and restoration of existing improvements that are in poor condition to a state that makes the property competitive again.

A. Financing Terms
D. Reclamation
G. Easement
J. Negative Amortization
M. Deed restriction
P. Gross Market Income
S. Expert Testimony
V. Commercial Property
Y. Economic Forces

B. Rehabilitation
E. Hypothetical Condition
H. Total Operating Expenses
K. Capitalization
N. Life tenant
Q. Hypothication
T. Present Value
W. Regression

C. Letter of Transmittal
F. Market Participants
I. Utility
L. Leased Fee Interest
O. Exposure Time
R. Price
U. Direct costs
X. Percentage Adjustments

K. Provide the word that best matches each clue.

1. _____ In condemnation, the amount of loss for which a property owner is compensated when his or her property is taken.

2. _____ One who is the right to occupancy and use of the property of another for a period of time according to a lease agreement.

3. _____ Net income that is left after the 4 agents of production have been paid.

4. _____ Typically result from a lawsuit in which a monetary judgment is awarded.

5. _____ Any claim or liability that affects our limits the title to property.

6. _____ An agreement put into words (written or spoken).

7. _____ Any rate used to convert income into value.

8. _____ An individual or other legal person designated in a will to settle the estate of the deceased person.

9. _____ Testimony of persons who are presumed to have special knowledge of, or skill in, a particular field due to education, experience, or study.

10. _____ Only one party makes a promise

11. _____ The rights of possession, transfer, lease, mortgage, improve.

12. _____ In appraising, a loss in property value from any cause

13. _____ Land that is not needed to serve or support the existing improvement.

14. _____ A comprehensive, long-range official plan that guides the physical growth and development of the community.

15. _____ A letter or statement that serves as a notice of delivery from the appraiser to the client of a report containing an opinion or conclusion concerning real estate

16. _____ Value to a particular individual. The present worth of anticipated future benefits.

17. _____ A form of ownership in which each owner possesses the exclusive right to use and occupy an allotted unit plus an undivided interest in common areas.

18. _____ The wearing away of surface land by natural causes.

19. _____ A method used to convert an estimate of a single year's income expectancy into an indication of value in one direct step

20. _____ One cause of depreciation.

21. _____ One of the four criteria the highest and best use of a property must meet.

22. _____ A method of estimating value in which the depreciated cost of the improvements on the improved property is calculated and deducted from the total sale price

23. _____ The right of government to take private property for public use upon payment of just compensation.

24. _____ The periodic income attributable to the interests in real property.

25. _____ Pledge of a described property interest as collateral or security for the repayment of a loan under certain terms and conditions.

A. Unilateral contract	B. Executor	C. Letter of Transmittal
D. Lessee	E. Extraction	F. Investment Value
G. Condominium	H. Expert Testimony	I. Surplus Productivity
J. Judgment liens	K. Capitalization Rate	L. Encumbrance
M. Depreciation	N. Express contract	O. Direct Capitalization
P. Legal Permissibility	Q. Erosion	R. Master Plan
S. Mortgage	T. Obsolescence	U. Cash Flow
V. Just Compensation	W. Eminent Domain	X. Excess Land
Y. Rights in real property		

L. Provide the word that best matches each clue.

1. _____ Total floor area of a building, excluding unenclosed area, measured from the exterior of the walls of the above-grade area.

2. _____ A limitation that passes with the land regardless of the owner.

3. _____ Method by which government can take private property.

4. _____ Property taxes or special assessments, has priority over other liens.

5. _____ Lien against a particular property owned by the debtor.

6. _____ Annual crops and plantings such as corn, wheat, and vegetables.

7. _____ A form of ownership in which each owner possesses the exclusive right to use and occupy an allotted unit plus an undivided interest in common areas.

8. _____ Ann agreement that is presumed to exist because of the parties' actions.

9. _____ Process of dividing one number (dividend) by another number (divisor) produces this result.

10. _____ first thing a developer considers in developing a property is the cost of land.

11. _____ A rate derived from a single year's NOI and the total property value.

12. _____ The employment of a site or holding to produce revenue or other benefits.

13. _____ Value of a superior property is adversely affected by its association with an inferior property of the same type.

14. _____ The readjustment of the value of an appreciated asset for tax purposes upon inheritance.

15. _____ Charge against property in which the property is the security for payment of the debt.

16. _____ Analyzing value of a property based on numerical data.

17. _____ A statistical measure that attempts to determine the strength of the relationship between one dependent variable and a series of other changing variables.

18. _____ Any communication, written or oral, of an appraisal or appraisal review that is transmitted to the client upon completion of an assignment.

19. _____ Any rate used to convert income into value.

20. _____ Data and analyses used in the assignment are summarized (i.e. less detail).

21. _____ Net income that is left after the 4 agents of production have been paid.

22. _____ A future possessor read interest in real estate that is given to a third-party and matures upon the termination of a limited or determinable be.

23. _____ The type and extent of research and analyses in appraisal or appraisal review assignment.

24. _____ A category of elements of comparison in the sales comparison approach

25. _____ A vacant or in proof parcel of land devoted to or available for use as a residence.

A. Scope of Work
B. Specific Lien
C. Remainder
D. Regression Analysis
E. Government lien
F. Physical Characteristics
G. Implied contract
H. Regression
I. Deed restriction
J. Capitalization Rate
K. Summary appraisal
L. Quotent
M. Step Up Depreciation
N. Land Use
O. Lien
P. Emblements
Q. Land
R. Residential Property
S. Report
T. Gross Building Area
U. Quantitative Analysis
V. Surplus Productivity
W. Overall rate
X. Condemnation
Y. Condominium

M. Provide the word that best matches each clue.

1. _____ The wear and tear that begins with the building is completed and placed into service.

2. _____ Method by which government can take private property.

3. _____ A part of an appraisal report in which the appraiser certifies that the work was completed according to the applicable standards.

4. _____ Trespassing on the domain of another.

5. _____ A plan, map, or chart of a city, town, section, or subdivision indicating the location and boundaries of individual properties.

6. _____ A tangible or intangible benefit of real property that enhances its attractiveness or increases the satisfaction of the user.

7. _____ A report that is prepared regularly, usually each month, and indicates the rent-paying status of each tenant.

8. _____ Value to a particular individual. The present worth of anticipated future benefits.

9. _____ Amount a particular purchaser agrees to pay and a particular seller agrees to accept under the circumstances surrounding their transaction.

10. _____ The total income attributable to real property at full occupancy before vacancy and operating expenses are deducted.

11. _____ The right to use another's land for a stated purpose.

12. _____ Only one party makes a promise

13. _____ Any communication, written or oral, of an appraisal or appraisal review that is transmitted to the client upon completion of an assignment.

14. _____ In law, just, rational, appropriate, ordinary, or usual in the circumstances.

15. _____ Any rate used to convert income into value.

16. _____ The last phase in the development of the value opinion in which two or more value indications derived from market data are resolved into a value opinion.

17. _____ One who is the right to occupancy and use of the property of another for a period of time according to a lease agreement.

18. _____ Impairment of condition; because of depreciation that reflects the loss in value due to wear and tear, disintegration, use in service, and the action of the elements.

19. _____ The amount of money borrowed from lender (mortgagee).

20. _____ Data that is analyzed through the process of comparison.

21. _____ One who conveys the rights of occupancy and use to others under lease agreement.

22. _____ Temporary use to which a site or improved property is put until it is ready to be put to its future highest and best use.

23. _____ Monetary worth of a property, good, or service to buyers and sellers at a given time.

24. _____ A private or public partnership that pools funds for the acquisition and development of real estate projects or other business ventures.

25. _____ Ann agreement that is presumed to exist because of the parties' actions.

A. Reasonable	B. Price	C. Lessor
D. Capitalization Rate	E. Principle	F. Physical Deterioration
G. Implied contract	H. Report	I. Value
J. Encroachment	K. Rent Roll	L. Potential Gross Income
M. Interim use	N. Plat	O. Certification
P. Lessee	Q. Investment Value	R. Deterioration
S. Easement	T. Unilateral contract	U. Syndication
V. Specific Data	W. Amenity	X. Condemnation
Y. Final Reconciliation		

N. Provide the word that best matches each clue.

1. _____ Divided or undivided rights in real estate that represent less than the whole.

2. _____ The impairment of functional capacity of a property according to market tastes and standards.

3. _____ The total annual income the rental property produces after subtracting vacancy losses and adding miscellaneous income.

4. _____ The process by which all roads are grouped into classes or systems according to the character of service they are intended to provide.

5. _____ Time it takes an interest in real property to sell on the market subsequent to the date of an appraisal.

6. _____ The time of property remains on the market.

7. _____ A plan, map, or chart of a city, town, section, or subdivision indicating the location and boundaries of individual properties.

8. _____ The readjustment of the value of an appreciated asset for tax purposes upon inheritance.

9. _____ The amount of vacant space needed in a market for its orderly operation.

10. _____ A condition which is contrary to what is known by the appraiser to exist on the effective date of the assignment results, but is used for the purpose of analysis.

11. _____ The number of years since a structure or bldg. was originally built (birth).

12. _____ The rights of an owner to possess, control, enjoy, sell, lease, mortgage, and dispose of the property.

13. _____ The sudden removal of land from the property of one owner to that of another, e.g., change in the course of a river.

14. _____ A contract in which the rights to use and occupy land or structures are transferred by the owner to another for a specified period of time in return for specified rent.

15. _____ Total payment is insufficient to pay interest due.

16. _____ Total area of finished above-grade residential space

17. _____ A financial statement that reflects the gross revenues, expenses, and net operating profit or loss of an investment over a fixed period.

18. _____ Right of government to raise revenue through assessments on valuable goods, products, and rights.

19. _____ Neighborhood phenomenon in which middle- and upper-income persons purchase neighborhood properties and renovate or rehabilitate them.

20. _____ The relative desirability of a property in comparison with similar or competing properties in the area.

21. _____ A right granted or taken for the construction, maintenance, and operation of the highway.

22. _____ Rights pertaining to properties abutting a lake or pond.

23. _____ A part of an appraisal report in which the appraiser certifies that the work was completed according to the applicable standards.

24. _____ An identified parcel or tract of land, including improvements.

25. _____ Principle that real property value is created and sustained when contrasting, opposing, or interacting elements are in a state of equilibrium.

A. Real Estate
B. Marketability
C. Plat
D. Balance
E. Exposure Time
F. Highway Easement
G. Bundle of rights
H. Hypothetical Condition
I. Partial Interest
J. Step Up Depreciation
K. Certification
L. Operating Statement
M. Gross Living Area
N. Taxation
O. Marketing time
P. Chronological age
Q. Lease
R. Negative Amortization
S. Littoral rights
T. Frictional Vacancy
U. Effective Gross Income
V. Functional Classification
W. Gentrification
X. Avulsion
Y. Functional Obsolesce

O. Provide the word that best matches each clue.

1. _____ The actual rental income specified in a lease.

2. _____ A shortened term for similar property sales, rentals, or operating expenses used for comparison in the valuation process.

3. _____ A type of renovation that involves modification or updating of existing improvements.

4. _____ A category of elements of comparison in the sales comparison approach

5. _____ Depriving an abutting owner of the inherent rights of ingress and to egress from the highway or street.

6. _____ The cost to restore an item of deferred maintenance to new or reasonably new condition.

7. _____ When the lessee (tenant) does not pay any costs of ownership and pays a given amount of rent per period.

8. _____ Process of dividing one number (dividend) by another number (divisor) produces this result.

9. _____ A market-derived figure that represents the amount an entrepreneur receives for their contribution.

10. _____ A borrower has possession of the property.

11. _____ A financial statement that reflects the gross revenues, expenses, and net operating profit or loss of an investment over a fixed period.

12. _____ One who owns an interest in real property for his or her own lifetime.

13. _____ An identified parcel or tract of land, including improvements.

14. _____ The right to construct, operate, and maintain a pipeline over the lands of others within prescribed geographical limits.

15. _____ Value of a superior property is adversely affected by its association with an inferior property of the same type.

16. _____ The party of parties who engage an appraiser in a specific assignment.

17. _____ An ownership interest for the possessory interest has been granted to another by creation of a contractual landlord-tenant relationship.

18. _____ One of the four criteria the highest and best use of a property must meet; the selected land-use must yield the highest value of the possible uses.

19. _____ Improvements on and off the site that make it suitable for its intended use or development.

20. _____ Information that is gathered in its original form by the analyst.

21. _____ The difference between an improvements total economic life and its remaining economic life.

22. _____ The right of government to take private property for public use upon payment of just compensation.

23. _____ The quantity left over.

24. _____ Created by agreement during the property owner's lifetime

25. _____ A part of an appraisal report in which the appraiser certifies that the work was completed according to the applicable standards.

A. Quotent
D. Hypothication
G. Remodeling
J. Residual

B. Client
E. Comparables
H. Site Improvements
K. Leased Fee Interest

C. Eminent Domain
F. Operating Statement
I. Effective age
L. Certification

M. Gross lease   N. Physical Characteristics   O. Maximum Productivity
P. Real Estate   Q. Regression   R. Cost to Cure
S. Life tenant   T. Entrepreneurial profit   U. Loss of Access
V. Contract rent   W. Living trust   X. Primary Data
Y. Pipeline Easement

P. Provide the word that best matches each clue.

1. _____ Has no legal force or binding effect and cannot be enforced in a court of law.

2. _____ Guiding control of the money supply in the economy.

3. _____ A type of renovation that involves modification or updating of existing improvements.

4. _____ Zoning regulations that designate the distance a building must be set back from the front, rear, and sides of the property lines.

5. _____ The process of valuing a universe of properties as of a given date using standard methodology, employing common data, and allowing for statistical testing.

6. _____ A vacant or in proof parcel of land devoted to or available for use as a residence.

7. _____ An easement for the construction, maintenance, and operation of a full line, usually for the transmission of electric power.

8. _____ Amount paid for an income producing property.

9. _____ The relative desirability of a property in comparison with similar or competing properties in the area.

10. _____ Easement that is attached to, benefits, and passes with the conveyance of the dominant estate. Burdens the servient estate.

11. _____ The estimated period during which improvements will continue to provide utility.

12. _____ The degree, nature, or extent of interest that a person has in land.

13. _____ The value of a particular component is measured in terms of the amount it adds to the value of the whole property.

14. _____ The yield rate used to convert future payments or receipts into present value; usually considered to be a synonym for yield rate.

15. _____ A condition which is contrary to what is known by the appraiser to exist on the effective date of the assignment results, but is used for the purpose of analysis.

16. _____ The process by which all roads are grouped into classes or systems according to the character of service they are intended to provide.

17. _____ land that is improved so that is ready to be used for a specific purpose.

18. _____ An identified parcel or tract of land, including improvements.

19. _____ Income derived from the operation of a business or real property

20. _____ A process for examining the productive attributes of the specific property, its demand and supply, and its geographic market area.

21. _____ Rights pertaining to properties abutting a lake or pond.

22. _____ One who is the right to occupancy and use of the property of another for a period of time according to a lease agreement.

23. _____ An agreement in which all the elements of a contract are present and, therefore, legally enforceable.

24. _____ Time it takes an interest in real property to sell on the market subsequent to the date of an appraisal.

25. _____ Conclusions of the appraisal are stated, but the data or analyses used in the appraisal to develop these conclusions do not need to be included in the report.

A. Residential Property
D. Marketing time
G. Monetary Policy
J. Remaining Useful Life
M. Contribution
P. Pole Line Easement
S. Market Price
V. Void contract
Y. Easement appurtenant

B. Discount Rate
E. Mass Appraisal
H. Lessee
K. Littoral rights
N. Remodeling
Q. Operating Income
T. Site
W. Real Estate

C. Marketability Analysis
F. Restricted use appraisal
I. Estate in land
L. Functional Classification
O. Setback
R. Valid contract
U. Hypothetical Condition
X. Marketability

A. Provide the word that best matches each clue.

1. INTERIM USE — Temporary use to which a site or improved property is put until it is ready to be put to its future highest and best use.

2. BOMA STANDARD — The standard method of measurement for office buildings as defined by the Building Owners and Managers Association.

3. POLICE POWER — When the government regulates the land use for the good of the public.

4. EMBLEMENTS — Annual crops and plantings such as corn, wheat, and vegetables.

5. OVERALL RATE — A rate derived from a single year's NOI and the total property value.

6. PROGRESSION — Value of an inferior property is enhanced by its association with better properties of the same type.

7. SPECIFIC DATA — Data that is analyzed through the process of comparison.

8. COST APPROACH — an estimate of replacement cost of a structure, less depreciation, plus land value.

9. LOSS OF ACCESS — Depriving an abutting owner of the inherent rights of ingress and to egress from the highway or street.

10. QUOTENT — Process of dividing one number (dividend) by another number (divisor) produces this result.

11. BALANCE — Principle that real property value is created and sustained when contrasting, opposing, or interacting elements are in a state of equilibrium.

12. REAL ESTATE — An identified parcel or tract of land, including improvements.

13. ORAL APPRAISAL REPORT — A report that is transmitted orally.

14. RAIL EASEMENT — The right for the construction, maintenance, and operation of a rail line on a property.

15. EXTERNAL OBSOLESCENCE — An element of depreciation; and diminution in value caused by negative externalities and generally incurable on the part of the owner, landlord, or tenant.

16. PRESENT VALUE — The value of a future payment or series of future payments discounted to the current date or to time period zero.

17. ZONING — Public regulation of the character and extent of real estate use though police power.

18. DEPRECIATION — In appraising, a loss in property value from any cause

19. PROXIMITY DAMAGE — Damages that is caused by the remainder's proximity to the improvement being constructed.

20. LAND USE — The employment of a site or holding to produce revenue or other benefits.

21. COMPETENCE — The state of having the requisite or adequate ability or qualities to perform the specific assignment and produce credible assignment results.

22. ATTACHMENT — Seizure of property by court order.

23. CHRONOLOGICAL AGE — The number of years since a structure or bldg. was originally built (birth).

24. LIVING TRUST — Created by agreement during the property owner's lifetime

25. REPRODUCTION COST — Dollar amount required to construct an exact duplicate of the subject improvements, at current prices.

A. Real Estate
B. Balance
C. Interim use
D. Cost Approach
E. Police power
F. Competence
G. Proximity Damage
H. Living trust
I. Oral Appraisal Report
J. Loss of Access
K. Quotient
L. Specific Data
M. Land Use
N. BOMA Standard
O. Present Value
P. Reproduction Cost
Q. Attachment
R. Depreciation
S. Zoning
T. Chronological age
U. Overall rate
V. External Obsolescence
W. Emblements
X. Rail Easement
Y. Progression

B. Provide the word that best matches each clue.

1. LESSOR — One who conveys the rights of occupancy and use to others under lease agreement.

2. SEASONAL DWELLING — A dwelling not intended for year-round use, e.g., a vacation home.

3. LIS PENDENS — Legal term signifying pending litigation that can affect ownership title to real estate.

4. DETERIORATION — Impairment of condition; because of depreciation that reflects the loss in value due to wear and tear, disintegration, use in service, and the action of the elements.

5. RESTRICTED USE APPRAISAL — Conclusions of the appraisal are stated, but the data or analyses used in the appraisal to develop these conclusions do not need to be included in the report.

6. MONETARY POLICY — Guiding control of the money supply in the economy.

7. ORAL APPRAISAL REPORT — A report that is transmitted orally.

8. COMPETITION — A rivalry between buyers or between sellers.

9. ESTATE IN LAND   The degree, nature, or extent of interest that a person has in land.

10. BALANCE   Principle that real property value is created and sustained when contrasting, opposing, or interacting elements are in a state of equilibrium.

11. FRICTIONAL VACANCY   The amount of vacant space needed in a market for its orderly operation.

12. EFFECTIVE GROSS INCOME   The total annual income the rental property produces after subtracting vacancy losses and adding miscellaneous income.

13. TITLE   Combination of all elements that constitute proof of ownership.

14. LETTER OF TRANSMITTAL   A letter or statement that serves as a notice of delivery from the appraiser to the client of a report containing an opinion or conclusion concerning real estate

15. MARKET ANALYSIS   Study of real estate market conditions for specific types of property.

16. GENERAL LIEN   A lien against all of the property owned by the debtor.

17. RENOVATION   The process in which older structures or historic buildings are modernized, remodeled, or restored.

18. PROBATE   The legal process of settling an estate after a person has died.

19. RISK RATE   The annual rate of return on capital that is commensurate with the risk assumed by the investor; the rate of interest or yield necessary to attract capital.

20. CONSTANT   When a series of different "multiplicands" are multiplied by the same multiplier it is known as.

21. EASEMENT   The right to use another's land for a stated purpose.

22. PARTIAL INTEREST   Divided or undivided rights in real estate that represent less than the whole.

23. PRINCIPLE   The amount of money borrowed from lender (mortgagee).

24. NEGATIVE AMORTIZATION   Total payment is insufficient to pay interest due.

25. COST TO CURE   The cost to restore an item of deferred maintenance to new or reasonably new condition.

A. Market Analysis
B. Oral Appraisal Report
C. Renovation
D. Letter of Transmittal
E. Estate in land
F. Seasonal Dwelling
G. Frictional Vacancy
H. Lis Pendens
I. Partial Interest
J. Principle
K. Restricted use appraisal
L. Risk Rate
M. Easement
N. Title
O. Monetary Policy
P. Effective Gross Income
Q. Lessor
R. Deterioration
S. Balance
T. Negative Amortization
U. Cost to Cure
V. Probate
W. General Lien
X. Competition

C. Provide the word that best matches each clue.

1. DESIRE — Purchaser's wish for an item to satisfy human needs or individual wants beyond essential life-support needs.

2. MARKETING TIME — Time it takes an interest in real property to sell on the market subsequent to the date of an appraisal.

3. HYPOTHICATION — A borrower has possession of the property.

4. APPRAISAL — The act or process of developing an opinion of value.

5. EXCESS LAND — Land that is not needed to serve or support the existing improvement.

6. HYPOTHETICAL CONDITION — A condition which is contrary to what is known by the appraiser to exist on the effective date of the assignment results, but is used for the purpose of analysis.

7. FULL TAKING — The entire taking of the full real property interest of a parcel for public use under the power of eminent domain; requires the payment of compensation.

8. GOING CONCERN VALUE — When the value of a business plus the amount of real property is sought.

9. MARKET PARTICIPANTS — The parties involved in the transfer of property rights. Includes buyers, sellers, lessors, lessees, and brokers and their agents.

10. DESK REVIEW — An appraisal review in which the reviewer's scope of work does not include an inspection of the subject property.

11. LITTORAL RIGHTS — Rights pertaining to properties abutting a lake or pond.

12. DISCOUNT RATE — The yield rate used to convert future payments or receipts into present value; usually considered to be a synonym for yield rate.

13. HIGHWAY EASEMENT — A right granted or taken for the construction, maintenance, and operation of the highway.

14. LEGAL PERMISSIBILITY — One of the four criteria the highest and best use of a property must meet.

15. CONTRIBUTORY VALUE — The change in the value of a property as a whole, resulting from the addition or deletion of a property component.

16. SITE — land that is improved so that is ready to be used for a specific purpose.

17. CONDEMNATION — Method by which government can take private property.

18. BROWNFIELD — Industrial or commercial site that is abandoned or underused because it suffers from real or perceived continuing contamination.

19. TENANCY IN COMMON — Estate owned by 2 or more persons, each of whom has an equal undivided interest. Unlike Joint Tenancy and Tenancy by Entirety, No right of survivorship.

20. CAPITAL — goods, such as equipment (machinery and tools), bldgs., and infrastructure.

21. REMAINDER — A future possessor read interest in real estate that is given to a third-party and matures upon the termination of a limited or determinable be.

22. QUALITATIVE ANALYSIS — Is used for elements that cannot be given a numerical value.

23. SPECIFIC LIEN — Lien against a particular property owned by the debtor.

24. PLOTTAGE — An increase in value when extra utility is created by combining smaller parcels under single ownership.

25. PROXIMITY DAMAGE — Damages that is caused by the remainder's proximity to the improvement being constructed.

A. Going concern value	B. Specific Lien	C. Littoral rights
D. Market Participants	E. Plottage	F. Capital
G. Site	H. Hypothetical Condition	I. Remainder
J. Qualitative analysis	K. Legal Permissibility	L. Tenancy in Common
M. Proximity Damage	N. Discount Rate	O. Excess Land
P. Marketing time	Q. Hypothication	R. Appraisal
S. Condemnation	T. Desk Review	U. Contributory Value
V. Desire	W. Highway Easement	X. Brownfield
Y. Full Taking		

D. Provide the word that best matches each clue.

1. REVITALIZATION — A stage in a market area's life cycle characterized by renewal, redevelopment, modernization, and increasing demand.

2. JUST COMPENSATION — In condemnation, the amount of loss for which a property owner is compensated when his or her property is taken.

3. PERSONAL REPRESENTATIVE — An individual or other legal person designated in a will to settle the estate of a deceased person.

4. LEASE — A contract in which the rights to use and occupy land or structures are transferred by the owner to another for a specified period of time in return for specified rent.

5. PROBATE — The legal process of settling an estate after a person has died.

6. LIMITING CONDITION — A condition that limits the use of a report.

7. CASH FLOW — The periodic income attributable to the interests in real property.

8. EASEMENT IN GROSS   Easement that is not attached or appurtenant to any particular estate; does not run with the land nor is it transferred through the conveyance of title.

9. REAL PROPERTY   The interests, benefits, and rights inherent in ownership of real estate.

10. DRIVE BY APPRAISAL   An appraisal report in which the scope of work includes an exterior-only viewing of the subject property.

11. SYNDICATION   A private or public partnership that pools funds for the acquisition and development of real estate projects or other business ventures.

12. CONDEMNATION   Method by which government can take private property.

13. ESTATE TAX   A tax on the estate or wealth of the deceased person that is usually computed as a percentage of the market value of the assets of the estate.

14. TESTATE   The condition of dying with a valid will.

15. INTESTATE   The condition of dying without a will.

16. LIEN   Charge against property in which the property is the security for payment of the debt.

17. VALUE IN EXCHANGE   Price an economic good will attract in the competitive market.

18. DESK REVIEW   An appraisal review in which the reviewer's scope of work does not include an inspection of the subject property.

19. INTERIM USE   Temporary use to which a site or improved property is put until it is ready to be put to its future highest and best use.

20. SUBSURFACE RIGHTS   Rights to the use and profits of the underground portion of a designated property.

21. REMAINING USEFUL LIFE   The estimated period during which improvements will continue to provide utility.

22. ATTACHMENT   Seizure of property by court order.

23. TITLE   Combination of all elements that constitute proof of ownership.

24. MASS APPRAISAL   The process of valuing a universe of properties as of a given date using standard methodology, employing common data, and allowing for statistical testing.

25. REAL ESTATE   An identified parcel or tract of land, including improvements.

A. Drive by Appraisal	B. Mass Appraisal	C. Revitalization
D. Desk Review	E. Cash Flow	F. Just Compensation
G. Estate Tax	H. Subsurface rights	I. Easement in gross
J. Probate	K. Interim use	L. Syndication

M. Attachment
P. Real Estate
S. Intestate
V. Remaining Useful Life
Y. Real Property

N. Personal Representative
Q. Lien
T. Value in Exchange
W. Lease

O. Limiting Condition
R. Condemnation
U. Title
X. Testate

E. Provide the word that best matches each clue.

1. ABSORPTION RATE — Estimate of the rate at which a particular class of properties will sell in a particular geographic area.

2. TESTATE — The condition of dying with a valid will.

3. USEFUL LIFE — The period of time over which a structure may reasonably be expected to perform the function for which it was designed.

4. MARKET PRICE — Amount paid for an income producing property.

5. LABOR — comprises of all costs required to construct and market the product as land alone or with improvements.

6. JUST COMPENSATION — In condemnation, the amount of loss for which a property owner is compensated when his or her property is taken.

7. PROPERTY TAX — Any tax on ownership or possession of property and is measured by the number of units or value of such property.

8. QUALITATIVE ANALYSIS — Is used for elements that cannot be given a numerical value.

9. SUMMARY APPRAISAL — Data and analyses used in the assignment are summarized (i.e. less detail).

10. LIFE ESTATE — Total rights of use, occupancy and control, limited to the lifetime of the designated party, i.e. life tenant.

11. REPLACEMENT ALLOWANCE — An allowance that provides for the periodic replacement of building components that wear out more rapidly than the building itself.

12. QUANTITATIVE ANALYSIS — Analyzing value of a property based on numerical data.

13. GROSS MARKET INCOME — Annual amount of total revenue that a property would generate if it were occupied all throughout the year.

14. CONTRACT RENT — The actual rental income specified in a lease.

15. CONSTANT — When a series of different "multiplicands" are multiplied by the same multiplier it is known as.

16. FINAL OPINION OF VALUE — The opinion of value derived from the reconciliation of value indications and stated in the appraisal report

17. PERCENTAGE LEASE — Most commonly found in retail business. This lease has a base rent which is fixed and an excess rent, this is most commonly based on the percentage of the sales.

18. PHYSICAL DETERIORATION — The wear and tear that begins with the building is completed and placed into service.

19. ESCHEAT — Going to the State. The process that should a property be abandoned, it reverts back to the state.

20. LOSS OF ACCESS — Depriving an abutting owner of the inherent rights of ingress and to egress from the highway or street.

21. UNITS OF COMPARISON — Price per cubic foot, front foot, and per apartment.

22. REPLACEMENT COST — Dollar amount required to reconstruct a bldg. or other improvement, which have the same or equivalent utility as the original.

23. LAND USE — The employment of a site or holding to produce revenue or other benefits.

24. COST TO CURE — The cost to restore an item of deferred maintenance to new or reasonably new condition.

25. REMAINDER — A future possessor read interest in real estate that is given to a third-party and matures upon the termination of a limited or determinable be.

A. Life estate
B. Physical Deterioration
C. Just Compensation
D. Qualitative analysis
E. Absorption rate
F. Summary appraisal
G. Gross Market Income
H. Labor
I. Property Tax
J. Contract rent
K. Constant
L. Percentage lease
M. Replacement Cost
N. Units of comparison
O. Land Use
P. Market Price
Q. Replacement Allowance
R. Remainder
S. Cost to Cure
T. Escheat
U. Final Opinion of Value
V. Quantitative Analysis
W. Loss of Access
X. Useful life
Y. Testate

F. Provide the word that best matches each clue.

1. SANDWICH LEASE — A lease in which an intermediate, or sandwich, leaseholder is the lessee of one party and the lessor of another.

2. GROSS MARKET INCOME — Annual amount of total revenue that a property would generate if it were occupied all throughout the year.

3. MARKETABILITY — The relative desirability of a property in comparison with similar or competing properties in the area.

4. RENT ROLL — A report that is prepared regularly, usually each month, and indicates the rent-paying status of each tenant.

5. MASTER PLAN — A comprehensive, long-range official plan that guides the physical growth and development of the community.

6. ASSESSED VALUE — The value of a property according to the tax rolls in ad valorem taxation.

7. SCARCITY — The present or anticipated undersupply of an item relative to the demand for it. Conditions of scarcity contribute to value.

8. ENCROACHMENT — Trespassing on the domain of another.

9. DECLINE — A stage of diminishing demand in a market areas life cycle.

10. CONTRACT RENT — The actual rental income specified in a lease.

11. INVESTMENT VALUE — Value to a particular individual. The present worth of anticipated future benefits.

12. EROSION — The wearing away of surface land by natural causes.

13. RATE OF RETURN — The ratio of income or yield to the original investment.

14. TRENDS — A series of related changes brought about by a chain of causes and effects.

15. CERTIFICATION — A part of an appraisal report in which the appraiser certifies that the work was completed according to the applicable standards.

16. REMODELING — A type of renovation that involves modification or updating of existing improvements.

17. OPERATING EXPENSE RATIO — The ratio of total operating expenses to effective gross income

18. AMENITY — A tangible or intangible benefit of real property that enhances its attractiveness or increases the satisfaction of the user.

19. PROGRESSION — Value of an inferior property is enhanced by its association with better properties of the same type.

20. DRIVE BY APPRAISAL — An appraisal report in which the scope of work includes an exterior-only viewing of the subject property.

21. COST TO CURE — The cost to restore an item of deferred maintenance to new or reasonably new condition.

22. GOVERNMENT LIEN — Property taxes or special assessments, has priority over other liens.

23. PHYSICAL POSSIBILITY — One of the criteria for highest and best use of a property must meet.

24. SPECIFIC DATA — Data that is analyzed through the process of comparison.

25. CAPITALIZATION RATE — Any rate used to convert income into value.

A. Assessed Value
D. Erosion
G. Master Plan
J. Decline
M. Remodeling
P. Rate of return
S. Specific Data
V. Amenity
Y. Operating Expense Ratio

B. Government lien
E. Capitalization Rate
H. Contract rent
K. Trends
N. Drive by Appraisal
Q. Gross Market Income
T. Certification
W. Scarcity

C. Rent Roll
F. Physical Possibility
I. Encroachment
L. Cost to Cure
O. Sandwich lease
R. Marketability
U. Progression
X. Investment Value

G. Provide the word that best matches each clue.

1. MARKETABILITY ANALYSIS — A process for examining the productive attributes of the specific property, its demand and supply, and its geographic market area.

2. CONTRIBUTION — The value of a particular component is measured in terms of the amount it adds to the value of the whole property.

3. LIS PENDENS — Legal term signifying pending litigation that can affect ownership title to real estate.

4. MARKET VALUE — The most probable price at which real estate would sell.

5. CONTRIBUTORY VALUE — The change in the value of a property as a whole, resulting from the addition or deletion of a property component.

6. ABSORPTION RATE — Estimate of the rate at which a particular class of properties will sell in a particular geographic area.

7. FIXED EXPENSE — Operating expenses that generally do not vary with occupancy and that prudent management will pay whether the properties occupied or vacant.

8. LIEN — Charge against property in which the property is the security for payment of the debt.

9. NEGATIVE AMORTIZATION — Total payment is insufficient to pay interest due.

10. EXPRESS CONTRACT — An agreement put into words (written or spoken).

11. GENTRIFICATION — Neighborhood phenomenon in which middle- and upper-income persons purchase neighborhood properties and renovate or rehabilitate them.

12. ENTREPRENEURIAL INCENTIVE — The amount entrepreneur expects to receive for his or her contribution to the project.

13. LESSOR — One who conveys the rights of occupancy and use to others under lease agreement.

14. GROWTH — A stage in a market areas life cycle in which the market area gains public favor and acceptance.

15. OPERATING EXPENSES   The periodic expenditures necessary to maintain the real property and continue production of the effective gross income, assuming prudent and competent management.

16. GROSS MARKET INCOME   Annual amount of total revenue that a property would generate if it were occupied all throughout the year.

17. DEPRECIATION   In appraising, a loss in property value from any cause

18. FULL TAKING   The entire taking of the full real property interest of a parcel for public use under the power of eminent domain; requires the payment of compensation.

19. CAPITALIZATION RATE   Any rate used to convert income into value.

20. LESSEE   One who is the right to occupancy and use of the property of another for a period of time according to a lease agreement.

21. REGRESSION ANALYSIS   A statistical measure that attempts to determine the strength of the relationship between one dependent variable and a series of other changing variables.

22. EMINENT DOMAIN   The right of government to take private property for public use upon payment of just compensation.

23. DESKTOP APPRAISAL   An appraisal report in which the appraiser's scope of work does not include an inspection of the subject property or comparables.

24. RIGHTS IN REAL PROPERTY   The rights of possession, transfer, lease, mortgage, improve.

25. INVESTMENT VALUE   Value to a particular individual. The present worth of anticipated future benefits.

A. Lis Pendens
B. Desktop Appraisal
C. Lien
D. Operating Expenses
E. Capitalization Rate
F. Investment Value
G. Absorption rate
H. Gentrification
I. Contribution
J. Express contract
K. Lessor
L. Entrepreneurial Incentive
M. Lessee
N. Marketability Analysis
O. Contributory Value
P. Rights in real property
Q. Market Value
R. Full Taking
S. Growth
T. Fixed Expense
U. Gross Market Income
V. Depreciation
W. Negative Amortization
X. Regression Analysis
Y. Eminent Domain

H. Provide the word that best matches each clue.

1. ENCROACHMENT   Trespassing on the domain of another.

2. REVERSION   A lump sum benefit that an investor receives or expects to receive upon the termination of an investment; also called reversionary benefit.

3. REGRESSION — Value of a superior property is adversely affected by its association with an inferior property of the same type.

4. RANKING ANALYSIS — An ordinal technique for analyzing data, commonly used in the analysis of comparable sales.

5. ADVERSE POSSESSION — Involuntary transfer of property takes place when a party makes a property claim by taking possession over a period of years.

6. GROWTH — A stage in a market areas life cycle in which the market area gains public favor and acceptance.

7. CONSERVATION EASEMENT — An interest in real property restricting future land-use to preservation, conservation, wildlife habitat, or some combination of those uses.

8. PRICE — Amount a particular purchaser agrees to pay and a particular seller agrees to accept under the circumstances surrounding their transaction.

9. FIXED EXPENSE — Operating expenses that generally do not vary with occupancy and that prudent management will pay whether the properties occupied or vacant.

10. LOCATION — The relative position of the property to competitive properties and other value influences in its market area

11. HOUSING STARTS — Newly constructed housing units; includes both single-family and multifamily domiciles.

12. ZONING — Public regulation of the character and extent of real estate use though police power.

13. FUNCTIONAL CLASSIFICATION — The process by which all roads are grouped into classes or systems according to the character of service they are intended to provide.

14. ECONOMIC LIFE — The period over time which a structure may be competitive in the market.

15. ATTACHMENT — Seizure of property by court order.

16. OPERATING INCOME — Income derived from the operation of a business or real property

17. LIS PENDENS — Legal term signifying pending litigation that can affect ownership title to real estate.

18. SUMMARY APPRAISAL — Data and analyses used in the assignment are summarized (i.e. less detail).

19. LIMITING CONDITION — A condition that limits the use of a report.

20. UNITS OF COMPARISON — Price per cubic foot, front foot, and per apartment.

21. PHYSICAL POSSIBILITY — One of the criteria for highest and best use of a property must meet.

22. RIGHTS IN REAL PROPERTY — The rights of possession, transfer, lease, mortgage, improve.

23. CONFORMITY _____ The more a property or its components are in harmony with the surrounding properties or components, the greater the contributory value.

24. EFFECTIVE DATE _____ The date on which the analyses, opinions, and advice in an appraisal, review, or consulting service apply.

25. CONSEQUENTIAL DAMAGES _____ Damage to property arising as a consequence of a taking over and above direct damages.

A. Fixed Expense	B. Attachment	C. Growth
D. Adverse possession	E. Physical Possibility	F. Ranking Analysis
G. Encroachment	H. Zoning	I. Limiting Condition
J. Economic life	K. Rights in real property	L. Conservation Easement
M. Lis Pendens	N. Functional Classification	O. Reversion
P. Effective Date	Q. Housing Starts	R. Units of comparison
S. Price	T. Consequential Damages	U. Conformity
V. Location	W. Summary appraisal	X. Regression
Y. Operating Income		

I. Provide the word that best matches each clue.

1. EXECUTOR _____ An individual or other legal person designated in a will to settle the estate of the deceased person.

2. USEFUL LIFE _____ The period of time over which a structure may reasonably be expected to perform the function for which it was designed.

3. PROPERTY CLASS _____ In accounting, a category for property under the modified accelerated cost recovery system.

4. ENTREPRENEURIAL INCENTIVE _____ The amount entrepreneur expects to receive for his or her contribution to the project.

5. EFFECTIVE GROSS INCOME _____ The total annual income the rental property produces after subtracting vacancy losses and adding miscellaneous income.

6. VOID CONTRACT _____ Has no legal force or binding effect and cannot be enforced in a court of law.

7. SPECIFIC DATA _____ Data that is analyzed through the process of comparison.

8. EROSION _____ The wearing away of surface land by natural causes.

9. OVERALL RATE _____ A rate derived from a single year's NOI and the total property value.

10. APPRAISAL _____ The act or process of developing an opinion of value.

11. NEGATIVE AMORTIZATION _____ Total payment is insufficient to pay interest due.

12. HOUSING STARTS   Newly constructed housing units; includes both single-family and multifamily domiciles.

13. EASEMENT IN GROSS   Easement that is not attached or appurtenant to any particular estate; does not run with the land nor is it transferred through the conveyance of title.

14. ATTACHMENT   Seizure of property by court order.

15. REHABILITATION   The repair and restoration of existing improvements that are in poor condition to a state that makes the property competitive again.

16. VOLUNTARY LIENS   Created intentionally by property owner's actions. i.e. mortgage

17. MONETARY POLICY   Guiding control of the money supply in the economy.

18. CASH FLOW   The periodic income attributable to the interests in real property.

19. UNITS OF COMPARISON   Price per cubic foot, front foot, and per apartment.

20. PERSONAL REPRESENTATIVE   An individual or other legal person designated in a will to settle the estate of a deceased person.

21. MORTGAGE LIENS   Voluntary and one of the most common types of liens.

22. PHYSICAL POSSIBILITY   One of the criteria for highest and best use of a property must meet.

23. FEE SIMPLE ESTATE   Absolute ownership unencumbered by any other interest or estate.

24. DESK REVIEW   An appraisal review in which the reviewer's scope of work does not include an inspection of the subject property.

25. FIXED EXPENSE   Operating expenses that generally do not vary with occupancy and that prudent management will pay whether the properties occupied or vacant.

A. Units of comparison
B. Erosion
C. Void contract
D. Personal Representative
E. Useful life
F. Cash Flow
G. Housing Starts
H. Monetary Policy
I. Mortgage liens
J. Desk Review
K. Entrepreneurial Incentive
L. Negative Amortization
M. Property Class
N. Fee Simple Estate
O. Fixed Expense
P. Executor
Q. Specific Data
R. Easement in gross
S. Rehabilitation
T. Voluntary liens
U. Physical Possibility
V. Overall rate
W. Appraisal
X. Effective Gross Income
Y. Attachment

J. Provide the word that best matches each clue.

1. MARKET PARTICIPANTS   The parties involved in the transfer of property rights. Includes buyers, sellers, lessors, lessees, and brokers and their agents.

2. ECONOMIC FORCES   Supply and demand for housing, economic activity.

3. NEGATIVE AMORTIZATION — Total payment is insufficient to pay interest due.

4. COMMERCIAL PROPERTY — Income-producing property such as office and retail buildings.

5. EXPERT TESTIMONY — Testimony of persons who are presumed to have special knowledge of, or skill in, a particular field due to education, experience, or study.

6. UTILITY — Ability of a product to satisfy a human want, need, or desire.

7. RECLAMATION — Any method of bringing wasted natural resources into productive use.

8. TOTAL OPERATING EXPENSES — Sum of all fixed and variable operating expenses and reserve for replacement.

9. PRESENT VALUE — The value of a future payment or series of future payments discounted to the current date or to time period zero.

10. EXPOSURE TIME — The time of property remains on the market.

11. LIFE TENANT — One who owns an interest in real property for his or her own lifetime.

12. DIRECT COSTS — These are hard cost expenditures for the labor and materials used in the construction of improvements.

13. FINANCING TERMS — The manner in which a transaction was financed.

14. HYPOTHETICAL CONDITION — A condition which is contrary to what is known by the appraiser to exist on the effective date of the assignment results, but is used for the purpose of analysis.

15. HYPOTHICATION — A borrower has possession of the property.

16. CAPITALIZATION — The conversion of income into value.

17. LEASED FEE INTEREST — An ownership interest for the possessory interest has been granted to another by creation of a contractual landlord-tenant relationship.

18. GROSS MARKET INCOME — Annual amount of total revenue that a property would generate if it were occupied all throughout the year.

19. PRICE — Amount a particular purchaser agrees to pay and a particular seller agrees to accept under the circumstances surrounding their transaction.

20. PERCENTAGE ADJUSTMENTS — Adjustments for differences between the subject and comparable properties expressed as a percentage of the sale price of the comparable property.

21. DEED RESTRICTION — A limitation that passes with the land regardless of the owner.

22. LETTER OF TRANSMITTAL — A letter or statement that serves as a notice of delivery from the appraiser to the client of a report containing an opinion or conclusion concerning real estate

23. EASEMENT — The right to use another's land for a stated purpose.

24. REGRESSION — Value of a superior property is adversely affected by its association with an inferior property of the same type.

25. REHABILITATION — The repair and restoration of existing improvements that are in poor condition to a state that makes the property competitive again.

A. Financing Terms
D. Reclamation
G. Easement
J. Negative Amortization
M. Deed restriction
P. Gross Market Income
S. Expert Testimony
V. Commercial Property
Y. Economic Forces

B. Rehabilitation
E. Hypothetical Condition
H. Total Operating Expenses
K. Capitalization
N. Life tenant
Q. Hypothication
T. Present Value
W. Regression

C. Letter of Transmittal
F. Market Participants
I. Utility
L. Leased Fee Interest
O. Exposure Time
R. Price
U. Direct costs
X. Percentage Adjustments

K. Provide the word that best matches each clue.

1. JUST COMPENSATION — In condemnation, the amount of loss for which a property owner is compensated when his or her property is taken.

2. LESSEE — One who is the right to occupancy and use of the property of another for a period of time according to a lease agreement.

3. SURPLUS PRODUCTIVITY — Net income that is left after the 4 agents of production have been paid.

4. JUDGMENT LIENS — Typically result from a lawsuit in which a monetary judgment is awarded.

5. ENCUMBRANCE — Any claim or liability that affects our limits the title to property.

6. EXPRESS CONTRACT — An agreement put into words (written or spoken).

7. CAPITALIZATION RATE — Any rate used to convert income into value.

8. EXECUTOR — An individual or other legal person designated in a will to settle the estate of the deceased person.

9. EXPERT TESTIMONY — Testimony of persons who are presumed to have special knowledge of, or skill in, a particular field due to education, experience, or study.

10. UNILATERAL CONTRACT — Only one party makes a promise

11. RIGHTS IN REAL PROPERTY — The rights of possession, transfer, lease, mortgage, improve.

12. DEPRECIATION	In appraising, a loss in property value from any cause
13. EXCESS LAND	Land that is not needed to serve or support the existing improvement.
14. MASTER PLAN	A comprehensive, long-range official plan that guides the physical growth and development of the community.
15. LETTER OF TRANSMITTAL	A letter or statement that serves as a notice of delivery from the appraiser to the client of a report containing an opinion or conclusion concerning real estate
16. INVESTMENT VALUE	Value to a particular individual. The present worth of anticipated future benefits.
17. CONDOMINIUM	A form of ownership in which each owner possesses the exclusive right to use and occupy an allotted unit plus an undivided interest in common areas.
18. EROSION	The wearing away of surface land by natural causes.
19. DIRECT CAPITALIZATION	A method used to convert an estimate of a single year's income expectancy into an indication of value in one direct step
20. OBSOLESCENCE	One cause of depreciation.
21. LEGAL PERMISSIBILITY	One of the four criteria the highest and best use of a property must meet.
22. EXTRACTION	A method of estimating value in which the depreciated cost of the improvements on the improved property is calculated and deducted from the total sale price
23. EMINENT DOMAIN	The right of government to take private property for public use upon payment of just compensation.
24. CASH FLOW	The periodic income attributable to the interests in real property.
25. MORTGAGE	Pledge of a described property interest as collateral or security for the repayment of a loan under certain terms and conditions.

A. Unilateral contract
B. Executor
C. Letter of Transmittal
D. Lessee
E. Extraction
F. Investment Value
G. Condominium
H. Expert Testimony
I. Surplus Productivity
J. Judgment liens
K. Capitalization Rate
L. Encumbrance
M. Depreciation
N. Express contract
O. Direct Capitalization
P. Legal Permissibility
Q. Erosion
R. Master Plan
S. Mortgage
T. Obsolescence
U. Cash Flow
V. Just Compensation
W. Eminent Domain
X. Excess Land
Y. Rights in real property

L. Provide the word that best matches each clue.

1. GROSS BUILDING AREA — Total floor area of a building, excluding unenclosed area, measured from the exterior of the walls of the above-grade area.

2. DEED RESTRICTION — A limitation that passes with the land regardless of the owner.

3. CONDEMNATION — Method by which government can take private property.

4. GOVERNMENT LIEN — Property taxes or special assessments, has priority over other liens.

5. SPECIFIC LIEN — Lien against a particular property owned by the debtor.

6. EMBLEMENTS — Annual crops and plantings such as corn, wheat, and vegetables.

7. CONDOMINIUM — A form of ownership in which each owner possesses the exclusive right to use and occupy an allotted unit plus an undivided interest in common areas.

8. IMPLIED CONTRACT — Ann agreement that is presumed to exist because of the parties' actions.

9. QUOTENT — Process of dividing one number (dividend) by another number (divisor) produces this result.

10. LAND — first thing a developer considers in developing a property is the cost of land.

11. OVERALL RATE — A rate derived from a single year's NOI and the total property value.

12. LAND USE — The employment of a site or holding to produce revenue or other benefits.

13. REGRESSION — Value of a superior property is adversely affected by its association with an inferior property of the same type.

14. STEP UP DEPRECIATION — The readjustment of the value of an appreciated asset for tax purposes upon inheritance.

15. LIEN — Charge against property in which the property is the security for payment of the debt.

16. QUANTITATIVE ANALYSIS — Analyzing value of a property based on numerical data.

17. REGRESSION ANALYSIS — A statistical measure that attempts to determine the strength of the relationship between one dependent variable and a series of other changing variables.

18. REPORT — Any communication, written or oral, of an appraisal or appraisal review that is transmitted to the client upon completion of an assignment.

19. CAPITALIZATION RATE — Any rate used to convert income into value.

20. SUMMARY APPRAISAL — Data and analyses used in the assignment are summarized (i.e. less detail).

21. SURPLUS PRODUCTIVITY — Net income that is left after the 4 agents of production have been paid.

22. REMAINDER — A future possessor read interest in real estate that is given to a third-party and matures upon the termination of a limited or determinable be.

23. SCOPE OF WORK — The type and extent of research and analyses in appraisal or appraisal review assignment.

24. PHYSICAL CHARACTERISTICS — A category of elements of comparison in the sales comparison approach

25. RESIDENTIAL PROPERTY — A vacant or in proof parcel of land devoted to or available for use as a residence.

A. Scope of Work
B. Specific Lien
C. Remainder
D. Regression Analysis
E. Government lien
F. Physical Characteristics
G. Implied contract
H. Regression
I. Deed restriction
J. Capitalization Rate
K. Summary appraisal
L. Quotent
M. Step Up Depreciation
N. Land Use
O. Lien
P. Emblements
Q. Land
R. Residential Property
S. Report
T. Gross Building Area
U. Quantitative Analysis
V. Surplus Productivity
W. Overall rate
X. Condemnation
Y. Condominium

M. Provide the word that best matches each clue.

1. PHYSICAL DETERIORATION — The wear and tear that begins with the building is completed and placed into service.

2. CONDEMNATION — Method by which government can take private property.

3. CERTIFICATION — A part of an appraisal report in which the appraiser certifies that the work was completed according to the applicable standards.

4. ENCROACHMENT — Trespassing on the domain of another.

5. PLAT — A plan, map, or chart of a city, town, section, or subdivision indicating the location and boundaries of individual properties.

6. AMENITY — A tangible or intangible benefit of real property that enhances its attractiveness or increases the satisfaction of the user.

7. RENT ROLL — A report that is prepared regularly, usually each month, and indicates the rent-paying status of each tenant.

8. INVESTMENT VALUE — Value to a particular individual. The present worth of anticipated future benefits.

9. PRICE — Amount a particular purchaser agrees to pay and a particular seller agrees to accept under the circumstances surrounding their transaction.

10. POTENTIAL GROSS INCOME — The total income attributable to real property at full occupancy before vacancy and operating expenses are deducted.

11. EASEMENT — The right to use another's land for a stated purpose.

12. UNILATERAL CONTRACT — Only one party makes a promise

13. REPORT — Any communication, written or oral, of an appraisal or appraisal review that is transmitted to the client upon completion of an assignment.

14. REASONABLE — In law, just, rational, appropriate, ordinary, or usual in the circumstances.

15. CAPITALIZATION RATE — Any rate used to convert income into value.

16. FINAL RECONCILIATION — The last phase in the development of the value opinion in which two or more value indications derived from market data are resolved into a value opinion.

17. LESSEE — One who is the right to occupancy and use of the property of another for a period of time according to a lease agreement.

18. DETERIORATION — Impairment of condition; because of depreciation that reflects the loss in value due to wear and tear, disintegration, use in service, and the action of the elements.

19. PRINCIPLE — The amount of money borrowed from lender (mortgagee).

20. SPECIFIC DATA — Data that is analyzed through the process of comparison.

21. LESSOR — One who conveys the rights of occupancy and use to others under lease agreement.

22. INTERIM USE — Temporary use to which a site or improved property is put until it is ready to be put to its future highest and best use.

23. VALUE — Monetary worth of a property, good, or service to buyers and sellers at a given time.

24. SYNDICATION — A private or public partnership that pools funds for the acquisition and development of real estate projects or other business ventures.

25. IMPLIED CONTRACT — Ann agreement that is presumed to exist because of the parties' actions.

A. Reasonable
B. Price
C. Lessor
D. Capitalization Rate
E. Principle
F. Physical Deterioration
G. Implied contract
H. Report
I. Value
J. Encroachment
K. Rent Roll
L. Potential Gross Income
M. Interim use
N. Plat
O. Certification
P. Lessee
Q. Investment Value
R. Deterioration
S. Easement
T. Unilateral contract
U. Syndication
V. Specific Data
W. Amenity
X. Condemnation
Y. Final Reconciliation

N. Provide the word that best matches each clue.

1. PARTIAL INTEREST — Divided or undivided rights in real estate that represent less than the whole.

2. FUNCTIONAL OBSOLESCE — The impairment of functional capacity of a property according to market tastes and standards.

3. EFFECTIVE GROSS INCOME — The total annual income the rental property produces after subtracting vacancy losses and adding miscellaneous income.

4. FUNCTIONAL CLASSIFICATION — The process by which all roads are grouped into classes or systems according to the character of service they are intended to provide.

5. MARKETING TIME — Time it takes an interest in real property to sell on the market subsequent to the date of an appraisal.

6. EXPOSURE TIME — The time of property remains on the market.

7. PLAT — A plan, map, or chart of a city, town, section, or subdivision indicating the location and boundaries of individual properties.

8. STEP UP DEPRECIATION — The readjustment of the value of an appreciated asset for tax purposes upon inheritance.

9. FRICTIONAL VACANCY — The amount of vacant space needed in a market for its orderly operation.

10. HYPOTHETICAL CONDITION — A condition which is contrary to what is known by the appraiser to exist on the effective date of the assignment results, but is used for the purpose of analysis.

11. CHRONOLOGICAL AGE — The number of years since a structure or bldg. was originally built (birth).

12. BUNDLE OF RIGHTS — The rights of an owner to possess, control, enjoy, sell, lease, mortgage, and dispose of the property.

13. AVULSION — The sudden removal of land from the property of one owner to that of another, e.g., change in the course of a river.

14. LEASE — A contract in which the rights to use and occupy land or structures are transferred by the owner to another for a specified period of time in return for specified rent.

15. NEGATIVE AMORTIZATION — Total payment is insufficient to pay interest due.

16. GROSS LIVING AREA — Total area of finished above-grade residential space

17. OPERATING STATEMENT — A financial statement that reflects the gross revenues, expenses, and net operating profit or loss of an investment over a fixed period.

18. TAXATION — Right of government to raise revenue through assessments on valuable goods, products, and rights.

19. GENTRIFICATION _____ Neighborhood phenomenon in which middle- and upper-income persons purchase neighborhood properties and renovate or rehabilitate them.

20. MARKETABILITY _____ The relative desirability of a property in comparison with similar or competing properties in the area.

21. HIGHWAY EASEMENT _____ A right granted or taken for the construction, maintenance, and operation of the highway.

22. LITTORAL RIGHTS _____ Rights pertaining to properties abutting a lake or pond.

23. CERTIFICATION _____ A part of an appraisal report in which the appraiser certifies that the work was completed according to the applicable standards.

24. REAL ESTATE _____ An identified parcel or tract of land, including improvements.

25. BALANCE _____ Principle that real property value is created and sustained when contrasting, opposing, or interacting elements are in a state of equilibrium.

A. Real Estate	B. Marketability	C. Plat
D. Balance	E. Exposure Time	F. Highway Easement
G. Bundle of rights	H. Hypothetical Condition	I. Partial Interest
J. Step Up Depreciation	K. Certification	L. Operating Statement
M. Gross Living Area	N. Taxation	O. Marketing time
P. Chronological age	Q. Lease	R. Negative Amortization
S. Littoral rights	T. Frictional Vacancy	U. Effective Gross Income
V. Functional Classification	W. Gentrification	X. Avulsion
Y. Functional Obsolesce		

O. Provide the word that best matches each clue.

1. CONTRACT RENT _____ The actual rental income specified in a lease.

2. COMPARABLES _____ A shortened term for similar property sales, rentals, or operating expenses used for comparison in the valuation process.

3. REMODELING _____ A type of renovation that involves modification or updating of existing improvements.

4. PHYSICAL CHARACTERISTICS _____ A category of elements of comparison in the sales comparison approach

5. LOSS OF ACCESS _____ Depriving an abutting owner of the inherent rights of ingress and to egress from the highway or street.

6. COST TO CURE _____ The cost to restore an item of deferred maintenance to new or reasonably new condition.

7. GROSS LEASE _____ When the lessee (tenant) does not pay any costs of ownership and pays a given amount of rent per period.

8. QUOTENT   Process of dividing one number (dividend) by another number (divisor) produces this result.

9. ENTREPRENEURIAL PROFIT   A market-derived figure that represents the amount an entrepreneur receives for their contribution.

10. HYPOTHICATION   A borrower has possession of the property.

11. OPERATING STATEMENT   A financial statement that reflects the gross revenues, expenses, and net operating profit or loss of an investment over a fixed period.

12. LIFE TENANT   One who owns an interest in real property for his or her own lifetime.

13. REAL ESTATE   An identified parcel or tract of land, including improvements.

14. PIPELINE EASEMENT   The right to construct, operate, and maintain a pipeline over the lands of others within prescribed geographical limits.

15. REGRESSION   Value of a superior property is adversely affected by its association with an inferior property of the same type.

16. CLIENT   The party of parties who engage an appraiser in a specific assignment.

17. LEASED FEE INTEREST   An ownership interest for the possessory interest has been granted to another by creation of a contractual landlord-tenant relationship.

18. MAXIMUM PRODUCTIVITY   One of the four criteria the highest and best use of a property must meet; the selected land-use must yield the highest value of the possible uses.

19. SITE IMPROVEMENTS   Improvements on and off the site that make it suitable for its intended use or development.

20. PRIMARY DATA   Information that is gathered in its original form by the analyst.

21. EFFECTIVE AGE   The difference between an improvements total economic life and its remaining economic life.

22. EMINENT DOMAIN   The right of government to take private property for public use upon payment of just compensation.

23. RESIDUAL   The quantity left over.

24. LIVING TRUST   Created by agreement during the property owner's lifetime

25. CERTIFICATION   A part of an appraisal report in which the appraiser certifies that the work was completed according to the applicable standards.

A. Quotent	B. Client	C. Eminent Domain
D. Hypothication	E. Comparables	F. Operating Statement
G. Remodeling	H. Site Improvements	I. Effective age
J. Residual	K. Leased Fee Interest	L. Certification

M. Gross lease
P. Real Estate
S. Life tenant
V. Contract rent
Y. Pipeline Easement

N. Physical Characteristics
Q. Regression
T. Entrepreneurial profit
W. Living trust

O. Maximum Productivity
R. Cost to Cure
U. Loss of Access
X. Primary Data

P. Provide the word that best matches each clue.

1. VOID CONTRACT — Has no legal force or binding effect and cannot be enforced in a court of law.

2. MONETARY POLICY — Guiding control of the money supply in the economy.

3. REMODELING — A type of renovation that involves modification or updating of existing improvements.

4. SETBACK — Zoning regulations that designate the distance a building must be set back from the front, rear, and sides of the property lines.

5. MASS APPRAISAL — The process of valuing a universe of properties as of a given date using standard methodology, employing common data, and allowing for statistical testing.

6. RESIDENTIAL PROPERTY — A vacant or in proof parcel of land devoted to or available for use as a residence.

7. POLE LINE EASEMENT — An easement for the construction, maintenance, and operation of a full line, usually for the transmission of electric power.

8. MARKET PRICE — Amount paid for an income producing property.

9. MARKETABILITY — The relative desirability of a property in comparison with similar or competing properties in the area.

10. EASEMENT APPURTENANT — Easement that is attached to, benefits, and passes with the conveyance of the dominant estate. Burdens the servient estate.

11. REMAINING USEFUL LIFE — The estimated period during which improvements will continue to provide utility.

12. ESTATE IN LAND — The degree, nature, or extent of interest that a person has in land.

13. CONTRIBUTION — The value of a particular component is measured in terms of the amount it adds to the value of the whole property.

14. DISCOUNT RATE — The yield rate used to convert future payments or receipts into present value; usually considered to be a synonym for yield rate.

15. HYPOTHETICAL CONDITION — A condition which is contrary to what is known by the appraiser to exist on the effective date of the assignment results, but is used for the purpose of analysis.

16. FUNCTIONAL CLASSIFICATION   The process by which all roads are grouped into classes or systems according to the character of service they are intended to provide.

17. SITE   land that is improved so that is ready to be used for a specific purpose.

18. REAL ESTATE   An identified parcel or tract of land, including improvements.

19. OPERATING INCOME   Income derived from the operation of a business or real property

20. MARKETABILITY ANALYSIS   A process for examining the productive attributes of the specific property, its demand and supply, and its geographic market area.

21. LITTORAL RIGHTS   Rights pertaining to properties abutting a lake or pond.

22. LESSEE   One who is the right to occupancy and use of the property of another for a period of time according to a lease agreement.

23. VALID CONTRACT   An agreement in which all the elements of a contract are present and, therefore, legally enforceable.

24. MARKETING TIME   Time it takes an interest in real property to sell on the market subsequent to the date of an appraisal.

25. RESTRICTED USE APPRAISAL   Conclusions of the appraisal are stated, but the data or analyses used in the appraisal to develop these conclusions do not need to be included in the report.

A. Residential Property	B. Discount Rate	C. Marketability Analysis
D. Marketing time	E. Mass Appraisal	F. Restricted use appraisal
G. Monetary Policy	H. Lessee	I. Estate in land
J. Remaining Useful Life	K. Littoral rights	L. Functional Classification
M. Contribution	N. Remodeling	O. Setback
P. Pole Line Easement	Q. Operating Income	R. Valid contract
S. Market Price	T. Site	U. Hypothetical Condition
V. Void contract	W. Real Estate	X. Marketability
Y. Easement appurtenant		

Word Search

A. Find the hidden words. The words have been placed horizontally, vertically, or diagonally. When you locate a word, draw an ellipse around it.

R	E	G	R	E	S	S	I	O	N	M	L	I	B	L	Z	J	E	C	N	X	R	T
Z	Q	U	A	N	T	I	T	A	T	I	V	E	A	N	A	L	Y	S	I	S	E	A
E	N	X	J	J	M	C	B	O	X	L	D	I	V	E	R	O	S	I	O	N	N	D
T	Y	C	W	R	E	M	A	I	N	D	E	R	I	N	T	E	R	E	S	T	T	T
P	K	T	P	A	T	Z	Z	M	C	O	S	T	T	O	C	U	R	E	W	C	R	E
L	T	S	S	J	R	M	A	R	K	E	T	P	R	I	C	E	E	F	L	O	X	
K	Q	H	C	A	P	I	T	A	L	I	Z	A	T	I	O	N	R	A	T	E	L	Q
C	O	N	S	E	R	V	A	T	I	O	N	E	A	S	E	M	E	N	T	N	L	B
U	N	I	T	S	O	F	C	O	M	P	A	R	I	S	O	N	J	P	V	W	G	K
T	U	I	I	Q	N	C	O	R	U	G	S	P	S	C	A	R	C	I	T	Y	D	K
A	P	K	S	N	E	N	C	I	Y	T	D	G	R	O	S	S	L	E	A	S	E	L
P	H	Y	S	I	C	A	L	D	E	T	E	R	I	O	R	A	T	I	O	N	Y	D
H	H	I	F	I	Y	Y	I	K	E	F	F	E	C	T	I	V	E	D	A	T	E	B
B	R	C	W	F	Q	K	E	P	A	K	Q	R	E	A	S	O	N	A	B	L	E	I
A	L	D	T	G	G	L	N	K	V	O	L	U	N	T	A	R	Y	L	I	E	N	S
O	N	B	E	K	K	N	T	Y	M	A	S	S	A	P	P	R	A	I	S	A	L	N

1. Any rate used to convert income into value.
2. The date on which the analyses, opinions, and advice in an appraisal, review, or consulting service apply.
3. Amount paid for an income producing property.
4. The party of parties who engage an appraiser in a specific assignment.
5. The cost to restore an item of deferred maintenance to new or reasonably new condition.
6. The wearing away of surface land by natural causes.
7. An interest in real property restricting future land-use to preservation, conservation, wildlife habitat, or some combination of those uses.
8. The process of valuing a universe of properties as of a given date using standard methodology, employing common data, and allowing for statistical testing.
9. Analyzing value of a property based on numerical data.
10. Created intentionally by property owner's actions. i.e. mortgage
11. The present or anticipated undersupply of an item relative to the demand for it. Conditions of scarcity contribute to value.
12. Price per cubic foot, front foot, and per apartment.
13. Person who is entitled to an estate after a prior estate or interest has expired
14. In law, just, rational, appropriate, ordinary, or usual in the circumstances.
15. A report that is prepared regularly, usually each month, and indicates the rent-paying status of each tenant.
16. Value of a superior property is adversely affected by its association with an inferior property of the same type.
17. The wear and tear that begins with the building is completed and placed into service.
18. When the lessee (tenant) does not pay any costs of ownership and pays a given amount of rent per period.

A. Capitalization Rate
B. Gross lease
C. Reasonable
D. Cost to Cure
E. Remainder interest
F. Scarcity
G. Erosion
H. Units of comparison
I. Regression
J. Client
K. Mass Appraisal
L. Voluntary liens
M. Effective Date
N. Rent Roll
O. Market Price
P. Quantitative Analysis
Q. Physical Deterioration
R. Conservation Easement

B. Find the hidden words. The words have been placed horizontally, vertically, or diagonally. When you locate a word, draw an ellipse around it.

H	S	U	R	F	A	C	E	R	I	G	H	T	S	E	L	Q	N	I	B	K	H	H
S	S	I	T	E	O	D	G	R	O	S	S	L	I	V	I	N	G	A	R	E	A	C
B	M	A	R	K	E	T	P	R	I	C	E	H	F	U	L	L	T	A	K	I	N	G
V	M	A	R	K	E	T	A	B	I	L	I	T	Y	A	N	A	L	Y	S	I	S	H
W	F	R	I	P	A	R	I	A	N	R	I	G	H	T	S	L	B	S	N	Z	M	O
P	Y	L	V	C	M	C	T	G	E	R	M	C	B	I	Z	Z	T	W	L	K	A	W
P	D	A	S	S	E	S	S	E	D	V	A	L	U	E	R	T	B	G	L	Y	Q	A
U	L	M	V	M	P	C	A	J	U	D	P	D	U	T	D	D	B	T	U	D	B	D
P	B	S	T	E	P	U	P	D	E	P	R	E	C	I	A	T	I	O	N	W	S	L
S	B	M	U	G	A	M	I	P	V	H	O	U	S	I	N	G	S	T	A	R	T	S
D	M	D	T	K	B	F	T	M	I	X	B	A	D	J	U	S	T	M	E	N	T	S
P	U	T	I	L	I	T	Y	X	R	E	A	L	E	S	T	A	T	E	E	S	E	N
V	O	I	D	C	O	N	T	R	A	C	T	Y	Q	W	V	A	L	U	E	L	Z	U
E	J	Y	W	Z	X	C	I	L	N	I	E	Y	G	Q	J	Q	C	K	I	J	J	N
D	E	E	M	I	N	E	N	T	D	O	M	A	I	N	I	C	B	N	N	S	T	K
E	C	O	N	T	R	I	B	U	T	O	R	Y	V	A	L	U	E	S	Y	K	L	E

1. The right of government to take private property for public use upon payment of just compensation.
2. The entire taking of the full real property interest of a parcel for public use under the power of eminent domain; requires the payment of compensation.
3. Total area of finished above-grade residential space
4. The change in the value of a property as a whole, resulting from the addition or deletion of a property component.
5. The legal process of settling an estate after a person has died.
6. Has no legal force or binding effect and cannot be enforced in a court of law.
7. Rights pertaining to properties touching a river or stream.
8. Amount paid for an income producing property.
9. land that is improved so that is ready to be used for a specific purpose.
10. Ability of a product to satisfy a human want, need, or desire.
11. Changes made to basic data to facilitate comparison or understanding.
12. The readjustment of the value of an appreciated asset for tax purposes upon inheritance.
13. Land, water, and anything attached to the land-either naturally or placed by human hands.
14. A process for examining the productive attributes of the specific property, its demand and supply, and its geographic market area.
15. An identified parcel or tract of land, including improvements.
16. Newly constructed housing units; includes both single -family and multifamily domiciles.
17. Monetary worth of a property, good, or service to buyers and sellers at a given time.
18. The value of a property according to the tax rolls in ad valorem taxation.

A. Riparian rights
B. Contributory Value
C. Housing Starts
D. Full Taking
E. Eminent Domain
F. Value
G. Site
H. Assessed Value
I. Utility
J. Adjustments
K. Gross Living Area
L. Marketability Analysis
M. Real Estate
N. Void contract
O. Market Price
P. Surface rights
Q. Step Up Depreciation
R. Probate

C. Find the hidden words. The words have been placed horizontally, vertically, or diagonally. When you locate a word, draw an ellipse around it.

H	F	W	J	A	E	L	C	C	A	S	H	E	Q	U	I	V	A	L	E	N	T	O
I	G	P	H	Y	S	I	C	A	L	P	O	S	S	I	B	I	L	I	T	Y	M	O
G	D	I	N	M	T	D	G	R	E	V	I	T	A	L	I	Z	A	T	I	O	N	P
H	K	Q	G	U	A	N	R	X	V	F	I	X	E	D	E	X	P	E	N	S	E	O
W	Z	U	T	T	T	Y	O	T	N	R	Y	R	O	Y	A	L	T	Y	E	X	E	L
A	O	Z	J	B	E	A	S	P	C	P	N	K	F	E	G	H	P	I	I	E	A	R
Y	N	R	H	A	I	V	S	L	I	F	E	E	S	T	A	T	E	F	S	I	T	Q
E	I	M	Y	W	N	E	L	M	A	R	K	E	T	V	A	L	U	E	E	P	T	H
A	N	R	P	B	L	P	E	F	E	K	H	I	D	P	D	O	M	R	E	F	A	J
S	G	U	M	G	A	W	A	L	E	D	J	R	Z	P	E	R	Q	G	B	P	C	Z
E	P	Z	G	S	N	Z	S	N	G	Z	S	R	Q	D	E	W	Z	I	S	N	H	K
M	R	J	K	F	D	K	E	X	F	O	F	U	Q	R	D	X	O	Z	N	B	M	E
E	M	O	R	T	G	A	G	E	L	I	E	N	S	Y	Q	V	Z	Z	X	T	E	N
N	F	I	N	A	N	C	I	A	L	F	E	A	S	I	B	I	L	I	T	Y	N	M
T	F	G	R	O	W	T	H	V	R	E	N	O	V	A	T	I	O	N	A	H	T	Y
E	X	T	E	R	N	A	L	O	B	S	O	L	E	S	C	E	N	C	E	D	W	J

1. A stage in a market areas life cycle in which the market area gains public favor and acceptance.
2. When the lessee (tenant) does not pay any costs of ownership and pays a given amount of rent per period.
3. Seizure of property by court order.
4. The most probable price at which real estate would sell.
5. Total rights of use, occupancy and control, limited to the lifetime of the designated party, i.e. life tenant.
6. One of the four criteria the highest and best use of a property must meet.
7. Voluntary and one of the most common types of liens.
8. The degree, nature, or extent of interest that a person has in land.
9. The process in which older structures or historic buildings are modernized, remodeled, or restored.
10. Written, legal instrument that conveys an estate or interest in real property to someone else, assuming it is executed and delivered.
11. A stage in a market area's life cycle characterized by renewal, redevelopment, modernization, and increasing demand.
12. An element of depreciation; and diminution in value caused by negative externalities and generally incurable on the part of the owner, landlord, or tenant.
13. Operating expenses that generally do not vary with occupancy and that prudent management will pay whether the properties occupied or vacant.
14. One of the criteria for highest and best use of a property must meet.
15. Public regulation of the character and extent of real estate use though police power.
16. A right granted or taken for the construction, maintenance, and operation of the highway.
17. Money paid to an owner of real property or mineral rights for the right to deplete natural resource.
18. The price of a property with above- or below-market financing expressed in terms of the price that would have been paid in an all-cash sale.

A. Physical Possibility
B. Renovation
C. Financial Feasibility
D. Royalty
E. Highway Easement
F. Revitalization
G. External Obsolescence
H. Mortgage liens
I. Cash Equivalent
J. Attachment
K. Gross lease
L. Zoning
M. Market Value
N. Deed
O. Fixed Expense
P. Growth
Q. Estate in land
R. Life estate

D. Find the hidden words. The words have been placed horizontally, vertically, or diagonally. When you locate a word, draw an ellipse around it.

F	O	K	O	P	H	Y	S	I	C	A	L	P	O	S	S	I	B	I	L	I	T	Y
E	I	M	S	I	N	G	L	E	F	A	M	I	L	Y	H	O	U	S	E	L	H	L
S	J	A	N	E	G	A	T	I	V	E	A	M	O	R	T	I	Z	A	T	I	O	N
T	L	E	T	T	E	R	O	F	T	R	A	N	S	M	I	T	T	A	L	T	T	C
A	E	I	Y	D	U	W	P	R	P	R	O	G	R	E	S	S	I	O	N	A	J	N
T	M	X	L	A	S	C	O	N	D	E	M	N	A	T	I	O	N	F	N	X	R	N
E	F	U	N	C	T	I	O	N	A	L	O	B	S	O	L	E	S	C	E	A	B	E
I	T	Z	R	Q	P	D	K	R	O	N	S	T	K	A	N	C	E	E	H	T	H	S
N	P	I	P	E	L	I	N	E	E	A	S	E	M	E	N	T	W	A	X	I	Q	X
L	M	L	E	A	S	E	D	F	E	E	I	N	T	E	R	E	S	T	S	O	C	Y
A	Q	U	A	L	I	T	A	T	I	V	E	A	N	A	L	Y	S	I	S	N	R	M
N	S	X	K	C	A	P	I	T	A	L	I	Z	A	T	I	O	N	R	A	T	E	I
D	G	M	E	S	F	A	B	S	O	R	P	T	I	O	N	R	A	T	E	Z	U	A
T	E	B	Z	F	D	I	E	F	F	E	C	T	I	V	E	D	A	T	E	N	G	U
L	X	S	A	L	V	A	G	E	V	A	L	U	E	E	X	E	C	U	T	O	R	Z
T	D	E	F	E	R	R	E	D	M	A	I	N	T	E	N	A	N	C	E	Z	S	R

1. Right of government to raise revenue through assessments on valuable goods, products, and rights.
2. Any rate used to convert income into value.
3. The degree, nature, or extent of interest that a person has in land.
4. Estimate of the rate at which a particular class of properties will sell in a particular geographic area.
5. Method by which government can take private property.
6. One of the criteria for highest and best use of a property must meet.
7. An ownership interest for the possessory interest has been granted to another by creation of a contractual landlord-tenant relationship.
8. An individual or other legal person designated in a will to settle the estate of the deceased person.
9. The right to construct, operate, and maintain a pipeline over the lands of others within prescribed geographical limits.
10. The dwelling that is designated for occupancy by one family.
11. The impairment of functional capacity of a property according to market tastes and standards.
12. A letter or statement that serves as a notice of delivery from the appraiser to the client of a report containing an opinion or conclusion concerning real estate
13. The date on which the analyses, opinions, and advice in an appraisal, review, or consulting service apply.
14. Total payment is insufficient to pay interest due.
15. The price expected for a whole property (e.g., a house) or a part of a property (e.g., a plumbing fixture) that is removed from the premises usually for use elsewhere.
16. Is used for elements that cannot be given a numerical value.
17. Needed repairs or replacement of items that should have taken place during the course of normal maintenance.
18. Value of an inferior property is enhanced by its association with better properties of the same type.

A. Negative Amortization
B. Qualitative analysis
C. Physical Possibility
D. Absorption rate
E. Condemnation
F. Taxation
G. Single Family House
H. Leased Fee Interest
I. Functional Obsolesce
J. Progression
K. Letter of Transmittal
L. Capitalization Rate
M. Effective Date
N. Deferred Maintenance
O. Estate in land
P. Pipeline Easement
Q. Salvage Value
R. Executor

E. Find the hidden words. The words have been placed horizontally, vertically, or diagonally. When you locate a word, draw an ellipse around it.

L	O	S	S	O	F	A	C	C	E	S	S	R	P	Q	C	V	G	B	M	Q	E	V
R	Z	O	S	Y	N	D	I	C	A	T	I	O	N	C	L	T	B	Z	E	M	A	V
R	E	M	A	I	N	I	N	G	E	C	O	N	O	M	I	C	L	I	F	E	S	A
W	R	E	A	L	E	S	T	A	T	E	M	A	R	K	E	T	M	N	Z	P	S	L
F	E	E	S	I	M	P	L	E	E	S	T	A	T	E	N	E	G	X	M	M	E	U
J	N	U	N	I	L	A	T	E	R	A	L	C	O	N	T	R	A	C	T	N	S	E
M	V	O	I	D	C	O	N	T	R	A	C	T	B	N	K	E	E	N	C	O	S	I
J	A	R	M	S	L	E	N	G	T	H	A	H	R	N	R	S	S	V	L	I	E	N
Z	P	M	V	F	E	P	R	O	X	I	M	I	T	Y	D	A	M	A	G	E	D	E
P	A	R	Z	D	A	D	V	I	E	N	N	O	J	X	V	Q	J	H	D	N	V	X
S	X	Q	O	F	R	A	N	K	I	N	G	A	N	A	L	Y	S	I	S	T	A	C
F	I	N	A	N	C	I	A	L	F	E	A	S	I	B	I	L	I	T	Y	Q	L	H
J	X	L	E	T	T	E	R	O	F	T	R	A	N	S	M	I	T	T	A	L	U	A
A	Q	V	J	U	D	M	N	Z	O	F	E	Z	N	A	E	D	J	Y	D	Y	E	N
H	Y	P	O	T	H	I	C	A	T	I	O	N	D	N	B	Q	X	D	B	L	Y	G
G	M	M	K	D	W	R	E	F	A	I	R	M	A	R	K	E	T	V	A	L	U	E

1. The price at which the property would change hands between a willing buyer and a willing seller and both having reasonable knowledge of relevant facts.
2. Price an economic good will attract in the competitive market.
3. The party of parties who engage an appraiser in a specific assignment.
4. A borrower has possession of the property.
5. Charge against property in which the property is the security for payment of the debt.
6. The value of a property according to the tax rolls in ad valorem taxation.
7. The estimated period during which improvements will continue to represent the highest and best use of the property.
8. Has no legal force or binding effect and cannot be enforced in a court of law.
9. One of the four criteria the highest and best use of a property must meet.
10. Depriving an abutting owner of the inherent rights of ingress and to egress from the highway or street.
11. An ordinal technique for analyzing data, commonly used in the analysis of comparable sales.
12. Damages that is caused by the remainder's proximity to the improvement being constructed.
13. A transaction in which the buyers and sellers of a product act independently and have no relationship to each other.
14. Only one party makes a promise
15. A private or public partnership that pools funds for the acquisition and development of real estate projects or other business ventures.
16. Buyers and sellers of particular real estate and the transactions that occur among them.
17. A letter or statement that serves as a notice of delivery from the appraiser to the client of a report containing an opinion or conclusion concerning real estate
18. Absolute ownership unencumbered by any other interest or estate.

A. Proximity Damage
B. Lien
C. Unilateral contract
D. Real Estate Market
E. Financial Feasibility
F. Value in Exchange
G. Syndication
H. Assessed Value
I. Remaining Economic Life
J. Letter of Transmittal
K. Client
L. Void contract
M. Ranking Analysis
N. Hypothication
O. Fee Simple Estate
P. Fair Market Value
Q. Arms Length
R. Loss of Access

F. Find the hidden words. The words have been placed horizontally, vertically, or diagonally. When you locate a word, draw an ellipse around it.

O	F	U	N	C	T	I	O	N	A	L	O	B	S	O	L	E	S	C	E	T	J	D
N	E	T	L	E	A	S	E	K	S	U	R	F	A	C	E	R	I	G	H	T	S	T
X	I	S	S	U	P	R	A	S	U	R	F	A	C	E	R	I	G	H	T	S	K	P
J	B	K	S	F	Y	X	C	U	S	B	A	L	A	N	C	E	X	A	K	B	B	I
S	S	P	D	I	R	E	C	T	C	A	P	I	T	A	L	I	Z	A	T	I	O	N
J	D	R	E	M	A	I	N	I	N	G	U	S	E	F	U	L	L	I	F	E	M	Z
I	N	D	I	R	E	C	T	C	O	S	T	S	U	C	F	U	V	S	U	E	I	F
S	D	I	S	T	R	E	S	S	S	A	L	E	M	O	B	W	V	U	G	L	G	U
X	R	E	D	E	V	E	L	O	P	M	E	N	T	N	M	R	S	Y	B	D	J	K
R	A	I	L	E	A	S	E	M	E	N	T	E	Q	F	C	B	L	X	C	E	Q	M
L	D	E	E	D	R	E	S	T	R	I	C	T	I	O	N	D	E	H	Q	C	K	S
I	Y	E	C	O	N	O	M	I	C	L	I	F	E	R	Z	E	N	Y	L	L	D	C
J	P	M	D	M	V	U	J	J	Z	R	C	Q	A	M	E	U	E	I	V	I	I	B
S	A	L	V	A	G	E	V	A	L	U	E	M	H	I	C	Y	K	A	B	N	F	X
G	E	Z	Y	C	H	P	J	U	D	G	M	E	N	T	L	I	E	N	S	E	N	Z
Q	V	A	L	I	D	C	O	N	T	R	A	C	T	Y	I	V	Y	R	S	Q	R	X

1. A method used to convert an estimate of a single year's income expectancy into an indication of value in one direct step
2. The more a property or its components are in harmony with the surrounding properties or components, the greater the contributory value.
3. Soft cost expenditures that are necessary components but are not typically part of the construction contract.
4. The period over time which a structure may be competitive in the market.
5. The estimated period during which improvements will continue to provide utility.
6. Right to undisturbed use and control of designated air space above a specific land area within stated elevations.
7. A stage of diminishing demand in a market areas life cycle.
8. Typically result from a lawsuit in which a monetary judgment is awarded.
9. Land, water, and anything attached to the land-either naturally or placed by human hands.
10. A lease in which the landlord passes on all expenses to the tenant.
11. The development or improvement of cleared or undeveloped land in an urban renewal area.
12. A limitation that passes with the land regardless of the owner.
13. An agreement in which all the elements of a contract are present and, therefore, legally enforceable.
14. The right for the construction, maintenance, and operation of a rail line on a property.
15. Principle that real property value is created and sustained when contrasting, opposing, or interacting elements are in a state of equilibrium.
16. The price expected for a whole property (e.g., a house) or a part of a property (e.g., a plumbing fixture) that is removed from the premises usually for use elsewhere.
17. A sale involving a seller acting under undue distress.
18. The impairment of functional capacity of a property according to market tastes and standards.

A. Valid contract
B. Economic life
C. Rail Easement
D. Net Lease
E. Deed restriction
F. Decline
G. Redevelopment
H. Surface rights
I. Salvage Value
J. Distress Sale
K. Balance
L. Functional Obsolesce
M. Direct Capitalization
N. Judgment liens
O. Conformity
P. Remaining Useful Life
Q. Supra surface rights
R. Indirect costs

G. Find the hidden words. The words have been placed horizontally, vertically, or diagonally. When you locate a word, draw an ellipse around it.

Z	S	V	I	I	H	C	W	T	V	I	H	J	J	X	S	D	Q	Z	P	R	K	D
M	W	X	P	F	K	O	E	P	W	X	B	P	V	Z	V	F	G	G	W	L	E	Q
B	E	C	O	N	O	M	I	C	F	O	R	C	E	S	D	Z	O	N	I	N	G	C
B	D	D	L	D	K	P	T	Q	E	H	W	G	Y	K	C	W	R	D	Z	K	F	U
O	X	W	I	X	D	E	E	C	O	N	O	M	I	C	L	I	F	E	J	S	S	F
F	M	L	C	S	I	T	V	D	G	B	M	M	D	L	K	N	D	P	G	V	D	A
T	B	R	E	Q	S	E	X	H	N	G	S	E	T	B	A	C	K	G	F	A	A	X
Z	C	J	P	V	T	N	F	S	A	N	D	W	I	C	H	L	E	A	S	E	P	Z
Q	Q	Q	O	N	R	C	R	E	A	L	E	S	T	A	T	E	M	A	R	K	E	T
H	U	J	W	B	I	E	C	O	S	T	U	H	R	N	O	S	L	E	V	U	V	N
Q	A	U	E	G	C	B	I	L	A	T	E	R	A	L	C	O	N	T	R	A	C	T
L	C	O	R	L	T	L	O	S	S	O	F	A	C	C	E	S	S	L	U	U	A	G
E	K	D	K	E	S	U	B	S	U	R	F	A	C	E	R	I	G	H	T	S	J	D
X	M	E	L	E	M	E	N	T	S	O	F	C	O	M	P	A	R	I	S	O	N	M
Z	O	N	P	R	E	S	E	R	V	A	T	I	O	N	E	A	S	E	M	E	N	T
M	E	G	R	O	S	S	B	U	I	L	D	I	N	G	A	R	E	A	N	X	N	A

1. Relevant characteristics used to compare and adjust the property prices.
2. The state of having the requisite or adequate ability or qualities to perform the specific assignment and produce credible assignment results.
3. Total dollar expenditure to develop an improvement.
4. Supply and demand for housing, economic activity.
5. Buyers and sellers of particular real estate and the transactions that occur among them.
6. A lease in which an intermediate, or sandwich, leaseholder is the lessee of one party and the lessor of another.
7. Zoning regulations that designate the distance a building must be set back from the front, rear, and sides of the property lines.
8. Right or interest in property.
9. Type of market are characterized by homogeneous land use. e.g., apt., commercial, industrial, agricultural

10. The period over time which a structure may be competitive in the market.
11. Rights to the use and profits of the underground portion of a designated property.
12. A promise made in exchange for another promise.
13. When the government regulates the land use for the good of the public.
14. Total floor area of a building, excluding unenclosed area, measured from the exterior of the walls of the above-grade area.
15. A voluntary legal agreement that becomes part of the chain of title thereby protecting a historic, archaeological, or cultural resource.
16. Depriving an abutting owner of the inherent rights of ingress and to egress from the highway or street.
17. Public regulation of the character and extent of real estate use though police power.

A. Loss of Access
B. Zoning
C. Economic life
D. Bilateral contract
E. Real Estate Market
F. Subsurface rights
G. Estate
H. Gross Building Area
I. Sandwich lease
J. Elements of comparison
K. Cost
L. Preservation Easement
M. District
N. Police power
O. Economic Forces
P. Setback
Q. Competence

H. Find the hidden words. The words have been placed horizontally, vertically, or diagonally. When you locate a word, draw an ellipse around it.

K	B	T	L	E	G	A	L	P	E	R	M	I	S	S	I	B	I	L	I	T	Y	I
P	W	A	J	B	E	T	E	N	A	N	C	Y	I	N	C	O	M	M	O	N	C	G
X	P	X	A	N	Q	H	J	I	I	T	R	L	R	P	D	O	U	S	Y	Q	O	J
X	N	A	G	T	Q	F	V	U	G	A	C	F	X	A	W	L	M	Y	G	D	S	V
F	D	T	W	P	S	L	F	B	C	R	D	N	W	Z	C	A	M	E	N	I	T	Y
U	T	I	Z	B	N	O	B	E	X	P	O	S	U	R	E	T	I	M	E	T	A	O
Q	U	O	T	E	N	T	G	U	S	C	A	R	C	I	T	Y	P	H	C	I	P	T
S	N	N	N	S	J	J	E	X	T	Q	T	E	I	Z	R	A	A	S	U	R	P	S
Y	E	N	E	I	G	H	B	O	R	H	O	O	D	P	H	E	K	I	I	J	R	X
V	X	Y	T	X	M	A	R	K	E	T	V	A	L	U	E	L	A	T	I	H	O	S
K	P	C	M	O	N	E	T	A	R	Y	P	O	L	I	C	Y	I	E	X	U	A	X
K	P	H	Y	S	I	C	A	L	P	O	S	S	I	B	I	L	I	T	Y	O	C	O
U	P	M	R	E	M	A	I	N	D	E	R	I	N	T	E	R	E	S	T	K	H	Q
V	N	X	F	O	Y	A	V	Z	Y	S	U	K	S	T	A	B	I	L	I	T	Y	L
O	R	E	H	A	B	I	L	I	T	A	T	I	O	N	Q	S	S	B	G	C	W	W
S	N	F	I	N	A	L	O	P	I	N	I	O	N	O	F	V	A	L	U	E	G	A

1. A tangible or intangible benefit of real property that enhances its attractiveness or increases the satisfaction of the user.
2. Process of dividing one number (dividend) by another number (divisor) produces this result.
3. Complementary land uses; inhabitants, buildings, or business enterprises.
4. an estimate of replacement cost of a structure, less depreciation, plus land value.
5. The opinion of value derived from the reconciliation of value indications and stated in the appraisal report
6. Right of government to raise revenue through assessments on valuable goods, products, and rights.
7. Person who is entitled to an estate after a prior estate or interest has expired
8. Guiding control of the money supply in the economy.
9. Estate owned by 2 or more persons, each of whom has an equal undivided interest. Unlike Joint Tenancy and Tenancy by Entirety, No right of survivorship.
10. Stage in market area's life cycle. The market area experiences equilibrium without market gains or losses.
11. The most probable price at which real estate would sell.
12. land that is improved so that is ready to be used for a specific purpose.
13. One of the four criteria the highest and best use of a property must meet.
14. The time of property remains on the market.
15. The present or anticipated undersupply of an item relative to the demand for it. Conditions of scarcity contribute to value.
16. One of the criteria for highest and best use of a property must meet.
17. The repair and restoration of existing improvements that are in poor condition to a state that makes the property competitive again.

A. Cost Approach
B. Physical Possibility
C. Market Value
D. Exposure Time
E. Rehabilitation
F. Quotent
G. Site
H. Legal Permissibility
I. Remainder interest
J. Amenity
K. Stability
L. Taxation
M. Neighborhood
N. Final Opinion of Value
O. Monetary Policy
P. Scarcity
Q. Tenancy in Common

I. Find the hidden words. The words have been placed horizontally, vertically, or diagonally. When you locate a word, draw an ellipse around it.

C	U	U	D	U	F	D	E	S	K	R	E	V	I	E	W	K	S	N	D	C	X	D
O	C	T	T	S	K	U	C	J	E	E	Z	N	Z	A	L	Y	C	B	X	L	E	O
M	N	Z	R	E	F	S	T	H	T	M	Y	G	A	V	A	S	O	I	H	G	J	P
P	R	N	P	F	Y	H	R	W	A	A	I	T	M	O	B	N	P	S	B	T	R	E
E	W	B	I	U	Z	J	E	Q	X	I	C	F	Y	J	O	L	E	V	E	T	E	R
T	G	R	W	L	S	H	N	P	A	N	I	L	M	Y	R	D	O	H	E	F	A	A
E	F	Q	F	L	P	X	D	M	T	D	E	T	K	I	X	P	F	G	L	P	L	T
N	F	N	M	I	S	P	S	N	I	E	L	E	S	S	O	R	W	V	S	V	P	I
C	L	L	L	F	L	P	J	V	O	R	B	M	X	A	H	E	O	W	X	R	R	N
E	P	M	G	E	N	U	R	J	N	W	W	G	L	R	P	P	R	S	J	Y	O	G
K	D	M	B	T	E	A	M	W	D	I	L	H	A	Q	O	A	K	A	A	O	P	I
E	R	E	A	L	E	S	T	A	T	E	M	A	R	K	E	T	A	T	B	O	E	N
P	J	Y	V	A	L	U	E	I	N	E	X	C	H	A	N	G	E	E	L	X	R	C
F	Q	U	A	N	T	I	T	A	T	I	V	E	A	N	A	L	Y	S	I	S	T	O
Q	I	C	A	P	I	T	A	L	I	Z	A	T	I	O	N	R	A	T	E	U	Y	M
S	P	H	Y	S	I	C	A	L	P	O	S	S	I	B	I	L	I	T	Y	L	Q	E

1. Price an economic good will attract in the competitive market.
2. The state of having the requisite or adequate ability or qualities to perform the specific assignment and produce credible assignment results.
3. The period of time over which a structure may reasonably be expected to perform the function for which it was designed.
4. The type and extent of research and analyses in appraisal or appraisal review assignment.
5. One who conveys the rights of occupancy and use to others under lease agreement.
6. Buyers and sellers of particular real estate and the transactions that occur among them.
7. Analyzing value of a property based on numerical data.
8. comprises of all costs required to construct and market the product as land alone or with improvements.
9. Income derived from the operation of a business or real property
10. A future possessor read interest in real estate that is given to a third-party and matures upon the termination of a limited or determinable be.
11. An appraisal review in which the reviewer's scope of work does not include an inspection of the subject property.
12. One of the criteria for highest and best use of a property must meet.
13. Right of government to raise revenue through assessments on valuable goods, products, and rights.
14. Any rate used to convert income into value.
15. The interests, benefits, and rights inherent in ownership of real estate.
16. A series of related changes brought about by a chain of causes and effects.

A. Capitalization Rate
B. Remainder
C. Operating Income
D. Competence
E. Taxation
F. Desk Review
G. Real Estate Market
H. Physical Possibility
I. Quantitative Analysis
J. Real Property
K. Scope of Work
L. Value in Exchange
M. Lessor
N. Labor
O. Useful life
P. Trends

J. Find the hidden words. The words have been placed horizontally, vertically, or diagonally. When you locate a word, draw an ellipse around it.

V	Z	P	N	A	D	V	E	R	S	E	P	O	S	S	E	S	S	I	O	N	W	W
S	U	P	R	A	S	U	R	F	A	C	E	R	I	G	H	T	S	J	D	A	X	C
G	T	A	S	V	R	K	V	W	L	U	W	G	S	I	B	I	D	L	E	S	N	W
N	O	T	L	I	X	L	O	Q	F	D	T	J	A	H	R	N	X	I	P	S	E	E
A	K	Y	X	G	P	Z	L	U	D	D	D	R	N	F	S	A	W	T	R	E	T	J
I	U	K	C	H	F	L	U	G	D	C	T	P	O	E	K	X	H	T	E	M	L	T
X	Q	H	E	M	O	T	N	R	E	N	O	V	A	T	I	O	N	O	C	B	E	H
N	O	M	A	R	K	E	T	V	A	C	A	N	C	Y	P	O	Q	R	I	L	A	Z
L	H	F	D	U	Y	D	A	P	L	A	T	S	L	Z	L	W	A	A	A	A	S	N
O	E	N	C	U	M	B	R	A	N	C	E	Y	G	Q	X	Z	C	L	T	G	E	F
C	D	H	V	I	Z	S	Y	P	O	L	I	C	E	P	O	W	E	R	I	E	X	Q
P	M	U	E	H	Z	H	L	D	J	P	F	F	H	S	Q	O	G	I	O	T	O	H
C	O	M	M	E	R	C	I	A	L	P	R	O	P	E	R	T	Y	G	N	Z	Q	Q
W	F	E	M	A	R	K	E	T	V	A	L	U	E	B	W	Y	P	H	E	A	N	I
W	K	R	E	M	A	I	N	D	E	R	I	N	T	E	R	E	S	T	F	J	G	Y
Z	N	N	J	P	R	E	S	E	N	T	V	A	L	U	E	X	A	S	U	K	R	G

1. Involuntary transfer of property takes place when a party makes a property claim by taking possession over a period of years.
2. Created intentionally by property owner's actions. i.e. mortgage
3. The combining of 2 or more parcels into one ownership (tract).
4. Rights pertaining to properties abutting a lake or pond.
5. Income-producing property such as office and retail buildings.
6. In appraising, a loss in property value from any cause
7. Any claim or liability that affects our limits the title to property.
8. The overall vacancy rate that occurs as a result of the interaction of supply and demand of a particular property type in a particular region or market.
9. The most probable price at which real estate would sell.
10. A lease in which the landlord passes on all expenses to the tenant.
11. The process in which older structures or historic buildings are modernized, remodeled, or restored.
12. The value of a future payment or series of future payments discounted to the current date or to time period zero.
13. Person who is entitled to an estate after a prior estate or interest has expired
14. Right to undisturbed use and control of designated air space above a specific land area within stated elevations.
15. When the government regulates the land use for the good of the public.
16. A plan, map, or chart of a city, town, section, or subdivision indicating the location and boundaries of individual properties.

A. Remainder interest
B. Assemblage
C. Voluntary liens
D. Plat
E. Net Lease
F. Encumbrance
G. Depreciation
H. Commercial Property
I. Market Value
J. Renovation
K. Littoral rights
L. Police power
M. Present Value
N. Supra surface rights
O. Adverse possession
P. Market Vacancy

K. Find the hidden words. The words have been placed horizontally, vertically, or diagonally. When you locate a word, draw an ellipse around it.

C	G	D	P	R	M	A	R	K	E	T	A	B	I	L	I	T	Y	Y	V	X	Y	C
X	L	E	U	L	H	F	R	Y	W	F	J	W	M	Q	I	L	D	H	A	Z	R	F
K	I	M	P	L	I	E	D	C	O	N	T	R	A	C	T	Q	E	S	P	M	E	Y
W	Y	R	X	O	G	I	L	E	A	N	J	T	X	S	I	V	O	L	P	X	C	G
T	N	G	F	V	H	O	Y	T	S	G	G	L	H	N	I	T	H	Y	U	Q	L	D
A	L	H	P	V	W	C	J	J	G	W	O	C	T	V	G	E	J	R	R	L	A	E
C	A	K	R	L	A	E	M	I	N	E	N	T	D	O	M	A	I	N	T	T	M	E
G	X	L	K	K	Y	P	O	R	A	N	G	E	O	F	V	A	L	U	E	P	A	D
U	W	V	L	X	E	L	D	L	E	I	N	T	E	S	T	A	T	E	N	R	T	W
E	E	N	Q	B	A	J	L	I	S	P	E	N	D	E	N	S	Z	B	A	W	I	W
Q	P	T	W	V	S	O	E	T	E	S	T	A	T	E	X	Z	W	G	N	Z	O	M
Y	M	A	R	K	E	T	P	A	R	T	I	C	I	P	A	N	T	S	C	Y	N	K
S	L	F	H	Q	M	V	S	V	H	P	S	A	F	E	R	A	T	E	E	T	H	J
A	L	N	R	T	E	E	H	B	P	B	X	A	C	C	R	E	T	I	O	N	Z	N
P	E	R	S	O	N	A	L	R	E	P	R	E	S	E	N	T	A	T	I	V	E	F
V	P	E	R	P	T	R	Q	R	N	W	P	E	M	B	L	E	M	E	N	T	S	F

1. Annual crops and plantings such as corn, wheat, and vegetables.
2. Any method of bringing wasted natural resources into productive use.
3. Written, legal instrument that conveys an estate or interest in real property to someone else, assuming it is executed and delivered.
4. In final reconciliation, the range in which the final market value opinion of a property may fall; usually stated as the interval between a high and low value limit.
5. The condition of dying with a valid will.
6. Something that has been added or appended to a property and has since become an inherent part of the property.
7. A right granted or taken for the construction, maintenance, and operation of the highway.
8. The right of government to take private property for public use upon payment of just compensation.
9. The relative desirability of a property in comparison with similar or competing properties in the area.
10. Ann agreement that is presumed to exist because of the parties' actions.
11. Legal term signifying pending litigation that can affect ownership title to real estate.
12. An increase in dry land created by the gradual accumulation of waterborne solid material over formerly riparian land.
13. An individual or other legal person designated in a will to settle the estate of a deceased person.
14. The condition of dying without a will.
15. The minimum rate of return on invested capital.
16. The parties involved in the transfer of property rights. Includes buyers, sellers, lessors, lessees, and brokers and their agents.

A. Marketability
D. Market Participants
G. Range of Value
J. Implied contract
M. Lis Pendens
P. Accretion
B. Reclamation
E. Safe Rate
H. Appurtenance
K. Eminent Domain
N. Deed
C. Intestate
F. Testate
I. Personal Representative
L. Highway Easement
O. Emblements

L. Find the hidden words. The words have been placed horizontally, vertically, or diagonally. When you locate a word, draw an ellipse around it.

R	E	P	L	A	C	E	M	E	N	T	A	L	L	O	W	A	N	C	E	U	R	W
Y	O	G	U	W	L	O	Y	K	T	I	S	T	R	I	C	J	H	I	C	I	E	Q
X	F	D	S	T	E	P	U	P	D	E	P	R	E	C	I	A	T	I	O	N	M	X
D	P	S	J	X	S	R	C	O	K	K	D	D	B	V	D	C	Z	F	G	V	O	K
W	W	Z	W	A	S	H	O	E	P	G	C	E	D	Z	T	L	J	U	R	E	D	G
V	P	N	C	F	O	E	I	G	F	B	O	S	E	F	C	K	M	L	I	S	E	G
Y	H	P	K	U	R	T	B	V	L	H	L	I	K	P	M	M	V	L	E	T	L	Q
X	U	R	U	E	A	S	E	M	E	N	T	R	O	T	C	N	P	T	K	M	I	B
Z	T	M	C	O	M	P	E	T	E	N	C	E	K	E	K	J	R	A	K	E	N	U
F	R	I	C	T	I	O	N	A	L	V	A	C	A	N	C	Y	T	K	A	N	G	J
S	A	V	U	L	A	S	S	E	M	B	L	A	G	E	B	S	J	I	Y	T	T	P
N	G	O	I	N	G	C	O	N	C	E	R	N	V	A	L	U	E	N	P	V	D	S
V	C	O	N	T	R	I	B	U	T	O	R	Y	V	A	L	U	E	G	I	A	G	D
I	N	T	E	R	N	A	L	R	A	T	E	O	F	R	E	T	U	R	N	L	R	U
P	O	T	E	N	T	I	A	L	G	R	O	S	S	I	N	C	O	M	E	U	L	O
S	U	R	P	L	U	S	P	R	O	D	U	C	T	I	V	I	T	Y	Y	E	Z	K

1. One who conveys the rights of occupancy and use to others under lease agreement.
2. The entire taking of the full real property interest of a parcel for public use under the power of eminent domain; requires the payment of compensation.
3. An allowance that provides for the periodic replacement of building components that wear out more rapidly than the building itself.
4. The change in the value of a property as a whole, resulting from the addition or deletion of a property component.
5. Value to a particular individual. The present worth of anticipated future benefits.
6. The readjustment of the value of an appreciated asset for tax purposes upon inheritance.
7. Net income that is left after the 4 agents of production have been paid.
8. The total income attributable to real property at full occupancy before vacancy and operating expenses are deducted.
9. The combining of 2 or more parcels into one ownership (tract).
10. Purchaser's wish for an item to satisfy human needs or individual wants beyond essential life-support needs.
11. The right to use another's land for a stated purpose.
12. The annualized yield or rate of return on capital that is generated or capable of being generated within an investment or portfolio over a period of ownership.
13. A type of renovation that involves modification or updating of existing improvements.
14. The state of having the requisite or adequate ability or qualities to perform the specific assignment and produce credible assignment results.
15. When the value of a business plus the amount of real property is sought.
16. The amount of vacant space needed in a market for its orderly operation.

A. Remodeling
D. Going concern value
G. Replacement Allowance
J. Step Up Depreciation
M. Full Taking
P. Assemblage

B. Easement
E. Surplus Productivity
H. Contributory Value
K. Lessor
N. Internal Rate of Return

C. Potential Gross Income
F. Investment Value
I. Frictional Vacancy
L. Competence
O. Desire

M. Find the hidden words. The words have been placed horizontally, vertically, or diagonally. When you locate a word, draw an ellipse around it.

B	C	E	U	V	L	E	S	S	O	R	D	U	H	C	N	X	H	C	O	S	R	B
A	W	O	P	E	R	A	T	I	N	G	E	X	P	E	N	S	E	R	A	T	I	O
X	P	H	Q	V	O	P	E	R	A	T	I	N	G	S	T	A	T	E	M	E	N	T
B	O	Q	C	A	P	I	T	A	L	I	Z	A	T	I	O	N	I	O	H	M	X	V
A	A	Q	E	E	X	M	S	M	A	R	K	E	T	A	N	A	L	Y	S	I	S	H
B	F	Y	A	V	O	L	U	N	T	A	R	Y	L	I	E	N	S	E	P	Y	C	K
O	B	N	E	I	G	H	B	O	R	H	O	O	D	C	V	U	L	J	S	H	M	L
R	E	M	O	D	E	L	I	N	G	T	V	A	A	M	B	N	C	N	X	C	K	E
I	F	L	X	B	V	O	I	D	A	B	L	E	C	O	N	T	R	A	C	T	J	B
K	L	X	Y	V	T	F	G	E	V	M	P	Z	H	O	G	E	X	O	D	B	W	P
M	P	A	I	R	E	D	D	A	T	A	A	N	A	L	Y	S	I	S	L	R	X	M
O	A	M	R	Y	L	B	H	X	C	F	T	V	H	C	A	S	H	F	L	O	W	X
R	D	E	S	K	T	O	P	A	P	P	R	A	I	S	A	L	L	N	L	X	U	Z
E	L	E	M	E	N	T	S	O	F	C	O	M	P	A	R	I	S	O	N	G	Z	M
B	O	M	A	S	T	A	N	D	A	R	D	F	Q	U	O	T	E	N	T	Z	N	V
K	D	E	B	T	C	O	V	E	R	A	G	E	R	A	T	I	O	N	E	V	S	S

1. Two or more sales are compared to derive an indication of the size of the adjustment for a single characteristic.
2. The ratio of total operating expenses to effective gross income
3. Relevant characteristics used to compare and adjust the property prices.
4. Complementary land uses; inhabitants, buildings, or business enterprises.
5. The conversion of income into value.
6. One who conveys the rights of occupancy and use to others under lease agreement.
7. Ratio of NOI to annual debt service.
8. Technically valid but gives one or more parties the power to legally void the agreement and thus cancel performance.
9. Process of dividing one number (dividend) by another number (divisor) produces this result.
10. A type of renovation that involves modification or updating of existing improvements.
11. An appraisal report in which the appraiser's scope of work does not include an inspection of the subject property or comparables.
12. The periodic income attributable to the interests in real property.
13. Created intentionally by property owner's actions. i.e. mortgage
14. A financial statement that reflects the gross revenues, expenses, and net operating profit or loss of an investment over a fixed period.
15. Study of real estate market conditions for specific types of property.
16. The standard method of measurement for office buildings as defined by the Building Owners and Managers Association.

A. Debt coverage ratio
B. Operating Expense Ratio
C. Lessor
D. Cash Flow
E. Desktop Appraisal
F. Elements of comparison
G. Paired data analysis
H. Capitalization
I. Quotent
J. Operating Statement
K. BOMA Standard
L. Market Analysis
M. Neighborhood
N. Voluntary liens
O. Voidable contract
P. Remodeling

N. Find the hidden words. The words have been placed horizontally, vertically, or diagonally. When you locate a word, draw an ellipse around it.

E	I	U	R	N	F	G	F	I	X	E	D	E	X	P	E	N	S	E	I	I	C	S
C	O	M	M	E	R	C	I	A	L	P	R	O	P	E	R	T	Y	D	V	N	I	U
Y	D	R	I	V	E	B	Y	A	P	P	R	A	I	S	A	L	Y	E	B	V	Y	F
A	S	O	T	M	E	S	M	O	M	N	O	A	X	C	P	S	J	T	Q	O	W	Y
R	N	Q	E	H	Q	X	E	O	X	I	P	Y	U	Z	D	L	W	E	P	L	A	Y
A	R	L	E	G	A	L	D	E	S	C	R	I	P	T	I	O	N	R	T	U	R	U
O	E	S	T	A	T	E	I	N	L	A	N	D	R	X	G	F	G	I	O	N	M	L
C	H	I	F	Y	P	F	O	V	I	Z	O	F	Z	C	D	C	L	O	H	T	S	N
A	O	R	A	L	A	P	P	R	A	I	S	A	L	R	E	P	O	R	T	A	L	X
X	A	U	W	Q	Q	S	R	Y	I	I	W	N	Q	L	U	F	V	A	R	R	E	B
C	R	R	E	P	O	O	U	C	O	S	T	D	T	Y	B	L	E	T	K	Y	N	I
L	B	Z	O	V	I	N	T	E	R	I	M	U	S	E	E	K	R	I	G	L	G	I
M	L	M	A	R	K	E	T	V	A	L	U	E	R	H	G	L	V	O	Y	I	T	U
G	I	J	U	S	T	C	O	M	P	E	N	S	A	T	I	O	N	N	P	E	H	H
B	B	X	S	I	N	G	L	E	F	A	M	I	L	Y	H	O	U	S	E	N	N	E
K	G	L	J	G	D	J	D	W	C	F	Y	H	A	Y	G	C	D	D	W	S	M	M

1. Impairment of condition; because of depreciation that reflects the loss in value due to wear and tear, disintegration, use in service, and the action of the elements.
2. The dwelling that is designated for occupancy by one family.
3. A description of land that identifies the real estate according to a system established or approved by law.
4. Income-producing property such as office and retail buildings.
5. The most probable price at which real estate would sell.
6. A transaction in which the buyers and sellers of a product act independently and have no relationship to each other.
7. Created by law, rather than by choice. i.e. property tax lien.
8. In condemnation, the amount of loss for which a property owner is compensated when his or her property is taken.
9. Temporary use to which a site or improved property is put until it is ready to be put to its future highest and best use.
10. A report that is transmitted orally.
11. Total dollar expenditure to develop an improvement.
12. Operating expenses that generally do not vary with occupancy and that prudent management will pay whether the properties occupied or vacant.
13. An appraisal report in which the scope of work includes an exterior-only viewing of the subject property.
14. The degree, nature, or extent of interest that a person has in land.

A. Commercial Property
B. Arms Length
C. Interim use
D. Cost
E. Involuntary liens
F. Deterioration
G. Fixed Expense
H. Market Value
I. Oral Appraisal Report
J. Drive by Appraisal
K. Just Compensation
L. Legal Description
M. Single Family House
N. Estate in land

O. Find the hidden words. The words have been placed horizontally, vertically, or diagonally. When you locate a word, draw an ellipse around it.

G	M	J	E	A	V	U	X	N	Y	Q	G	G	P	R	O	F	O	R	M	A	Z	X
S	I	N	G	L	E	F	A	M	I	L	Y	H	O	U	S	E	D	E	O	X	D	P
T	I	N	T	E	R	I	M	U	S	E	T	W	L	Y	H	Q	A	Y	Y	T	R	R
X	A	Y	Z	C	T	C	O	J	Y	E	A	S	E	M	E	N	T	P	H	H	B	U
Y	J	Z	Y	P	I	Y	J	X	M	T	N	F	S	T	F	T	Y	O	E	Z	O	S
I	Z	Y	D	C	T	L	J	U	Q	E	L	O	S	X	N	R	R	Z	Z	A	E	A
S	I	A	O	E	L	M	X	J	I	P	Z	A	O	C	I	M	L	Z	O	K	V	L
W	D	P	O	G	E	I	H	Y	H	G	N	B	R	Z	O	Z	H	G	N	I	L	V
T	Q	E	C	H	Y	P	O	T	H	I	C	A	T	I	O	N	A	F	I	R	E	A
J	F	P	E	R	C	E	N	T	A	G	E	L	E	A	S	E	L	B	N	S	H	G
D	D	A	C	T	U	P	R	O	X	I	M	I	T	Y	D	A	M	A	G	E	F	E
X	N	E	L	E	M	E	N	T	S	O	F	C	O	M	P	A	R	I	S	O	N	V
Q	C	Q	U	A	N	T	I	T	A	T	I	V	E	A	N	A	L	Y	S	I	S	A
V	N	A	L	C	S	E	C	O	N	D	A	R	Y	D	A	T	A	B	G	C	O	L
Q	F	R	A	O	L	E	A	S	E	H	O	L	D	I	N	T	E	R	E	S	T	U
J	P	E	Y	M	A	R	K	E	T	P	A	R	T	I	C	I	P	A	N	T	S	E

1. The dwelling that is designated for occupancy by one family.
2. Analyzing value of a property based on numerical data.
3. The tenant's possessory interest created by a lease.
4. A borrower has possession of the property.
5. Information that is not gathered in its original form by the analyst.
6. One who conveys the rights of occupancy and use to others under lease agreement.
7. Combination of all elements that constitute proof of ownership.
8. The right to use another's land for a stated purpose.
9. A projected income and expense statement for proposed development.
10. The parties involved in the transfer of property rights. Includes buyers, sellers, lessors, lessees, and brokers and their agents.
11. Temporary use to which a site or improved property is put until it is ready to be put to its future highest and best use.
12. The price expected for a whole property (e.g., a house) or a part of a property (e.g., a plumbing fixture) that is removed from the premises usually for use elsewhere.
13. Damages that is caused by the remainder's proximity to the improvement being constructed.
14. Relevant characteristics used to compare and adjust the property prices.
15. Public regulation of the character and extent of real estate use though police power.
16. Most commonly found in retail business. This lease has a base rent which is fixed and an excess rent, this is most commonly based on the percentage of the sales.

A. Percentage lease
D. Easement
G. Title
J. Salvage Value
M. Zoning
P. Leasehold Interest
B. Pro Forma
E. Quantitative Analysis
H. Elements of comparison
K. Secondary Data
N. Interim use
C. Lessor
F. Proximity Damage
I. Hypothication
L. Market Participants
O. Single Family House

P. Find the hidden words. The words have been placed horizontally, vertically, or diagonally. When you locate a word, draw an ellipse around it.

S	I	T	E	I	M	P	R	O	V	E	M	E	N	T	S	R	E	P	O	R	T	E
T	W	E	U	U	F	R	I	C	T	I	O	N	A	L	V	A	C	A	N	C	Y	M
V	L	Y	E	M	O	F	W	D	O	Z	F	R	Q	S	G	E	F	Z	E	R	Y	I
L	A	P	P	U	R	T	E	N	A	N	C	E	A	N	J	E	B	M	Y	U	U	N
Y	B	T	L	E	A	S	E	E	A	D	W	T	O	I	T	B	D	A	B	J	S	E
Y	L	R	O	R	F	P	C	X	Z	Y	Q	P	D	J	D	Y	J	R	D	T	B	N
D	X	H	O	U	S	I	N	G	S	T	A	R	T	S	M	S	C	K	E	I	L	T
K	C	A	P	I	T	A	L	I	Z	A	T	I	O	N	R	A	T	E	C	V	X	D
W	H	Y	E	R	F	Q	H	F	D	T	L	C	Q	H	B	E	F	T	L	P	E	O
U	S	E	F	U	L	L	I	F	E	F	V	E	S	K	A	F	U	A	I	M	T	M
O	G	F	U	U	F	A	R	A	M	M	D	N	R	D	Q	H	S	B	N	H	E	A
R	Y	C	V	F	Q	M	A	R	K	E	T	R	E	N	T	C	E	I	E	X	Y	I
Y	W	T	W	S	Z	Y	Y	Q	L	H	J	E	T	D	B	S	E	L	P	T	S	N
M	N	H	E	F	F	E	C	T	I	V	E	D	A	T	E	C	Q	I	D	J	O	D
C	V	T	B	O	P	K	Q	Y	D	S	I	C	V	X	H	T	I	T	S	E	Y	Y
O	D	S	U	B	S	U	R	F	A	C	E	R	I	G	H	T	S	Y	F	L	J	L

1. Something that has been added or appended to a property and has since become an inherent part of the property.
2. The relative desirability of a property in comparison with similar or competing properties in the area.
3. Amount a particular purchaser agrees to pay and a particular seller agrees to accept under the circumstances surrounding their transaction.
4. The date on which the analyses, opinions, and advice in an appraisal, review, or consulting service apply.
5. The right of government to take private property for public use upon payment of just compensation.
6. The period of time over which a structure may reasonably be expected to perform the function for which it was designed.
7. The most probable rent the property should bring in a competitive and open market reflecting all conditions and restrictions of the lease agreement.
8. Any rate used to convert income into value.
9. A contract in which the rights to use and occupy land or structures are transferred by the owner to another for a specified period of time in return for specified rent.
10. Newly constructed housing units; includes both single-family and multifamily domiciles.
11. The amount of vacant space needed in a market for its orderly operation.
12. Any communication, written or oral, of an appraisal or appraisal review that is transmitted to the client upon completion of an assignment.
13. A stage of diminishing demand in a market areas life cycle.
14. Rights to the use and profits of the underground portion of a designated property.
15. Improvements on and off the site that make it suitable for its intended use or development.

A. Marketability
E. Report
I. Lease
M. Useful life
B. Decline
F. Market Rent
J. Price
N. Appurtenance
C. Site Improvements
G. Subsurface rights
K. Housing Starts
O. Capitalization Rate
D. Effective Date
H. Frictional Vacancy
L. Eminent Domain

Q. Find the hidden words. The words have been placed horizontally, vertically, or diagonally. When you locate a word, draw an ellipse around it.

U	B	V	O	K	N	I	I	N	T	E	S	T	A	T	E	L	P	C	F	O	Q	B
S	F	L	B	A	L	A	N	C	E	B	K	C	O	S	T	K	R	J	U	W	U	D
U	R	P	O	T	E	N	T	I	A	L	G	R	O	S	S	I	N	C	O	M	E	E
R	K	P	R	E	S	E	R	V	A	T	I	O	N	E	A	S	E	M	E	N	T	E
F	P	R	O	X	I	M	I	T	Y	D	A	M	A	G	E	F	E	G	P	V	C	D
A	G	Y	W	W	H	D	Y	R	A	T	E	O	F	R	E	T	U	R	N	O	N	M
C	R	Q	F	A	I	R	M	A	R	K	E	T	V	A	L	U	E	D	D	O	W	S
E	D	C	O	R	A	L	A	P	P	R	A	I	S	A	L	R	E	P	O	R	T	V
R	A	P	E	R	C	E	N	T	A	G	E	A	D	J	U	S	T	M	E	N	T	S
I	T	E	S	T	A	T	E	A	P	P	R	A	I	S	A	L	R	C	Z	F	B	X
G	A	H	D	E	Z	H	C	H	S	F	Z	I	E	X	L	V	D	W	D	F	R	N
H	V	I	M	D	N	A	B	P	W	X	O	R	G	G	Y	H	K	I	S	J	A	W
T	W	R	J	Y	E	J	F	N	C	O	N	T	R	I	B	U	T	I	O	N	F	W
S	Z	K	K	E	Z	R	A	M	H	B	I	S	W	I	Q	Y	R	N	O	T	O	K
W	Q	Q	Z	Q	C	F	I	Q	W	B	N	Q	A	S	W	V	T	H	T	I	G	C
Z	E	Z	J	T	A	N	W	Q	T	R	G	L	C	T	T	E	I	O	V	D	Q	E

1. A voluntary legal agreement that becomes part of the chain of title thereby protecting a historic, archaeological, or cultural resource.
2. The total income attributable to real property at full occupancy before vacancy and operating expenses are deducted.
3. Written, legal instrument that conveys an estate or interest in real property to someone else, assuming it is executed and delivered.
4. The act or process of developing an opinion of value.
5. The ratio of income or yield to the original investment.
6. Public regulation of the character and extent of real estate use though police power.
7. Total dollar expenditure to develop an improvement.
8. Land, water, and anything attached to the land-either naturally or placed by human hands.
9. A report that is transmitted orally.
10. The price at which the property would change hands between a willing buyer and a willing seller and both having reasonable knowledge of relevant facts.
11. Principle that real property value is created and sustained when contrasting, opposing, or interacting elements are in a state of equilibrium.
12. Damages that is caused by the remainder's proximity to the improvement being constructed.
13. The condition of dying with a valid will.
14. The value of a particular component is measured in terms of the amount it adds to the value of the whole property.
15. Adjustments for differences between the subject and comparable properties expressed as a percentage of the sale price of the comparable property.
16. The condition of dying without a will.

A. Balance
B. Intestate
C. Rate of return
D. Zoning
E. Contribution
F. Preservation Easement
G. Potential Gross Income
H. Oral Appraisal Report
I. Proximity Damage
J. Surface rights
K. Deed
L. Percentage Adjustments
M. Appraisal
N. Fair Market Value
O. Cost
P. Testate

R. Find the hidden words. The words have been placed horizontally, vertically, or diagonally. When you locate a word, draw an ellipse around it.

Q	E	N	T	R	E	P	R	E	N	E	U	R	I	A	L	P	R	O	F	I	T	F
H	X	B	V	T	D	E	S	I	R	E	H	A	G	E	T	Q	M	Z	H	Q	J	E
V	U	G	H	Z	P	Q	C	C	P	Y	E	N	C	L	V	N	U	C	V	U	Y	R
C	J	S	K	G	J	C	G	E	B	E	Q	I	W	Y	J	G	R	H	Z	O	T	E
I	W	T	C	H	V	Z	F	F	O	E	S	C	H	E	A	T	F	E	S	T	X	O
L	I	T	T	O	R	A	L	R	I	G	H	T	S	O	J	G	Z	V	K	E	X	Z
C	O	N	D	E	M	N	A	T	I	O	N	W	U	P	X	E	N	K	N	N	Z	X
X	C	A	W	R	E	H	O	U	S	I	N	G	S	T	A	R	T	S	B	T	G	H
Y	O	W	Q	K	D	E	A	U	F	I	S	C	A	L	P	O	L	I	C	Y	R	I
A	S	Z	P	R	I	M	A	R	Y	D	A	T	A	X	U	L	W	W	H	S	Y	V
R	T	P	O	T	E	N	T	I	A	L	G	R	O	S	S	I	N	C	O	M	E	U
A	G	G	U	W	S	X	E	F	E	X	P	O	S	U	R	E	T	I	M	E	T	O
L	A	I	T	E	N	A	N	C	Y	I	N	C	O	M	M	O	N	M	Q	K	W	K
W	B	N	A	Z	D	C	O	S	T	T	O	C	U	R	E	P	A	U	W	J	I	L
O	P	E	R	A	T	I	N	G	E	X	P	E	N	S	E	R	A	T	I	O	G	B
Q	P	A	I	R	E	D	D	A	T	A	A	N	A	L	Y	S	I	S	E	X	J	E

1. Two or more sales are compared to derive an indication of the size of the adjustment for a single characteristic.
2. Estate owned by 2 or more persons, each of whom has an equal undivided interest. Unlike Joint Tenancy and Tenancy by Entirety, No right of survivorship.
3. Management of government receipts and expenditures.
4. Process of dividing one number (dividend) by another number (divisor) produces this result.
5. Rights pertaining to properties abutting a lake or pond.
6. A market-derived figure that represents the amount an entrepreneur receives for their contribution.
7. Newly constructed housing units; includes both single-family and multifamily domiciles.
8. The ratio of total operating expenses to effective gross income
9. The cost to restore an item of deferred maintenance to new or reasonably new condition.
10. Total dollar expenditure to develop an improvement.
11. Going to the State. The process that should a property be abandoned, it reverts back to the state.
12. Information that is gathered in its original form by the analyst.
13. The total income attributable to real property at full occupancy before vacancy and operating expenses are deducted.
14. The time of property remains on the market.
15. Method by which government can take private property.
16. Purchaser's wish for an item to satisfy human needs or individual wants beyond essential life-support needs.

A. Escheat
B. Cost to Cure
C. Quotient
D. Condemnation
E. Operating Expense Ratio
F. Desire
G. Fiscal Policy
H. Littoral rights
I. Tenancy in Common
J. Cost
K. Primary Data
L. Potential Gross Income
M. Housing Starts
N. Exposure Time
O. Entrepreneurial profit
P. Paired data analysis

S. Find the hidden words. The words have been placed horizontally, vertically, or diagonally. When you locate a word, draw an ellipse around it.

B	A	D	V	E	R	S	E	P	O	S	S	E	S	S	I	O	N	T	D	V	D	G
J	I	K	N	L	R	E	C	O	N	C	I	L	I	A	T	I	O	N	K	I	I	C
P	R	E	S	E	R	V	A	T	I	O	N	E	A	S	E	M	E	N	T	N	S	O
D	R	H	C	S	L	I	V	I	N	G	T	R	U	S	T	L	P	V	T	H	C	M
E	M	F	G	S	R	H	S	C	I	W	K	D	F	Z	R	I	R	T	B	E	O	P
T	S	I	C	O	X	S	U	Q	V	E	M	K	E	B	F	A	I	L	I	R	U	E
E	E	Y	Q	R	S	W	J	R	V	Y	V	D	F	D	L	V	M	B	Y	I	N	T
R	G	L	I	F	E	T	E	N	A	N	T	A	K	D	S	V	A	U	L	T	T	E
I	P	W	D	F	R	D	U	F	D	T	Q	M	N	K	C	J	R	V	Y	A	R	N
O	L	C	T	Y	K	R	S	Q	J	G	V	A	V	W	S	N	Y	J	M	N	A	C
R	B	V	T	D	Z	R	E	Q	C	J	V	G	H	R	W	X	D	O	E	C	T	E
A	H	S	A	U	T	I	L	I	T	Y	M	E	E	E	K	P	A	I	X	E	E	Y
T	P	L	A	T	K	G	A	C	E	X	A	S	N	C	U	M	T	K	P	T	I	I
I	I	X	I	R	K	Y	G	S	A	M	E	N	I	T	Y	L	A	V	I	A	A	W
O	Q	I	O	Q	U	F	F	W	J	S	D	T	V	J	M	J	U	H	L	X	D	W
N	W	N	G	Q	G	O	I	N	G	C	O	N	C	E	R	N	V	A	L	U	E	M

1. Information that is gathered in its original form by the analyst.
2. In condemnation, the loss in value to the remainder in a partial taking of property.
3. One who owns an interest in real property for his or her own lifetime.
4. Created by agreement during the property owner's lifetime
5. When the value of a business plus the amount of real property is sought.
6. Involuntary transfer of property takes place when a party makes a property claim by taking possession over a period of years.
7. A tangible or intangible benefit of real property that enhances its attractiveness or increases the satisfaction of the user.
8. The state of having the requisite or adequate ability or qualities to perform the specific assignment and produce credible assignment results.
9. A voluntary legal agreement that becomes part of the chain of title thereby protecting a historic, archaeological, or cultural resource.
10. A plan, map, or chart of a city, town, section, or subdivision indicating the location and boundaries of individual properties.
11. Ability of a product to satisfy a human want, need, or desire.
12. A tax on the right to receive property by inheritance; as distinguished from estate tax.
13. One who conveys the rights of occupancy and use to others under lease agreement.
14. The process of reducing a range of value indications into an appropriate conclusion for that analysis.
15. Impairment of condition; because of depreciation that reflects the loss in value due to wear and tear, disintegration, use in service, and the action of the elements.
16. The yield rate used to convert future payments or receipts into present value; usually considered to be a synonym for yield rate.

A. Inheritance Tax
E. Damages
I. Primary Data
M. Amenity

B. Life tenant
F. Living trust
J. Reconciliation
N. Adverse possession

C. Utility
G. Deterioration
K. Going concern value
O. Discount Rate

D. Lessor
H. Plat
L. Competence
P. Preservation Easement

T. Find the hidden words. The words have been placed horizontally, vertically, or diagonally. When you locate a word, draw an ellipse around it.

A	D	O	O	H	V	X	E	W	U	G	V	Q	J	C	L	Y	F	E	X	O	P	T
C	O	M	M	E	R	C	I	A	L	P	R	O	P	E	R	T	Y	I	Q	N	X	W
Z	T	P	H	Y	S	I	C	A	L	D	E	T	E	R	I	O	R	A	T	I	O	N
U	H	Z	H	N	E	I	G	H	B	O	R	H	O	O	D	E	B	I	S	U	K	I
W	Q	M	S	C	Y	R	B	A	K	L	A	N	D	U	S	E	Y	I	E	C	T	X
P	H	Y	S	I	C	A	L	C	H	A	R	A	C	T	E	R	I	S	T	I	C	S
L	K	F	X	U	Y	A	E	D	Z	Z	W	I	E	B	D	E	U	W	B	B	Y	C
C	B	F	R	E	V	I	T	A	L	I	Z	A	T	I	O	N	S	W	A	V	V	O
P	E	A	R	N	E	S	T	M	O	N	E	Y	V	M	F	G	J	T	C	R	C	N
F	I	N	A	L	O	P	I	N	I	O	N	O	F	V	A	L	U	E	K	W	P	F
D	I	R	E	C	T	C	A	P	I	T	A	L	I	Z	A	T	I	O	N	J	V	O
M	J	S	Y	N	D	I	C	A	T	I	O	N	T	D	C	I	W	Z	H	T	N	R
F	R	Z	I	I	Z	F	X	M	A	R	K	E	T	A	B	I	L	I	T	Y	C	M
O	P	E	R	A	T	I	N	G	E	X	P	E	N	S	E	R	A	T	I	O	E	I
C	O	N	S	E	R	V	A	T	I	O	N	E	A	S	E	M	E	N	T	P	H	T
M	U	P	Y	L	J	I	N	V	E	S	T	M	E	N	T	V	A	L	U	E	A	Y

1. A category of elements of comparison in the sales comparison approach
2. The more a property or its components are in harmony with the surrounding properties or components, the greater the contributory value.
3. A private or public partnership that pools funds for the acquisition and development of real estate projects or other business ventures.
4. Value to a particular individual. The present worth of anticipated future benefits.
5. A method used to convert an estimate of a single year's income expectancy into an indication of value in one direct step
6. The wear and tear that begins with the building is completed and placed into service.
7. The ratio of total operating expenses to effective gross income
8. Complementary land uses; inhabitants, buildings, or business enterprises.

9. An interest in real property restricting future land-use to preservation, conservation, wildlife habitat, or some combination of those uses.
10. The relative desirability of a property in comparison with similar or competing properties in the area.
11. Zoning regulations that designate the distance a building must be set back from the front, rear, and sides of the property lines.
12. The opinion of value derived from the reconciliation of value indications and stated in the appraisal report
13. The employment of a site or holding to produce revenue or other benefits.
14. Part of the purchase price given to bind a bargain.
15. A stage in a market area's life cycle characterized by renewal, redevelopment, modernization, and increasing demand.
16. Income-producing property such as office and retail buildings.

A. Conformity
D. Earnest money
G. Marketability
J. Operating Expense Ratio
M. Physical Deterioration
P. Conservation Easement

B. Final Opinion of Value
E. Physical Characteristics
H. Direct Capitalization
K. Investment Value
N. Neighborhood

C. Syndication
F. Commercial Property
I. Land Use
L. Setback
O. Revitalization

A. Find the hidden words. The words have been placed horizontally, vertically, or diagonally. When you locate a word, draw an ellipse around it.

```
R E G R E S S I O N M L I B L Z J E C N X R T
Z Q U A N T I T A T I V E A N A L Y S I S E A
E N X J J M C B O X L D I V E R O S I O N N D
T Y C W R E M A I N D E R I N T E R E S T T T
P K T P A T Z Z M C O S T T O C U R E W C R E
L T S S S J R M A R K E T P R I C E E F L O X
K Q H C A P I T A L I Z A T I O N R A T E L Q
C O N S E R V A T I O N E A S E M E N T N U B
U N I T S O F C O M P A R I S O N J P V W G K
T U I I Q N C O R U G S P S C A R C I T Y D K
A P K S N E N C I Y T D G R O S S L E A S E L
P H Y S I C A L D E T E R I O R A T I O N Y D
H H I F I Y Y I K E F F E C T I V E D A T E B
B R C W F Q K E P A K Q R E A S O N A B L E I
A L D T G G L N K V O L U N T A R Y L I E N S
O N B E K K N T Y M A S S A P P R A I S A L N
```

1. Any rate used to convert income into value.
2. The date on which the analyses, opinions, and advice in an appraisal, review, or consulting service apply.
3. Amount paid for an income producing property.
4. The party of parties who engage an appraiser in a specific assignment.
5. The cost to restore an item of deferred maintenance to new or reasonably new condition.
6. The wearing away of surface land by natural causes.
7. An interest in real property restricting future land-use to preservation, conservation, wildlife habitat, or some combination of those uses.
8. The process of valuing a universe of properties as of a given date using standard methodology, employing common data, and allowing for statistical testing.
9. Analyzing value of a property based on numerical data.
10. Created intentionally by property owner's actions. i.e. mortgage
11. The present or anticipated undersupply of an item relative to the demand for it. Conditions of scarcity contribute to value.
12. Price per cubic foot, front foot, and per apartment.
13. Person who is entitled to an estate after a prior estate or interest has expired
14. In law, just, rational, appropriate, ordinary, or usual in the circumstances.
15. A report that is prepared regularly, usually each month, and indicates the rent-paying status of each tenant.
16. Value of a superior property is adversely affected by its association with an inferior property of the same type.
17. The wear and tear that begins with the building is completed and placed into service.
18. When the lessee (tenant) does not pay any costs of ownership and pays a given amount of rent per period.

A. Capitalization Rate
B. Gross lease
C. Reasonable
D. Cost to Cure
E. Remainder interest
F. Scarcity
G. Erosion
H. Units of comparison
I. Regression
J. Client
K. Mass Appraisal
L. Voluntary liens
M. Effective Date
N. Rent Roll
O. Market Price
P. Quantitative Analysis
Q. Physical Deterioration
R. Conservation Easement

B. Find the hidden words. The words have been placed horizontally, vertically, or diagonally. When you locate a word, draw an ellipse around it.

H	S	U	R	F	A	C	E	R	I	G	H	T	S	E	L	Q	N	I	B	K	H	H
S	S	I	T	E	O	D	G	R	O	S	S	L	I	V	I	N	G	A	R	E	A	C
B	M	A	R	K	E	T	P	R	I	C	E	H	F	U	L	L	T	A	K	I	N	G
V	M	A	R	K	E	T	A	B	I	L	I	T	Y	A	N	A	L	Y	S	I	S	H
W	F	R	I	P	A	R	I	A	N	R	I	G	H	T	S	L	B	S	N	Z	M	O
P	Y	L	V	C	M	C	T	G	E	R	M	C	B	I	Z	Z	T	W	L	K	A	W
P	D	A	S	S	E	S	S	E	D	V	A	L	U	E	R	T	B	G	L	Y	Q	A
U	L	M	V	M	P	C	A	J	U	D	P	D	U	T	D	D	B	T	U	D	B	D
P	B	S	T	E	P	U	P	D	E	P	R	E	C	I	A	T	I	O	N	W	S	L
S	B	M	U	G	A	M	I	P	V	H	O	U	S	I	N	G	S	T	A	R	T	S
D	M	D	T	K	B	F	T	M	I	X	B	A	D	J	U	S	T	M	E	N	T	S
P	U	T	I	L	I	T	Y	X	R	E	A	L	E	S	T	A	T	E	E	S	E	N
V	O	I	D	C	O	N	T	R	A	C	T	Y	Q	W	V	A	L	U	E	L	Z	U
E	J	Y	W	Z	X	C	I	L	N	I	E	Y	G	Q	J	Q	C	K	I	J	J	N
D	E	E	M	I	N	E	N	T	D	O	M	A	I	N	I	C	B	N	N	S	T	K
E	C	O	N	T	R	I	B	U	T	O	R	Y	V	A	L	U	E	S	Y	K	L	E

1. The right of government to take private property for public use upon payment of just compensation.
2. The entire taking of the full real property interest of a parcel for public use under the power of eminent domain; requires the payment of compensation.
3. Total area of finished above-grade residential space
4. The change in the value of a property as a whole, resulting from the addition or deletion of a property component.
5. The legal process of settling an estate after a person has died.
6. Has no legal force or binding effect and cannot be enforced in a court of law.
7. Rights pertaining to properties touching a river or stream.
8. Amount paid for an income producing property.
9. land that is improved so that is ready to be used for a specific purpose.
10. Ability of a product to satisfy a human want, need, or desire.
11. Changes made to basic data to facilitate comparison or understanding.
12. The readjustment of the value of an appreciated asset for tax purposes upon inheritance.
13. Land, water, and anything attached to the land-either naturally or placed by human hands.
14. A process for examining the productive attributes of the specific property, its demand and supply, and its geographic market area.
15. An identified parcel or tract of land, including improvements.
16. Newly constructed housing units; includes both single -family and multifamily domiciles.
17. Monetary worth of a property, good, or service to buyers and sellers at a given time.
18. The value of a property according to the tax rolls in ad valorem taxation.

A. Riparian rights
B. Contributory Value
C. Housing Starts
D. Full Taking
E. Eminent Domain
F. Value
G. Site
H. Assessed Value
I. Utility
J. Adjustments
K. Gross Living Area
L. Marketability Analysis
M. Real Estate
N. Void contract
O. Market Price
P. Surface rights
Q. Step Up Depreciation
R. Probate

C. Find the hidden words. The words have been placed horizontally, vertically, or diagonally. When you locate a word, draw an ellipse around it.

H	F	W	J	A	E	L	C	C	A	S	H	E	Q	U	I	V	A	L	E	N	T	O
I	G	P	H	Y	S	I	C	A	L	P	O	S	S	I	B	I	L	I	T	Y	M	O
G	D	I	N	M	T	D	G	R	E	V	I	T	A	L	I	Z	A	T	I	O	N	P
H	K	Q	G	U	A	N	R	X	V	F	I	X	E	D	E	X	P	E	N	S	E	O
W	Z	U	T	T	T	Y	O	T	N	R	Y	R	O	Y	A	L	T	Y	E	X	E	L
A	O	Z	J	B	E	A	S	P	C	P	N	K	F	E	G	H	P	I	I	E	A	R
Y	N	R	H	A	I	V	S	L	I	F	E	E	S	T	A	T	E	F	S	I	T	Q
E	I	M	Y	W	N	E	L	M	A	R	K	E	T	V	A	L	U	E	E	P	T	H
A	N	R	P	B	L	P	E	F	E	K	H	I	D	P	D	O	M	R	E	F	A	J
S	G	U	M	G	A	W	A	L	E	D	J	R	Z	P	E	R	Q	G	B	P	C	Z
E	P	Z	G	S	N	Z	S	N	G	Z	S	R	Q	D	E	W	Z	I	S	N	H	K
M	R	J	K	F	D	K	E	X	F	O	F	U	Q	R	D	X	O	Z	N	B	M	E
E	M	O	R	T	G	A	G	E	L	I	E	N	S	Y	Q	V	Z	Z	X	T	E	N
N	F	I	N	A	N	C	I	A	L	F	E	A	S	I	B	I	L	I	T	Y	N	M
T	F	G	R	O	W	T	H	V	R	E	N	O	V	A	T	I	O	N	A	H	U	Y
E	X	T	E	R	N	A	L	O	B	S	O	L	E	S	C	E	N	C	E	D	W	J

1. A stage in a market areas life cycle in which the market area gains public favor and acceptance.
2. When the lessee (tenant) does not pay any costs of ownership and pays a given amount of rent per period.
3. Seizure of property by court order.
4. The most probable price at which real estate would sell.
5. Total rights of use, occupancy and control, limited to the lifetime of the designated party, i.e. life tenant.
6. One of the four criteria the highest and best use of a property must meet.
7. Voluntary and one of the most common types of liens.
8. The degree, nature, or extent of interest that a person has in land.
9. The process in which older structures or historic buildings are modernized, remodeled, or restored.
10. Written, legal instrument that conveys an estate or interest in real property to someone else, assuming it is executed and delivered.
11. A stage in a market area's life cycle characterized by renewal, redevelopment, modernization, and increasing demand.
12. An element of depreciation; and diminution in value caused by negative externalities and generally incurable on the part of the owner, landlord, or tenant.
13. Operating expenses that generally do not vary with occupancy and that prudent management will pay whether the properties occupied or vacant.
14. One of the criteria for highest and best use of a property must meet.
15. Public regulation of the character and extent of real estate use though police power.
16. A right granted or taken for the construction, maintenance, and operation of the highway.
17. Money paid to an owner of real property or mineral rights for the right to deplete natural resource.
18. The price of a property with above- or below-market financing expressed in terms of the price that would have been paid in an all-cash sale.

A. Physical Possibility
B. Renovation
C. Financial Feasibility
D. Royalty
E. Highway Easement
F. Revitalization
G. External Obsolescence
H. Mortgage liens
I. Cash Equivalent
J. Attachment
K. Gross lease
L. Zoning
M. Market Value
N. Deed
O. Fixed Expense
P. Growth
Q. Estate in land
R. Life estate

D. Find the hidden words. The words have been placed horizontally, vertically, or diagonally. When you locate a word, draw an ellipse around it.

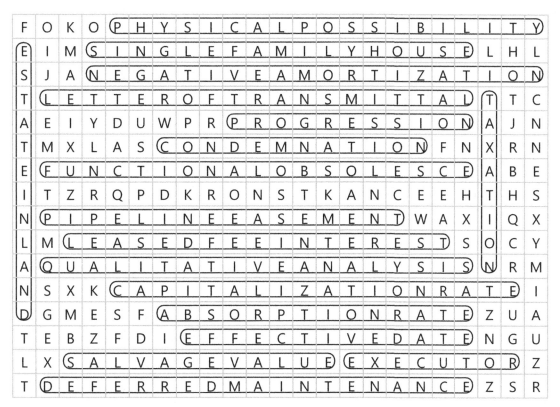

1. Right of government to raise revenue through assessments on valuable goods, products, and rights.
2. Any rate used to convert income into value.
3. The degree, nature, or extent of interest that a person has in land.
4. Estimate of the rate at which a particular class of properties will sell in a particular geographic area.
5. Method by which government can take private property.
6. One of the criteria for highest and best use of a property must meet.
7. An ownership interest for the possessory interest has been granted to another by creation of a contractual landlord-tenant relationship.
8. An individual or other legal person designated in a will to settle the estate of the deceased person.
9. The right to construct, operate, and maintain a pipeline over the lands of others within prescribed geographical limits.
10. The dwelling that is designated for occupancy by one family.

11. The impairment of functional capacity of a property according to market tastes and standards.
12. A letter or statement that serves as a notice of delivery from the appraiser to the client of a report containing an opinion or conclusion concerning real estate
13. The date on which the analyses, opinions, and advice in an appraisal, review, or consulting service apply.
14. Total payment is insufficient to pay interest due.
15. The price expected for a whole property (e.g., a house) or a part of a property (e.g., a plumbing fixture) that is removed from the premises usually for use elsewhere.
16. Is used for elements that cannot be given a numerical value.
17. Needed repairs or replacement of items that should have taken place during the course of normal maintenance.
18. Value of an inferior property is enhanced by its association with better properties of the same type.

A. Negative Amortization
B. Qualitative analysis
C. Physical Possibility
D. Absorption rate
E. Condemnation
F. Taxation
G. Single Family House
H. Leased Fee Interest
I. Functional Obsolesce
J. Progression
K. Letter of Transmittal
L. Capitalization Rate
M. Effective Date
N. Deferred Maintenance
O. Estate in land
P. Pipeline Easement
Q. Salvage Value
R. Executor

E. Find the hidden words. The words have been placed horizontally, vertically, or diagonally. When you locate a word, draw an ellipse around it.

L	O	S	S	O	F	A	C	C	E	S	S	R	P	Q	C	V	G	B	M	Q	E	V
R	Z	O	S	Y	N	D	I	C	A	T	I	O	N	C	L	T	B	Z	E	M	A	V
R	E	M	A	I	N	I	N	G	E	C	O	N	O	M	I	C	L	I	F	E	S	A
W	R	E	A	L	E	S	T	A	T	E	M	A	R	K	E	T	M	N	Z	P	S	L
F	E	E	S	I	M	P	L	E	E	S	T	A	T	E	N	E	G	X	M	M	E	U
J	N	U	N	I	L	A	T	E	R	A	L	C	O	N	T	R	A	C	T	N	S	E
M	V	O	I	D	C	O	N	T	R	A	C	T	B	N	K	E	E	N	C	O	S	I
J	A	R	M	S	L	E	N	G	T	H	A	H	R	N	R	S	S	V	L	I	E	N
Z	P	M	V	F	E	P	R	O	X	I	M	I	T	Y	D	A	M	A	G	E	D	E
P	A	R	Z	D	A	D	V	I	E	N	N	O	J	X	V	Q	J	H	D	N	V	X
S	X	Q	O	F	R	A	N	K	I	N	G	A	N	A	L	Y	S	I	S	T	A	C
F	I	N	A	N	C	I	A	L	F	E	A	S	I	B	I	L	I	T	Y	Q	L	H
J	X	L	E	T	T	E	R	O	F	T	R	A	N	S	M	I	T	T	A	L	U	A
A	Q	V	J	U	D	M	N	Z	O	F	E	Z	N	A	E	D	J	Y	D	Y	E	N
H	Y	P	O	T	H	I	C	A	T	I	O	N	D	N	B	Q	X	D	B	L	Y	G
G	M	M	K	D	W	R	E	F	A	I	R	M	A	R	K	E	T	V	A	L	U	E

1. The price at which the property would change hands between a willing buyer and a willing seller and both having reasonable knowledge of relevant facts.
2. Price an economic good will attract in the competitive market.
3. The party of parties who engage an appraiser in a specific assignment.
4. A borrower has possession of the property.
5. Charge against property in which the property is the security for payment of the debt.
6. The value of a property according to the tax rolls in ad valorem taxation.
7. The estimated period during which improvements will continue to represent the highest and best use of the property.
8. Has no legal force or binding effect and cannot be enforced in a court of law.
9. One of the four criteria the highest and best use of a property must meet.
10. Depriving an abutting owner of the inherent rights of ingress and to egress from the highway or street.
11. An ordinal technique for analyzing data, commonly used in the analysis of comparable sales.
12. Damages that is caused by the remainder's proximity to the improvement being constructed.
13. A transaction in which the buyers and sellers of a product act independently and have no relationship to each other.
14. Only one party makes a promise
15. A private or public partnership that pools funds for the acquisition and development of real estate projects or other business ventures.
16. Buyers and sellers of particular real estate and the transactions that occur among them.
17. A letter or statement that serves as a notice of delivery from the appraiser to the client of a report containing an opinion or conclusion concerning real estate
18. Absolute ownership unencumbered by any other interest or estate.

A. Proximity Damage
B. Lien
C. Unilateral contract
D. Real Estate Market
E. Financial Feasibility
F. Value in Exchange
G. Syndication
H. Assessed Value
I. Remaining Economic Life
J. Letter of Transmittal
K. Client
L. Void contract
M. Ranking Analysis
N. Hypothication
O. Fee Simple Estate
P. Fair Market Value
Q. Arms Length
R. Loss of Access

F. Find the hidden words. The words have been placed horizontally, vertically, or diagonally. When you locate a word, draw an ellipse around it.

```
O  F  U  N  C  T  I  O  N  A  L  O  B  S  O  L  E  S  C  E  T  J  D
N  E  T  L  E  A  S  E  K  S  U  R  F  A  C  E  R  I  G  H  T  S  T
X  I  S  S  U  P  R  A  S  U  R  F  A  C  E  R  I  G  H  T  S  K  P
J  B  K  S  F  Y  X  C  U  S  B  A  L  A  N  C  E  X  A  K  B  B  I
S  S  P  D  I  R  E  C  T  C  A  P  I  T  A  L  I  Z  A  T  I  O  N
J  D  R  E  M  A  I  N  I  N  G  U  S  E  F  U  L  L  I  F  E  M  Z
I  N  D  I  R  E  C  T  C  O  S  T  S  U  C  F  U  V  S  U  E  I  F
S  D  I  S  T  R  E  S  S  S  A  L  E  M  O  B  W  V  U  G  L  G  U
X  R  E  D  E  V  E  L  O  P  M  E  N  T  N  M  R  S  Y  B  D  J  K
R  A  I  L  E  A  S  E  M  E  N  T  E  Q  F  C  B  L  X  C  E  Q  M
L  D  E  E  D  R  E  S  T  R  I  C  T  I  O  N  D  E  H  Q  C  K  S
I  Y  E  C  O  N  O  M  I  C  L  I  F  E  R  Z  E  N  Y  L  L  D  C
J  P  M  D  M  V  U  J  J  J  Z  R  C  Q  A  M  E  U  E  I  V  I  B
S  A  L  V  A  G  E  V  A  L  U  E  M  H  I  C  Y  K  A  B  N  F  X
G  E  Z  Y  C  H  P  J  U  D  G  M  E  N  T  L  I  E  N  S  E  N  Z
Q  V  A  L  I  D  C  O  N  T  R  A  C  T  Y  I  V  Y  R  S  Q  R  X
```

1. A method used to convert an estimate of a single year's income expectancy into an indication of value in one direct step
2. The more a property or its components are in harmony with the surrounding properties or components, the greater the contributory value.
3. Soft cost expenditures that are necessary components but are not typically part of the construction contract.
4. The period over time which a structure may be competitive in the market.
5. The estimated period during which improvements will continue to provide utility.
6. Right to undisturbed use and control of designated air space above a specific land area within stated elevations.
7. A stage of diminishing demand in a market areas life cycle.
8. Typically result from a lawsuit in which a monetary judgment is awarded.
9. Land, water, and anything attached to the land-either naturally or placed by human hands.
10. A lease in which the landlord passes on all expenses to the tenant.
11. The development or improvement of cleared or undeveloped land in an urban renewal area.
12. A limitation that passes with the land regardless of the owner.
13. An agreement in which all the elements of a contract are present and, therefore, legally enforceable.
14. The right for the construction, maintenance, and operation of a rail line on a property.
15. Principle that real property value is created and sustained when contrasting, opposing, or interacting elements are in a state of equilibrium.
16. The price expected for a whole property (e.g., a house) or a part of a property (e.g., a plumbing fixture) that is removed from the premises usually for use elsewhere.
17. A sale involving a seller acting under undue distress.
18. The impairment of functional capacity of a property according to market tastes and standards.

A. Valid contract
B. Economic life
C. Rail Easement
D. Net Lease
E. Deed restriction
F. Decline
G. Redevelopment
H. Surface rights
I. Salvage Value
J. Distress Sale
K. Balance
L. Functional Obsolesce
M. Direct Capitalization
N. Judgment liens
O. Conformity
P. Remaining Useful Life
Q. Supra surface rights
R. Indirect costs

G. Find the hidden words. The words have been placed horizontally, vertically, or diagonally. When you locate a word, draw an ellipse around it.

Z	S	V	I	I	H	C	W	T	V	I	H	J	J	X	S	D	Q	Z	P	R	K	D
M	W	X	P	F	K	O	E	P	W	X	B	P	V	Z	V	F	G	G	W	L	E	Q
B	E	C	O	N	O	M	I	C	F	O	R	C	E	S	D	Z	O	N	I	N	G	C
B	D	D	L	D	K	P	T	Q	E	H	W	G	Y	K	C	W	R	D	Z	K	F	U
O	X	W	I	X	D	E	E	C	O	N	O	M	I	C	L	I	F	E	J	S	S	F
F	M	L	C	S	I	T	V	D	G	B	M	M	D	L	K	N	D	P	G	V	D	A
T	B	R	E	Q	S	E	X	H	N	G	S	E	T	B	A	C	K	G	F	A	A	X
Z	C	J	P	V	T	N	F	S	A	N	D	W	I	C	H	L	E	A	S	E	P	Z
Q	Q	Q	O	N	R	C	R	E	A	L	E	S	T	A	T	E	M	A	R	K	E	T
H	U	J	W	B	I	E	C	O	S	T	U	H	R	N	O	S	L	E	V	U	V	N
Q	A	U	E	G	C	B	I	L	A	T	E	R	A	L	C	O	N	T	R	A	C	T
L	C	O	R	L	T	L	O	S	S	O	F	A	C	C	E	S	S	L	U	U	A	G
E	K	D	K	E	S	U	B	S	U	R	F	A	C	E	R	I	G	H	T	S	J	D
X	M	E	L	E	M	E	N	T	S	O	F	C	O	M	P	A	R	I	S	O	N	M
Z	O	N	P	R	E	S	E	R	V	A	T	I	O	N	E	A	S	E	M	E	N	T
M	E	G	R	O	S	S	B	U	I	L	D	I	N	G	A	R	E	A	N	X	N	A

1. Relevant characteristics used to compare and adjust the property prices.
2. The state of having the requisite or adequate ability or qualities to perform the specific assignment and produce credible assignment results.
3. Total dollar expenditure to develop an improvement.
4. Supply and demand for housing, economic activity.
5. Buyers and sellers of particular real estate and the transactions that occur among them.
6. A lease in which an intermediate, or sandwich, leaseholder is the lessee of one party and the lessor of another.
7. Zoning regulations that designate the distance a building must be set back from the front, rear, and sides of the property lines.
8. Right or interest in property.
9. Type of market are characterized by homogeneous land use. e.g., apt., commercial, industrial, agricultural
10. The period over time which a structure may be competitive in the market.
11. Rights to the use and profits of the underground portion of a designated property.
12. A promise made in exchange for another promise.
13. When the government regulates the land use for the good of the public.
14. Total floor area of a building, excluding unenclosed area, measured from the exterior of the walls of the above-grade area.
15. A voluntary legal agreement that becomes part of the chain of title thereby protecting a historic, archaeological, or cultural resource.
16. Depriving an abutting owner of the inherent rights of ingress and to egress from the highway or street.
17. Public regulation of the character and extent of real estate use though police power.

A. Loss of Access
D. Bilateral contract
G. Estate
J. Elements of comparison
M. District
P. Setback

B. Zoning
E. Real Estate Market
H. Gross Building Area
K. Cost
N. Police power
Q. Competence

C. Economic life
F. Subsurface rights
I. Sandwich lease
L. Preservation Easement
O. Economic Forces

H. Find the hidden words. The words have been placed horizontally, vertically, or diagonally. When you locate a word, draw an ellipse around it.

K	B	T	L	E	G	A	L	P	E	R	M	I	S	S	I	B	I	L	I	T	Y	I
P	W	A	J	B	E	T	E	N	A	N	C	Y	I	N	C	O	M	M	O	N	C	G
X	P	X	A	N	Q	H	J	I	I	T	R	L	R	P	D	O	U	S	Y	Q	O	J
X	N	A	G	T	Q	F	V	U	G	A	C	F	X	A	W	L	M	Y	G	D	S	V
F	D	T	W	P	S	L	F	B	C	R	D	N	W	Z	C	A	M	E	N	I	T	Y
U	T	I	Z	B	N	O	B	E	X	P	O	S	U	R	E	T	I	M	E	T	A	O
Q	U	O	T	E	N	T	G	U	S	C	A	R	C	I	T	Y	P	H	C	I	P	T
S	N	N	N	S	J	J	E	X	T	Q	T	E	I	Z	R	A	A	S	U	R	P	S
Y	E	N	E	I	G	H	B	O	R	H	O	O	D	P	H	E	K	I	I	J	R	X
V	X	Y	T	X	M	A	R	K	E	T	V	A	L	U	E	L	A	T	I	H	O	S
K	P	C	M	O	N	E	T	A	R	Y	P	O	L	I	C	Y	I	E	X	U	A	X
K	P	H	Y	S	I	C	A	L	P	O	S	S	I	B	I	L	I	T	Y	O	C	O
U	P	M	R	E	M	A	I	N	D	E	R	I	N	T	E	R	E	S	T	K	H	Q
V	N	X	F	O	Y	A	V	Z	Y	S	U	K	S	T	A	B	I	L	I	T	Y	L
O	R	E	H	A	B	I	L	I	T	A	T	I	O	N	Q	S	S	B	G	C	W	W
S	N	F	I	N	A	L	O	P	I	N	I	O	N	O	F	V	A	L	U	E	G	A

1. A tangible or intangible benefit of real property that enhances its attractiveness or increases the satisfaction of the user.
2. Process of dividing one number (dividend) by another number (divisor) produces this result.
3. Complementary land uses; inhabitants, buildings, or business enterprises.
4. an estimate of replacement cost of a structure, less depreciation, plus land value.
5. The opinion of value derived from the reconciliation of value indications and stated in the appraisal report
6. Right of government to raise revenue through assessments on valuable goods, products, and rights.
7. Person who is entitled to an estate after a prior estate or interest has expired
8. Guiding control of the money supply in the economy.
9. Estate owned by 2 or more persons, each of whom has an equal undivided interest. Unlike Joint Tenancy and Tenancy by Entirety, No right of survivorship.
10. Stage in market area's life cycle. The market area experiences equilibrium without market gains or losses.
11. The most probable price at which real estate would sell.
12. land that is improved so that is ready to be used for a specific purpose.
13. One of the four criteria the highest and best use of a property must meet.
14. The time of property remains on the market.
15. The present or anticipated undersupply of an item relative to the demand for it. Conditions of scarcity contribute to value.
16. One of the criteria for highest and best use of a property must meet.
17. The repair and restoration of existing improvements that are in poor condition to a state that makes the property competitive again.

A. Cost Approach
E. Rehabilitation
I. Remainder interest
M. Neighborhood
Q. Tenancy in Common

B. Physical Possibility
F. Quotent
J. Amenity
N. Final Opinion of Value

C. Market Value
G. Site
K. Stability
O. Monetary Policy

D. Exposure Time
H. Legal Permissibility
L. Taxation
P. Scarcity

I. Find the hidden words. The words have been placed horizontally, vertically, or diagonally. When you locate a word, draw an ellipse around it.

C	U	U	D	U	F	D	E	S	K	R	E	V	I	E	W	K	S	N	D	C	X	D
O	C	T	T	S	K	U	C	J	E	E	Z	N	Z	A	L	Y	C	B	X	L	E	O
M	N	Z	R	E	F	S	T	H	T	M	Y	G	A	V	A	S	O	I	H	G	J	P
P	R	N	P	F	Y	H	R	W	A	A	I	T	M	O	B	N	P	S	B	T	R	E
E	W	B	I	U	Z	J	E	Q	X	I	C	F	Y	J	O	L	E	V	E	T	E	R
T	G	R	W	L	S	H	N	P	A	N	I	L	M	Y	R	D	O	H	E	F	A	A
E	F	Q	F	L	P	X	D	M	T	D	E	T	K	I	X	P	F	G	L	P	L	T
N	F	N	M	I	S	P	S	N	I	E	L	E	S	S	O	R	W	V	S	V	P	I
C	L	L	L	F	L	P	J	V	O	R	B	M	X	A	H	E	O	W	X	R	R	N
E	P	M	G	E	N	U	R	J	W	W	W	G	L	R	P	P	R	S	J	Y	O	G
K	D	M	B	T	E	A	M	W	D	I	L	H	A	Q	O	A	K	A	A	O	P	I
E	R	E	A	L	E	S	T	A	T	E	M	A	R	K	E	T	A	T	B	O	E	N
P	J	Y	V	A	L	U	E	I	N	E	X	C	H	A	N	G	E	E	L	X	R	C
F	Q	U	A	N	T	I	T	A	T	I	V	E	A	N	A	L	Y	S	I	S	S	T	O
Q	I	C	A	P	I	T	A	L	I	Z	A	T	I	O	N	R	A	T	E	U	Y	M
S	P	H	Y	S	I	C	A	L	P	O	S	S	I	B	I	L	I	T	Y	L	Q	E

1. Price an economic good will attract in the competitive market.
2. The state of having the requisite or adequate ability or qualities to perform the specific assignment and produce credible assignment results.
3. The period of time over which a structure may reasonably be expected to perform the function for which it was designed.
4. The type and extent of research and analyses in appraisal or appraisal review assignment.
5. One who conveys the rights of occupancy and use to others under lease agreement.
6. Buyers and sellers of particular real estate and the transactions that occur among them.
7. Analyzing value of a property based on numerical data.
8. comprises of all costs required to construct and market the product as land alone or with improvements.

9. Income derived from the operation of a business or real property
10. A future possessor read interest in real estate that is given to a third-party and matures upon the termination of a limited or determinable be.
11. An appraisal review in which the reviewer's scope of work does not include an inspection of the subject property.
12. One of the criteria for highest and best use of a property must meet.
13. Right of government to raise revenue through assessments on valuable goods, products, and rights.
14. Any rate used to convert income into value.
15. The interests, benefits, and rights inherent in ownership of real estate.
16. A series of related changes brought about by a chain of causes and effects.

A. Capitalization Rate
B. Remainder
C. Operating Income
D. Competence
E. Taxation
F. Desk Review
G. Real Estate Market
H. Physical Possibility
I. Quantitative Analysis
J. Real Property
K. Scope of Work
L. Value in Exchange
M. Lessor
N. Labor
O. Useful life
P. Trends

J. Find the hidden words. The words have been placed horizontally, vertically, or diagonally. When you locate a word, draw an ellipse around it.

```
V  Z  P  N  A  D  V  E  R  S  E  P  O  S  S  E  S  S  I  O  N  W  W
S  U  P  R  A  S  U  R  F  A  C  E  R  I  G  H  T  S  J  D  A  X  C
G  T  A  S  V  R  K  V  W  L  U  W  G  S  I  B  I  D  L  E  S  N  W
N  O  T  L  I  X  L  O  Q  F  D  T  J  A  H  R  N  X  I  P  S  E  E
A  K  Y  X  G  P  Z  L  U  D  D  D  R  N  F  S  A  W  T  R  E  T  J
I  U  K  C  H  F  L  U  G  D  C  T  P  O  E  K  X  H  T  E  M  L  T
X  Q  H  E  M  O  T  N  R  E  N  O  V  A  T  I  O  N  O  C  B  E  H
N  O  M  A  R  K  E  T  V  A  C  A  N  C  Y  P  O  Q  R  I  L  A  Z
L  H  F  D  U  Y  D  A  P  L  A  T  S  L  Z  L  W  A  A  A  A  S  N
O  E  N  C  U  M  B  R  A  N  C  E  Y  G  Q  X  Z  C  L  T  G  E  F
C  D  H  V  I  Z  S  Y  P  O  L  I  C  E  P  O  W  E  R  I  E  X  Q
P  M  U  E  H  Z  H  L  D  J  P  F  F  H  S  Q  O  G  I  O  T  O  H
C  O  M  M  E  R  C  I  A  L  P  R  O  P  E  R  T  Y  G  W  Z  Q  Q
W  F  E  M  A  R  K  E  T  V  A  L  U  E  B  W  Y  P  H  E  A  N  I
W  K  R  E  M  A  I  N  D  E  R  I  N  T  E  R  E  S  T  F  J  G  Y
Z  N  N  J  P  R  E  S  E  N  T  V  A  L  U  E  X  A  S  U  K  R  G
```

1. Involuntary transfer of property takes place when a party makes a property claim by taking possession over a period of years.
2. Created intentionally by property owner's actions. i.e. mortgage
3. The combining of 2 or more parcels into one ownership (tract).
4. Rights pertaining to properties abutting a lake or pond.
5. Income-producing property such as office and retail buildings.
6. In appraising, a loss in property value from any cause
7. Any claim or liability that affects our limits the title to property.
8. The overall vacancy rate that occurs as a result of the interaction of supply and demand of a particular property type in a particular region or market.
9. The most probable price at which real estate would sell.
10. A lease in which the landlord passes on all expenses to the tenant.
11. The process in which older structures or historic buildings are modernized, remodeled, or restored.
12. The value of a future payment or series of future payments discounted to the current date or to time period zero.
13. Person who is entitled to an estate after a prior estate or interest has expired
14. Right to undisturbed use and control of designated air space above a specific land area within stated elevations.
15. When the government regulates the land use for the good of the public.
16. A plan, map, or chart of a city, town, section, or subdivision indicating the location and boundaries of individual properties.

A. Remainder interest
E. Net Lease
I. Market Value
M. Present Value
B. Assemblage
F. Encumbrance
J. Renovation
N. Supra surface rights
C. Voluntary liens
G. Depreciation
K. Littoral rights
O. Adverse possession
D. Plat
H. Commercial Property
L. Police power
P. Market Vacancy

K. Find the hidden words. The words have been placed horizontally, vertically, or diagonally. When you locate a word, draw an ellipse around it.

```
C G D P R M A R K E T A B I L I T Y Y V X Y C
X L E U L H F R Y W F J W M Q I L D H A Z R F
K I M P L I E D C O N T R A C T Q E S P M E Y
W Y R X O G I L E A N J T X S I V O L P X C G
T N G F V H O Y T S G G L H N I T H Y U Q L D
A L H P V W C J J G W O C T V G E J R R L A E
C A K R L A E M I N E N T D O M A I N T T M E
G X L K K Y P O R A N G E O F V A L U E P A D
U W V L X E L D L E I N T E S T A T E N R T W
E E N Q B A J L I S P E N D E N S Z B A W I W
Q P T W V S O E T E S T A T E X Z W G N Z O M
Y M A R K E T P A R T I C I P A N T S C Y N K
S L F H Q M V S V H P S A F E R A T E E T H J
A L N R T E E H B P B X A C C R E T I O N Z N
P E R S O N A L R E P R E S E N T A T I V E F
V P E R P T R Q R N W P E M B L E M E N T S F
```

1. Annual crops and plantings such as corn, wheat, and vegetables.
2. Any method of bringing wasted natural resources into productive use.
3. Written, legal instrument that conveys an estate or interest in real property to someone else, assuming it is executed and delivered.
4. In final reconciliation, the range in which the final market value opinion of a property may fall; usually stated as the interval between a high and low value limit.
5. The condition of dying with a valid will.
6. Something that has been added or appended to a property and has since become an inherent part of the property.
7. A right granted or taken for the construction, maintenance, and operation of the highway.
8. The right of government to take private property for public use upon payment of just compensation.
9. The relative desirability of a property in comparison with similar or competing properties in the area.
10. Ann agreement that is presumed to exist because of the parties' actions.
11. Legal term signifying pending litigation that can affect ownership title to real estate.
12. An increase in dry land created by the gradual accumulation of waterborne solid material over formerly riparian land.
13. An individual or other legal person designated in a will to settle the estate of a deceased person.
14. The condition of dying without a will.
15. The minimum rate of return on invested capital.
16. The parties involved in the transfer of property rights. Includes buyers, sellers, lessors, lessees, and brokers and their agents.

A. Marketability
D. Market Participants
G. Range of Value
J. Implied contract
M. Lis Pendens
P. Accretion

B. Reclamation
E. Safe Rate
H. Appurtenance
K. Eminent Domain
N. Deed

C. Intestate
F. Testate
I. Personal Representative
L. Highway Easement
O. Emblements

L. Find the hidden words. The words have been placed horizontally, vertically, or diagonally. When you locate a word, draw an ellipse around it.

```
R E P L A C E M E N T A L L O W A N C E U R W
Y O G U W L O Y K T I S T R I C J H I C I E Q
X F D S T E P U P D E P R E C I A T I O N M X
D P S J X S R C O K K D D B V D C Z F G V O K
W W Z W A S H O E P G C E D Z T L J U R E D G
V P N C F O E I G F B O S E F C K M L I S E G
Y H P K U R T B V L H L I K P M M V L E T L Q
X U R U E A S E M E N T R O T C N P T K M I B
Z T M C O M P E T E N C E K E K J R A K E N U
F R I C T I O N A L V A C A N C Y T K A N G J
S A V U L A S S E M B L A G E B S J I Y T T P
N G O I N G C O N C E R N V A L U E N P V D S
V C O N T R I B U T O R Y V A L U E G I A G D
I N T E R N A L R A T E O F R E T U R N L R U
P O T E N T I A L G R O S S I N C O M E U L O
S U R P L U S P R O D U C T I V I T Y Y E Z K
```

1. One who conveys the rights of occupancy and use to others under lease agreement.
2. The entire taking of the full real property interest of a parcel for public use under the power of eminent domain; requires the payment of compensation.
3. An allowance that provides for the periodic replacement of building components that wear out more rapidly than the building itself.
4. The change in the value of a property as a whole, resulting from the addition or deletion of a property component.
5. Value to a particular individual. The present worth of anticipated future benefits.
6. The readjustment of the value of an appreciated asset for tax purposes upon inheritance.
7. Net income that is left after the 4 agents of production have been paid.
8. The total income attributable to real property at full occupancy before vacancy and operating expenses are deducted.
9. The combining of 2 or more parcels into one ownership (tract).
10. Purchaser's wish for an item to satisfy human needs or individual wants beyond essential life-support needs.
11. The right to use another's land for a stated purpose.
12. The annualized yield or rate of return on capital that is generated or capable of being generated within an investment or portfolio over a period of ownership.
13. A type of renovation that involves modification or updating of existing improvements.
14. The state of having the requisite or adequate ability or qualities to perform the specific assignment and produce credible assignment results.
15. When the value of a business plus the amount of real property is sought.
16. The amount of vacant space needed in a market for its orderly operation.

A. Remodeling
B. Easement
C. Potential Gross Income
D. Going concern value
E. Surplus Productivity
F. Investment Value
G. Replacement Allowance
H. Contributory Value
I. Frictional Vacancy
J. Step Up Depreciation
K. Lessor
L. Competence
M. Full Taking
N. Internal Rate of Return
O. Desire
P. Assemblage

M. Find the hidden words. The words have been placed horizontally, vertically, or diagonally. When you locate a word, draw an ellipse around it.

B	C	E	U	V	L	E	S	S	O	R	D	U	H	C	N	X	H	C	O	S	R	B
A	W	O	P	E	R	A	T	I	N	G	E	X	P	E	N	S	E	R	A	T	I	O
X	P	H	Q	V	O	P	E	R	A	T	I	N	G	S	T	A	T	E	M	E	N	T
B	O	Q	C	A	P	I	T	A	L	I	Z	A	T	I	O	N	I	O	H	M	X	V
A	A	Q	E	E	X	M	S	M	A	R	K	E	T	A	N	A	L	Y	S	I	S	H
B	F	Y	A	V	O	L	U	N	T	A	R	Y	L	I	E	N	S	E	P	Y	C	K
O	B	N	E	I	G	H	B	O	R	H	O	O	D	C	V	U	L	J	S	H	M	L
R	E	M	O	D	E	L	I	N	G	T	V	A	A	M	B	N	C	N	X	C	K	E
I	F	L	X	B	V	O	I	D	A	B	L	E	C	O	N	T	R	A	C	T	J	B
K	L	X	Y	V	T	F	G	E	V	M	P	Z	H	O	G	E	X	O	D	B	W	P
M	P	A	I	R	E	D	D	A	T	A	A	N	A	L	Y	S	I	S	L	R	X	M
O	A	M	R	Y	L	B	H	X	C	F	T	V	H	C	A	S	H	F	L	O	W	X
R	D	E	S	K	T	O	P	A	P	P	R	A	I	S	A	L	L	N	L	X	U	Z
E	L	E	M	E	N	T	S	O	F	C	O	M	P	A	R	I	S	O	N	G	Z	M
B	O	M	A	S	T	A	N	D	A	R	D	F	Q	U	O	T	E	N	T	Z	N	V
K	D	E	B	T	C	O	V	E	R	A	G	E	R	A	T	I	O	N	E	V	S	S

1. Two or more sales are compared to derive an indication of the size of the adjustment for a single characteristic.
2. The ratio of total operating expenses to effective gross income
3. Relevant characteristics used to compare and adjust the property prices.
4. Complementary land uses; inhabitants, buildings, or business enterprises.
5. The conversion of income into value.
6. One who conveys the rights of occupancy and use to others under lease agreement.
7. Ratio of NOI to annual debt service.
8. Technically valid but gives one or more parties the power to legally void the agreement and thus cancel performance.
9. Process of dividing one number (dividend) by another number (divisor) produces this result.
10. A type of renovation that involves modification or updating of existing improvements.
11. An appraisal report in which the appraiser's scope of work does not include an inspection of the subject property or comparables.
12. The periodic income attributable to the interests in real property.
13. Created intentionally by property owner's actions. i.e. mortgage
14. A financial statement that reflects the gross revenues, expenses, and net operating profit or loss of an investment over a fixed period.
15. Study of real estate market conditions for specific types of property.
16. The standard method of measurement for office buildings as defined by the Building Owners and Managers Association.

A. Debt coverage ratio
D. Cash Flow
G. Paired data analysis
J. Operating Statement
M. Neighborhood
P. Remodeling

B. Operating Expense Ratio
E. Desktop Appraisal
H. Capitalization
K. BOMA Standard
N. Voluntary liens

C. Lessor
F. Elements of comparison
I. Quotent
L. Market Analysis
O. Voidable contract

N. Find the hidden words. The words have been placed horizontally, vertically, or diagonally. When you locate a word, draw an ellipse around it.

E	I	U	R	N	F	G	F	I	X	E	D	E	X	P	E	N	S	E	I	I	C	S
C	O	M	M	E	R	C	I	A	L	P	R	O	P	E	R	T	Y	D	V	N	I	U
Y	D	R	I	V	E	B	Y	A	P	P	R	A	I	S	A	L	Y	E	B	V	Y	F
A	S	O	T	M	E	S	M	O	M	N	O	A	X	C	P	S	J	T	Q	O	W	Y
R	N	Q	E	H	Q	X	E	O	X	I	P	Y	U	Z	D	L	W	E	P	L	A	Y
A	R	L	E	G	A	L	D	E	S	C	R	I	P	T	I	O	N	R	T	U	R	U
O	E	S	T	A	T	E	I	N	L	A	N	D	R	X	G	F	G	I	O	N	M	L
C	H	I	F	Y	P	F	O	V	I	Z	O	F	Z	C	D	C	L	O	H	T	S	N
A	O	R	A	L	A	P	P	R	A	I	S	A	L	R	E	P	O	R	T	A	L	X
X	A	U	W	Q	Q	S	R	Y	I	I	W	N	Q	L	U	F	V	A	R	R	E	B
C	R	R	E	P	O	O	U	C	O	S	T	D	T	Y	B	L	E	T	K	Y	N	I
L	B	Z	O	V	I	N	T	E	R	I	M	U	S	E	E	K	R	I	G	L	G	I
M	L	M	A	R	K	E	T	V	A	L	U	E	R	H	G	L	V	O	Y	I	T	U
G	I	J	U	S	T	C	O	M	P	E	N	S	A	T	I	O	N	N	P	E	H	H
B	B	X	S	I	N	G	L	E	F	A	M	I	L	Y	H	O	U	S	E	N	N	E
K	G	L	J	G	D	J	D	W	C	F	Y	H	A	Y	G	C	D	D	W	S	M	M

1. Impairment of condition; because of depreciation that reflects the loss in value due to wear and tear, disintegration, use in service, and the action of the elements.
2. The dwelling that is designated for occupancy by one family.
3. A description of land that identifies the real estate according to a system established or approved by law.
4. Income-producing property such as office and retail buildings.
5. The most probable price at which real estate would sell.
6. A transaction in which the buyers and sellers of a product act independently and have no relationship to each other.
7. Created by law, rather than by choice. i.e. property tax lien.
8. In condemnation, the amount of loss for which a property owner is compensated when his or her property is taken.
9. Temporary use to which a site or improved property is put until it is ready to be put to its future highest and best use.
10. A report that is transmitted orally.
11. Total dollar expenditure to develop an improvement.
12. Operating expenses that generally do not vary with occupancy and that prudent management will pay whether the properties occupied or vacant.
13. An appraisal report in which the scope of work includes an exterior-only viewing of the subject property.
14. The degree, nature, or extent of interest that a person has in land.

A. Commercial Property
E. Involuntary liens
I. Oral Appraisal Report
M. Single Family House

B. Arms Length
F. Deterioration
J. Drive by Appraisal
N. Estate in land

C. Interim use
G. Fixed Expense
K. Just Compensation

D. Cost
H. Market Value
L. Legal Description

O. Find the hidden words. The words have been placed horizontally, vertically, or diagonally. When you locate a word, draw an ellipse around it.

```
G M J E A V U X N Y Q G G P R O F O R M A Z X
S I N G L E F A M I L Y H O U S E D E O X D P
T I N T E R I M U S E T W L Y H Q A Y Y T R R
X A Y Z C T C O J Y E A S E M E N T P H H B U
Y J Z Y P I Y J X M T N F S T F T Y O E Z O S
I Z Y D C T L J U Q E L O S X N R R Z Z A E A
S I A O E L M X J I P Z A O C I M L Z O K V L
W D P O G E I H Y H G N B R Z O Z H G N I L V
T Q E C H Y P O T H I C A T I O N A F I R E A
J F P E R C E N T A G E L E A S E L B N S H G
D D A C T U P R O X I M I T Y D A M A G E F E
X N E L E M E N T S O F C O M P A R I S O N V
Q C Q U A N T I T A T I V E A N A L Y S I S A
V N A L C S E C O N D A R Y D A T A B G C O L
Q F R A O L E A S E H O L D I N T E R E S T U
J P E Y M A R K E T P A R T I C I P A N T S E
```

1. The dwelling that is designated for occupancy by one family.
2. Analyzing value of a property based on numerical data.
3. The tenant's possessory interest created by a lease.
4. A borrower has possession of the property.
5. Information that is not gathered in its original form by the analyst.
6. One who conveys the rights of occupancy and use to others under lease agreement.
7. Combination of all elements that constitute proof of ownership.
8. The right to use another's land for a stated purpose.
9. A projected income and expense statement for proposed development.
10. The parties involved in the transfer of property rights. Includes buyers, sellers, lessors, lessees, and brokers and their agents.
11. Temporary use to which a site or improved property is put until it is ready to be put to its future highest and best use.
12. The price expected for a whole property (e.g., a house) or a part of a property (e.g., a plumbing fixture) that is removed from the premises usually for use elsewhere.
13. Damages that is caused by the remainder's proximity to the improvement being constructed.
14. Relevant characteristics used to compare and adjust the property prices.
15. Public regulation of the character and extent of real estate use though police power.
16. Most commonly found in retail business. This lease has a base rent which is fixed and an excess rent, this is most commonly based on the percentage of the sales.

A. Percentage lease
D. Easement
G. Title
J. Salvage Value
M. Zoning
P. Leasehold Interest

B. Pro Forma
E. Quantitative Analysis
H. Elements of comparison
K. Secondary Data
N. Interim use

C. Lessor
F. Proximity Damage
I. Hypothication
L. Market Participants
O. Single Family House

P. Find the hidden words. The words have been placed horizontally, vertically, or diagonally. When you locate a word, draw an ellipse around it.

```
S I T E I M P R O V E M E N T S R E P O R T E
T W E U U F R I C T I O N A L V A C A N C Y M
V L Y E M O F W D O Z F R Q S G E F Z E R Y I
L A P P U R T E N A N C E A N J E B M Y U U N
Y B T L E A S E E A D W T O I T B D A B J S E
Y L R O R F P C X Z Y Q P D J D Y J R D T B N
D X H O U S I N G S T A R T S M S C K E I L T
K C A P I T A L I Z A T I O N R A T E C V X D
W H Y E R F Q H F D T L C Q H B E F T L P E O
U S E F U L L I F E F V E S K A F U A I M T M
O G F U U F A R A M M D N R D Q H S B N H E A
R Y C V F Q M A R K E T R E N T C E I E X Y I
Y W T W S Z Y Y Q L H J E T D B S E L P T S N
M N H E F F E C T I V E D A T E C Q I D J O D
C V T B O P K Q Y D S I C V X H T I T S E Y Y
O D S U B S U R F A C E R I G H T S Y F L J L
```

1. Something that has been added or appended to a property and has since become an inherent part of the property.
2. The relative desirability of a property in comparison with similar or competing properties in the area.
3. Amount a particular purchaser agrees to pay and a particular seller agrees to accept under the circumstances surrounding their transaction.
4. The date on which the analyses, opinions, and advice in an appraisal, review, or consulting service apply.
5. The right of government to take private property for public use upon payment of just compensation.
6. The period of time over which a structure may reasonably be expected to perform the function for which it was designed.
7. The most probable rent the property should bring in a competitive and open market reflecting all conditions and restrictions of the lease agreement.
8. Any rate used to convert income into value.
9. A contract in which the rights to use and occupy land or structures are transferred by the owner to another for a specified period of time in return for specified rent.
10. Newly constructed housing units; includes both single-family and multifamily domiciles.
11. The amount of vacant space needed in a market for its orderly operation.
12. Any communication, written or oral, of an appraisal or appraisal review that is transmitted to the client upon completion of an assignment.
13. A stage of diminishing demand in a market areas life cycle.
14. Rights to the use and profits of the underground portion of a designated property.
15. Improvements on and off the site that make it suitable for its intended use or development.

A. Marketability
E. Report
I. Lease
M. Useful life
B. Decline
F. Market Rent
J. Price
N. Appurtenance
C. Site Improvements
G. Subsurface rights
K. Housing Starts
O. Capitalization Rate
D. Effective Date
H. Frictional Vacancy
L. Eminent Domain

Q. Find the hidden words. The words have been placed horizontally, vertically, or diagonally. When you locate a word, draw an ellipse around it.

U	B	V	O	K	N	I	I	N	T	E	S	T	A	T	E	L	P	C	F	O	Q	B
S	F	L	B	A	L	A	N	C	E	B	K	C	O	S	T	K	R	J	U	W	U	D
U	R	P	O	T	E	N	T	I	A	L	G	R	O	S	S	I	N	C	O	M	E	E
R	K	P	R	E	S	E	R	V	A	T	I	O	N	E	A	S	E	M	E	N	T	E
F	P	R	O	X	I	M	I	T	Y	D	A	M	A	G	E	F	E	G	P	V	C	D
A	G	Y	W	W	H	D	Y	R	A	T	E	O	F	R	E	T	U	R	N	O	N	M
C	R	Q	F	A	I	R	M	A	R	K	E	T	V	A	L	U	E	D	D	O	W	S
E	D	C	O	R	A	L	A	P	P	R	A	I	S	A	L	R	E	P	O	R	T	V
R	A	P	E	R	C	E	N	T	A	G	E	A	D	J	U	S	T	M	E	N	T	S
I	T	E	S	T	A	T	E	A	P	P	R	A	I	S	A	L	R	C	Z	F	B	X
G	A	H	D	E	Z	H	C	H	S	F	Z	I	E	X	L	V	D	W	D	F	R	N
H	V	I	M	D	N	A	B	P	W	X	O	R	G	G	Y	H	K	I	S	J	A	W
T	W	R	J	Y	E	J	F	N	C	O	N	T	R	I	B	U	T	I	O	N	F	W
S	Z	K	K	E	Z	R	A	M	H	B	I	S	W	I	Q	Y	R	N	O	T	O	K
W	Q	Q	Z	Q	C	F	I	Q	W	B	N	Q	A	S	W	V	T	H	T	I	G	C
Z	E	Z	J	T	A	N	W	Q	T	R	G	L	C	T	T	E	I	O	V	D	Q	E

1. A voluntary legal agreement that becomes part of the chain of title thereby protecting a historic, archaeological, or cultural resource.
2. The total income attributable to real property at full occupancy before vacancy and operating expenses are deducted.
3. Written, legal instrument that conveys an estate or interest in real property to someone else, assuming it is executed and delivered.
4. The act or process of developing an opinion of value.
5. The ratio of income or yield to the original investment.
6. Public regulation of the character and extent of real estate use though police power.
7. Total dollar expenditure to develop an improvement.
8. Land, water, and anything attached to the land-either naturally or placed by human hands.
9. A report that is transmitted orally.
10. The price at which the property would change hands between a willing buyer and a willing seller and both having reasonable knowledge of relevant facts.
11. Principle that real property value is created and sustained when contrasting, opposing, or interacting elements are in a state of equilibrium.
12. Damages that is caused by the remainder's proximity to the improvement being constructed.
13. The condition of dying with a valid will.
14. The value of a particular component is measured in terms of the amount it adds to the value of the whole property.
15. Adjustments for differences between the subject and comparable properties expressed as a percentage of the sale price of the comparable property.
16. The condition of dying without a will.

A. Balance
D. Zoning
G. Potential Gross Income
J. Surface rights
M. Appraisal
P. Testate

B. Intestate
E. Contribution
H. Oral Appraisal Report
K. Deed
N. Fair Market Value

C. Rate of return
F. Preservation Easement
I. Proximity Damage
L. Percentage Adjustments
O. Cost

R. Find the hidden words. The words have been placed horizontally, vertically, or diagonally. When you locate a word, draw an ellipse around it.

```
Q E N T R E P R E N E U R I A L P R O F I T F
H X B V T D E S I R E H A G E T Q M Z H Q J E
V U G H Z P Q C C P Y E N C L V N U C V U Y R
C J S K G J C G E B E Q I W Y J G R H Z O T E
I W T C H V Z F F O E S C H E A T F E S T X O
L I T T O R A L R I G H T S O J G Z V K E X Z
C O N D E M N A T I O N W U P X E N K N N Z X
X C A W R E H O U S I N G S T A R T S B U G H
Y O W Q K D E A U F I S C A L P O L I C Y R I
A S Z P R I M A R Y D A T A X U L W W H S Y V
R T P O T E N T I A L G R O S S I N C O M E U
A G G U W S X E F E X P O S U R E T I M E T O
L A I T E N A N C Y I N C O M M O N M Q K W K
W B N A Z D C O S T T O C U R E P A U W J I L
O P E R A T I N G E X P E N S E R A T I O G B
Q P A I R E D D A T A A N A L Y S I S E X J E
```

1. Two or more sales are compared to derive an indication of the size of the adjustment for a single characteristic.
2. Estate owned by 2 or more persons, each of whom has an equal undivided interest. Unlike Joint Tenancy and Tenancy by Entirety, No right of survivorship.
3. Management of government receipts and expenditures.
4. Process of dividing one number (dividend) by another number (divisor) produces this result.
5. Rights pertaining to properties abutting a lake or pond.
6. A market-derived figure that represents the amount an entrepreneur receives for their contribution.
7. Newly constructed housing units; includes both single -family and multifamily domiciles.
8. The ratio of total operating expenses to effective gross income

9. The cost to restore an item of deferred maintenance to new or reasonably new condition.
10. Total dollar expenditure to develop an improvement.
11. Going to the State. The process that should a property be abandoned, it reverts back to the state.
12. Information that is gathered in its original form by the analyst.
13. The total income attributable to real property at full occupancy before vacancy and operating expenses are deducted.
14. The time of property remains on the market.
15. Method by which government can take private property.
16. Purchaser's wish for an item to satisfy human needs or individual wants beyond essential life-support needs.

A. Escheat
D. Condemnation
G. Fiscal Policy
J. Cost
M. Housing Starts
P. Paired data analysis

B. Cost to Cure
E. Operating Expense Ratio
H. Littoral rights
K. Primary Data
N. Exposure Time

C. Quotent
F. Desire
I. Tenancy in Common
L. Potential Gross Income
O. Entrepreneurial profit

S. Find the hidden words. The words have been placed horizontally, vertically, or diagonally. When you locate a word, draw an ellipse around it.

B	A	D	V	E	R	S	E	P	O	S	S	E	S	S	I	O	N	T	D	V	D	G
J	I	K	N	L	R	E	C	O	N	C	I	L	I	A	T	I	O	N	K	I	I	C
P	R	E	S	E	R	V	A	T	I	O	N	E	A	S	E	M	E	N	T	N	S	O
D	R	H	C	S	L	I	V	I	N	G	T	R	U	S	T	L	P	V	T	H	C	M
E	M	F	G	S	R	H	S	C	I	W	K	D	F	Z	R	I	R	T	B	E	O	P
T	S	I	C	O	X	S	U	Q	V	E	M	K	E	B	F	A	I	L	I	R	U	E
E	E	Y	Q	R	S	W	J	R	V	Y	V	D	F	D	L	V	M	B	Y	I	N	T
R	G	L	I	F	E	T	E	N	A	N	T	A	K	D	S	V	A	U	L	T	T	E
I	P	W	D	F	R	D	U	F	D	T	Q	M	N	K	C	J	R	V	Y	A	R	N
O	L	C	T	Y	K	R	S	Q	J	G	V	A	V	W	S	N	Y	J	M	N	A	C
R	B	V	T	D	Z	R	E	Q	C	J	V	G	H	R	W	X	D	O	E	C	T	E
A	H	S	A	U	T	I	L	I	T	Y	M	E	E	E	K	P	A	I	X	E	E	Y
T	P	L	A	T	K	G	A	C	E	X	A	S	N	C	U	M	T	K	P	T	I	I
I	I	X	I	R	K	Y	G	S	A	M	E	N	I	T	Y	L	A	V	I	A	A	W
O	Q	I	O	Q	U	F	F	W	J	S	D	T	V	J	M	J	U	H	L	X	D	W
N	W	N	G	Q	G	O	I	N	G	C	O	N	C	E	R	N	V	A	L	U	E	M

1. Information that is gathered in its original form by the analyst.
2. In condemnation, the loss in value to the remainder in a partial taking of property.
3. One who owns an interest in real property for his or her own lifetime.
4. Created by agreement during the property owner's lifetime
5. When the value of a business plus the amount of real property is sought.
6. Involuntary transfer of property takes place when a party makes a property claim by taking possession over a period of years.
7. A tangible or intangible benefit of real property that enhances its attractiveness or increases the satisfaction of the user.
8. The state of having the requisite or adequate ability or qualities to perform the specific assignment and produce credible assignment results.
9. A voluntary legal agreement that becomes part of the chain of title thereby protecting a historic, archaeological, or cultural resource.
10. A plan, map, or chart of a city, town, section, or subdivision indicating the location and boundaries of individual properties.
11. Ability of a product to satisfy a human want, need, or desire.
12. A tax on the right to receive property by inheritance; as distinguished from estate tax.
13. One who conveys the rights of occupancy and use to others under lease agreement.
14. The process of reducing a range of value indications into an appropriate conclusion for that analysis.
15. Impairment of condition; because of depreciation that reflects the loss in value due to wear and tear, disintegration, use in service, and the action of the elements.
16. The yield rate used to convert future payments or receipts into present value; usually considered to be a synonym for yield rate.

A. Inheritance Tax
E. Damages
I. Primary Data
M. Amenity
B. Life tenant
F. Living trust
J. Reconciliation
N. Adverse possession
C. Utility
G. Deterioration
K. Going concern value
O. Discount Rate
D. Lessor
H. Plat
L. Competence
P. Preservation Easement

T. Find the hidden words. The words have been placed horizontally, vertically, or diagonally. When you locate a word, draw an ellipse around it.

```
A D O O H V X E W U G V Q J C L Y F E X O P T
C O M M E R C I A L P R O P E R T Y I Q N X W
Z T P H Y S I C A L D E T E R I O R A T I O N
U H Z H N E I G H B O R H O O D E B I S U K I
W Q M S C Y R B A K L A N D U S E Y I E C T X
P H Y S I C A L C H A R A C T E R I S T I C S
L K F X U Y A E D Z Z W I E B D E U W B B Y C
C B F R E V I T A L I Z A T I O N S W A V V O
P E A R N E S T M O N E Y V M F G J T C R C N
F I N A L O P I N I O N O F V A L U E K W P F
D I R E C T C A P I T A L I Z A T I O N J V O
M J S Y N D I C A T I O N T D C I W Z H T N R
F R Z I I Z F X M A R K E T A B I L I T Y C M
O P E R A T I N G E X P E N S E R A T I O E I
C O N S E R V A T I O N E A S E M E N T P H T
M U P Y L J I N V E S T M E N T V A L U E A Y
```

1. A category of elements of comparison in the sales comparison approach
2. The more a property or its components are in harmony with the surrounding properties or components, the greater the contributory value.
3. A private or public partnership that pools funds for the acquisition and development of real estate projects or other business ventures.
4. Value to a particular individual. The present worth of anticipated future benefits.
5. A method used to convert an estimate of a single year's income expectancy into an indication of value in one direct step
6. The wear and tear that begins with the building is completed and placed into service.
7. The ratio of total operating expenses to effective gross income
8. Complementary land uses; inhabitants, buildings, or business enterprises.
9. An interest in real property restricting future land-use to preservation, conservation, wildlife habitat, or some combination of those uses.
10. The relative desirability of a property in comparison with similar or competing properties in the area.
11. Zoning regulations that designate the distance a building must be set back from the front, rear, and sides of the property lines.
12. The opinion of value derived from the reconciliation of value indications and stated in the appraisal report
13. The employment of a site or holding to produce revenue or other benefits.
14. Part of the purchase price given to bind a bargain.
15. A stage in a market area's life cycle characterized by renewal, redevelopment, modernization, and increasing demand.
16. Income-producing property such as office and retail buildings.

A. Conformity
D. Earnest money
G. Marketability
J. Operating Expense Ratio
M. Physical Deterioration
P. Conservation Easement

B. Final Opinion of Value
E. Physical Characteristics
H. Direct Capitalization
K. Investment Value
N. Neighborhood

C. Syndication
F. Commercial Property
I. Land Use
L. Setback
O. Revitalization

Made in the USA
Columbia, SC
16 September 2020